T0366423

# SHAPING A CITY

# SHAPING A CITY

## ITHACA, NEW YORK, A DEVELOPER'S PERSPECTIVE

MACK TRAVIS

PUBLISHED IN ASSOCIATION WITH
**CORNELL UNIVERSITY PRESS**
ITHACA AND LONDON

First published 2018 by Cornell University Press

Printed in the United States of America

Library of Congress Cataloging-in-Publication Data

Names: Travis, Mack, author.
Title: Shaping a city : Ithaca, New York, a developer's perspective / Mack Travis.
Description: Ithaca : Cornell University Press, 2018. | Includes bibliographical references.
Identifiers: LCCN 2018039115 (print) | LCCN 2018040190 (ebook) | ISBN 9781501730153 (pdf) | ISBN 9781501730160 (epub/mobi) | ISBN 9781501730146 | ISBN 9781501730146 (cloth: alk. paper)
Subjects: LCSH: Real estate development—New York (State)—Ithaca—History. | City planning—New York (State)—Ithaca—History. | Urban renewal—New York (State)—Ithaca—History. | Central business districts—New York (State)—Ithaca—History. | Ithaca (N.Y.)—History. | Travis, Mack.
Classification: LCC HD268.I8 (ebook) | LCC HD268.I8 T73 2018 (print) | DDC 333.3309747/71—dc23
LC record available at https://lccn.loc.gov/2018039115

This book is dedicated to Gary Ferguson, executive director of the Downtown Ithaca Business Improvement District, who through his energy, vision, and perseverance has played a major role in inspiring the city of Ithaca to reshape itself.

To Matthys (Thys) Van Cort, who came to Ithaca in 1971 and served as our enlightened city planner for thirty-five years.

And to the many mayors, city staff, council members, developers, bankers, volunteers, and businesspeople who work to make Ithaca, New York, the successful city that it is.

When the Stranger says: "What is the meaning of this city?

Do you huddle close together because you love each other?"

What will you answer? "We all dwell together

To make money from each other"? or "This is a community"?

**T. S. Eliot, Chorus 3 from *The Rock*, 1934**

# CONTENTS

# ACKNOWLEDGMENTS

Many people have contributed to this story: Thys Van Cort, Ithaca's director of planning and development for over thirty-five years; Gary Ferguson, executive director of the Downtown Ithaca Business Improvement District; Michael Stamm, executive director of Tompkins County Area Development; Nels Bohn, executive director of the Ithaca Urban Renewal Agency; Andy Sciarabba, CPA and fellow developer; John Novarr, developer; Paul Mazzarella, executive director of Ithaca Neighborhood Housing Services; Carl Haynes, president of Tompkins Cortland Community College; Greg Hartz, president of the Tompkins Trust Company; Phyllissa DeSarno, Ithaca's economic development director; and the numerous members of Ithaca Common Council and volunteers on the zoning board, planning board, and Ithaca Landmarks Preservation Commission; as well as the mayors, politicians, and many colleagues and fellow developers who have generously shared their time and expertise.

I would also like to thank Della Mancuso, Rick Ball, Tony Sorhaindo, and Meg Custer, who have spent countless hours reviewing and editing the manuscript for accuracy and clarity prior to submission to Cornell University Press; and finally, my wife and business partner, Carol G. Travis, whose love and attention, wisdom and intuition, have been at the heart of every project we have undertaken.

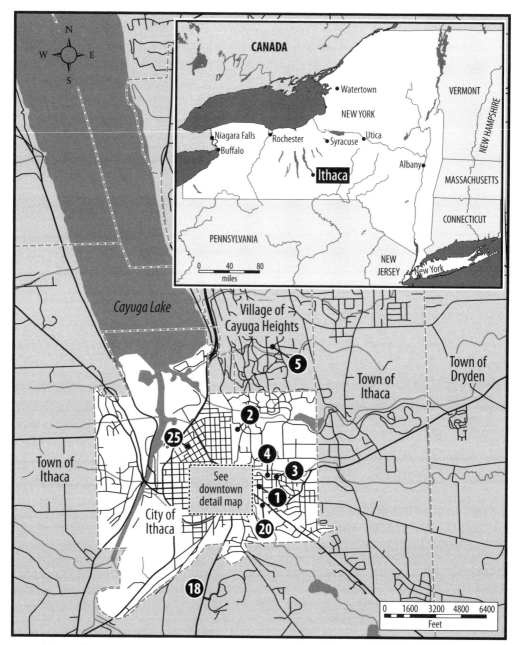

**Map 1.** Greater Ithaca, New York, area

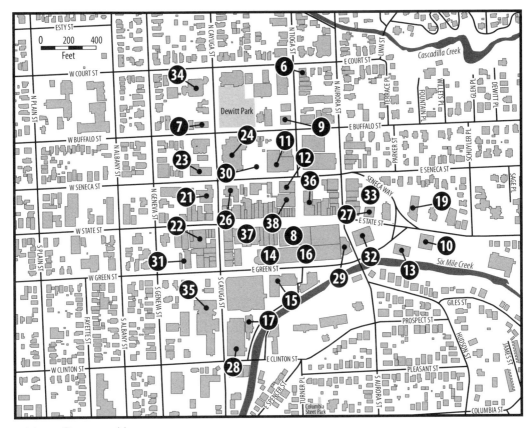

Map 2. Downtown Ithaca

## KEY

1  Eddy Street
2  Ravenwood
3  407 College Avenue
4  Eddygate
5  Westview
6  Westminster Hall
7  Cayuga Apartments
8  Center Ithaca
9  Acrographics
10  Gateway Center
11  Seneca Place
12  Tompkins Cortland Community College
13  Gateway Commons
14  Green Street Garage
15  Cayuga Green
16  Cinemapolis
17  Lofts @ Six Mile Creek
18  South Hill Business Campus
19  Challenge Industries

20  Collegetown Terrace
21  The Historic Clinton House
22  The State Theatre
23  Women's Community Building
24  Dewitt High School
25  INHS Hancock Street Affordable Housing
26  Masonic Temple
27  Carey Building
28  Coltivare
29  Ithaca Marriott hotel
30  Tompkins Financial Corporation headquarters
31  Press Bay Alley
32  City Center
33  Hilton Canopy hotel
34  The Old Library (Dewitt House)
35  Hotel Ithaca
36  Former First National Bank building
37  Harold's Square
38  Tompkins Center for History and Culture

# SHAPING A CITY

# INTRODUCTION

Why do some cities thrive and grow? Why do others languish and decline?

Our city—Ithaca, New York—is a small city now grown to thirty thousand residents. It is home to Cornell University and Ithaca College, global companies such as BorgWarner, numerous high-tech firms, a public library, a historic preservation society, many parks, and a large number of waterfalls. It is an intellectual, industrial haven that was carved out of the gorges and hills in the early 1800s and is set on Cayuga Lake, in the heart of the Finger Lakes district.

Today you can drive from one side of Ithaca to the other in less than ten minutes. If traffic is backed up for more than three minutes, it's considered a traffic jam. Twenty-one thousand students on East Hill at Cornell University, six thousand on South Hill at Ithaca College, and another twenty-five hundred at the downtown extension campus of Tompkins Cortland Community College together cause our population to double almost year-round and keep Ithaca young, exciting, and lively. The stability of these institutions of higher education, along with the glacial topography, five major waterfalls, and the local high-tech industries, have pushed Ithaca to the top of the list of desirable places to live, work, and raise a family. Ithaca is known as the "Enlightened City," so-called by *Utne Reader* in 1997. New York state senator George Winner, on a visit to Ithaca some years ago, referred to our city as the "Crown Jewel" in upstate New York.

Making a difference is not outside the realm of possibility in Ithaca. Ithaca is a small pond, and its opportunities and problems are not dissimilar to what most small US cities experience. It has sprawl in the outer regions, industries that have both supported and polluted, and suburban malls that have drawn vitality away from downtown. It has politics and bureaucracy, zoning, rules for historic preservation, developers, and gadflies. It has a department of planning and development and a local "BID," or business improvement district.

The merchants, tenants, property owners, mayors, and members of the Ithaca City Council have come together to create change in central downtown. Cornell University has joined forces with the city to bring hundreds of employees to the downtown. New theaters, parking garages, restaurants, hotels, and businesses—including many major apartment and office buildings—have all been developed within the last fifteen years.

What follows is the story of "shaping a city." Each generation has its turn to do this; it is no different in your city. Ithaca today has built on the successes and failures of those who have gone before, and it has added a planning juggernaut in the form of its business improvement district.

This story is written from the point of view of a real estate developer, property owner, and one of the founding members of our local business improvement district—or, as it is now called, the Downtown Ithaca Alliance.

The story I tell will give you a behind-the-scenes look at the projects and principles of development that have turned Ithaca from a quiet hamlet into a bustling and successful business hub with a small-city downtown that attracts researchers and start-ups. I will describe a city that draws full-time residents, from the bank president to the low-income wage earner, and is renowned for having more restaurants per capita than New York City. A city that is rated by numerous sources as one of the "best small cities in America."

Ithaca could be looked at as a case study for all cities. From understanding Ithaca, perhaps one can better understand one's own city and the forces at work for growth and economic sustainability. Who are the players? What needs to be done? What are the forces driving growth and development? How is it going to happen in your city, with your projects?

Having developed numerous real estate projects in Ithaca since the early 1970s, and having researched many cities in my role as president of Ithaca's business improvement district, I suggest that the forces at work in the development of Ithaca, New York, are to be found—and can be applied anywhere in our country—in cities both large and small.

# CHAPTER 1

# THE COMMONS (1971–75)
## A Pedestrian Mall

The years 1971 to 1975 were a watershed for Ithaca, New York. A transition was taking place that would affect Ithaca's downtown for the next four decades. The idea had started with urban renewal in the late '60s. The mayor and downtown business owners were determined to save downtown from economic collapse. A new shopping mall on the outskirts of town threatened to draw stores and customers from the main street of downtown to the suburbs. In 1971, urban consultants Parsons, Canfield, and Stein had been hired to help the city develop a plan. Their idea called for a small *pedestrian plaza* to be built in the heart of downtown at the intersection of Tioga and State Streets. A pedestrian plaza, they reasoned, might well be the financial salvation for downtown. A few full-scale pedestrian malls had already been built in cities like Boulder, Colorado, and Burlington, Vermont, to counteract the draw of the suburban malls and keep their downtowns as vibrant as possible in the face of growing competition.

In a series of public meetings led by the then mayor Ed Conley, it was decided: Ithaca would build not just the small pedestrian plaza recommended by the consultants, but a full-scale pedestrian mall replacing the main street on three full blocks in the heart of downtown. The city would bond to raise the money for its construction. The bonds would be paid back by charges to property owners in a special "assessment district" created within a two-block zone surrounding the area known as State and Tioga Streets, three blocks of which were selected to be restricted from vehicular traffic and would be designated as a pedestrian mall, the "Ithaca Commons."

When Thys (pronounced "Tace") Van Cort was interviewed and hired for the position of planning director in the fall of 1972, the city had already made the decision to build a pedestrian mall. His first major assignment: Get it done! The following is the story of how he did just that, how he—got it done!

The initial idea for a pedestrian mall had come from David Taube, a member of the board of Historic Ithaca and one of the principals at the local firm HOLT Architects. After consultation with the mayor and leaders on the planning board, Thys was directed to orchestrate the extensive search process for an architecture firm to design the pedestrian mall. This search resulted in hiring of the local firm led by Anton Egner—Egner Architectural Associates. Egner designated Bob Leathers, a well-known local architect, to be in charge of the job, and also retained Marvin Adleman, a professor of landscape architecture at Cornell, to assist with the project.

Immediately after hiring the new architect, Thys approached the mayor to suggest the formation of a client committee for the project. The committee's responsibilities would be to advise the architect on the design of the project, to help sell the project to the general public, to make sure that the various constituencies in downtown would have their voices heard in the design process, and to keep the public aware of the progress of the project. In addition, the committee was to advise Thys and the planning staff on the scheme that would be developed to pay for the pedestrian mall.

This committee was made up of representatives from the planning board, Common Council, and the board of public works, plus key members of the Downtown Businessmen's Association, the Downtown Businesswomen's Association, the Area Beautification Council, and Historic Ithaca. Mayor Conley appointed Thys to chair this Mall Steering Committee.

At first, Thys started holding closed meetings, which was possible then, because New York State did not yet have an "open meetings" law. However, this troubled him; he felt that having open meetings and press coverage was important, since this was a project that the committee would ultimately have to sell to the general public, the Common Council, and the board of public works. He discussed his concerns with members of the committee, and the decision was made that thereafter all meetings were to be open to the public and that the press should be invited.

As Thys described it, "There were two competing visions for the pedestrian mall—one was that it should be a museum piece to be enjoyed in silent reverence; the other was that it should be the center of a three-ring circus where stuff would happen, and people would come to have fun. This was my analysis, and as you can tell from my somewhat biased description, I was in the three-ring circus camp. The museum folks won out with the ban on dogs, but the circus people got the children's playground."

"Battles were fought," Thys said. "My department and I faced almost universal resistance from the other departments in city hall. The department of public works was certainly not in favor of such a harebrained idea, the legal department couldn't be bothered, and the controller was openly hostile. Compromises were made, but all in all the design process proceeded apace, and the design was completed by March of 1974, nine months after the architect was hired."

Thys continued, "The project was put out to bid in April 1974 by the board of public works. Bids were received in May and came in below budget. The base bid was just under $700,000, the low bidder being a firm which had an excellent reputation—Streeter Construction out of Elmira. Ultimately, the total cost of the mall, including soft costs such as architecture, engineering, legal, and financing, came in at $1.135 million. The mall was about 55,000 square feet, thus it was built for $12.70 a foot, hard cost."

Thys had taken the project to Common Council and the board of public works multiple times during the development process. Each time there was a risk that a down vote would stop it dead in its tracks. Any down vote could bring the project to a halt, so it had to be successful over and over again!

At the time the city started the design of the Ithaca Commons, there was no legal authorization under the laws of the state of New York that would allow borrowing for construction of a pedestrian mall. Municipalities in the state of New York cannot bond for any capital improvement without specific legislative authority being given for such borrowing by the New York State legislature. This meant that a city could bond for construction of a street, sidewalk, all kinds of buildings, sewers, water systems, parks, fire trucks, and so forth, but to bond for a pedestrian mall, according to state law, the project would have to be divided into its constituent parts: paving, sidewalks, electrical service, water mains, storm sewers, sanitary sewers, benches, pavilions, trees, and other plantings. Each of these components had its own period of probable usefulness. The term of the bonds for each of these elements would have been different. Thys found himself in a position where, to fund the project, he would have to write enabling legislation that would allow the city of Ithaca to *bond for the entire capital project.*

Thys described overcoming this hurdle: "I hired two very bright student interns for the summer of 1973. Wayne Merkelson and John Kirkpatrick took on the job of trying to develop both a financing scheme for the project and the legal authorization for its bonding. During the fall and winter these students researched what other enabling legislation looked like and drafted a law for consideration by the state legislature. By March 1974, when it seemed clear that this was more than just a harebrained idea, all of a sudden the city controller realized that we might actually pull this thing off. He then engaged the city's bond counsel in New York City to draft legislation. Looking back on it, our attempt at writing the legislation was rather amateurish but nonetheless a noble effort by a bunch of young go-getters. The legislation was sent to Albany, passed by both houses, and signed by the governor. Another huge hurdle had been overcome. We were again in business."

The last major piece was the design of the financial formula by which owners or merchants would be charged for the construction of the mall. The Common Council had decided early in the process that the downtown owners and merchants would have to pay the lion's share of the cost of the project. Thys recounted that he and his intrepid interns set about trying to come up with a scheme for this undertaking. There were all kinds of things they had to consider. Does the formula favor the big property owners or the small? How important was it that it be easy to administer versus equitable? For example, a benefit assessment based on foot traffic into each store would probably be the most equitable, as those who benefited most would pay the most. On the other hand, a formula based on foot traffic would be almost impossible to administer. Other bases of benefit would be far easier to administer. Those included lot size, front footage, or some percentage of assessed valuation. There are rules they had to know as well, and they were doing this without benefit of counsel. Benefit assessments cannot be based solely on assessed value; they could, however, be based on a formula that combines assessed value and another factor.

Thys said, "In the end we chose a formula that was easy to administer and, as it turned out, relatively regressive. We chose the formula based on front footage with a correction for depth. If you had a very deep store you would pay more than you would if you had a very shallow store, but the basis of the formula was front footage. There was also a correction for corner properties. In addition to charging those buildings along the Commons, there was a lesser charge for properties on the blocks leading up to the ends of the Commons, based on the notion that they too would benefit from the construction of this improvement but to a lesser extent than the projects directly fronting on the pedestrian mall. As it turns out," Thys added, "this was a relatively regressive formula favoring the large owners over the small property owners. We didn't really like that idea, but when we ran the numbers for a more progressive formula, the charges for the big owners were so high that we were afraid they would rebel and kill the project.

"I would note," he said, "that we did this work before the invention of computer spreadsheets. Every iteration of every scheme had to be calculated by hand with an adding machine. Wayne was great, he could punch the keys without looking at the keyboard! Dozens of iterations and tens of thousands of keystrokes later, we had a working formula.

"Our formula was accepted by the Common Council, and the tax benefit assessment was designed based on our formula. Eighty-five percent of the cost of the Commons was assigned to the tax benefit district. The other 15 percent was considered to be public improvements like sewers and water mains that the city would have paid for anyway."

Now Thys was at the eleventh hour with a great bid and the project fully funded when, he said, "suddenly a bunch of people got cold feet. Construction of a new two-story building for the Rothschild's Department Store and the 450-space Green Street parking garage was about to begin at exactly the same time as the pedestrian mall. People were concerned, particularly the merchants, that so much disruption would have extremely negative consequences for the businesses on State Street."

Thys and members of his committee lobbied heavily to move ahead, believing it was better to get the disruption over quickly rather than spread it out over several years. He was also extremely concerned—a concern that he shared with the mayor and the rest of the leadership— that if they did not go now with a good bid, the project would never get done. If they had to wait and bid it again the following year, the city would probably not get as good a bid, and the opposition to the project might have grown.

Thys tells how he and Mayor Conley went to a tumultuous meeting where one speaker after another condemned the project, or the timing, or both, as well as attacking them personally, but they stuck to their guns. A few days later they went back to the Common Council, where one of the council members predicted that half the businesses surrounding the construction site would be closed by the end of construction. At the final hour, a vote was held and the council approved the project. Construction started, and three blocks of the street in the heart of downtown were demolished in a matter of days.

Then the city was sued. The grounds for the suit were that Thys and his committee had not given legal notice that the street was going to be closed. As Thys says, "The judge, seeing that the street was already torn out, sensibly ruled that there might not have been legal notice within the letter of the law, but that the actual notice such as newspaper articles, letters to all the property owners and merchants, etc., constituted an abundant and sufficient actual notice." They were free to proceed.

Construction started in June of 1974. Less than six months later, by Thanksgiving, the project was 85 percent complete, all the paving was in, and everything was buttoned up for the winter. All that remained to be done in the spring was the completion of some of the pavilions, some of the benches, and plant materials.

Miraculously few stores closed in downtown during the construction process. Merchants were enthusiastic about the possibility of a pedestrian mall as a way to improve their business. The public maintained loyalty to their favorite stores and continued to brave the walkways and gravel piles caused by the construction. Only two businesses closed during construction, and Thys said that it was the consensus among the merchants that these businesses closed because they were not good retailers, for the street was never closed for business throughout the entire construction period.

The years 1971 to 1975 were indeed watershed years for Ithaca. The Ithaca Commons has had a positive impact on downtown vitality year after year. It changed Ithaca's downtown for the next four decades and beyond. It is truly representative of the fits and starts often surrounding progress on public-private projects still today. It was built in a spirit of cooperation and, when necessary, with intense drive and belief in the good that would result. It was Thys's first project in a career that would extend for another thirty-five years as Ithaca's director of planning and development.

Closing off the central three blocks of State and Tioga Streets, installing paving, benches, pavilions, trees, a fountain, meant that business could be conducted as one walked along the Commons, shopped in the specialty stores, and ate in the restaurants. Children could play on the playground and in the fountain. Performers could entertain in the pavilions. No dogs. No bikes. But it was as pleasant and welcoming a place as one could imagine.

It took two years total to complete the project. Most of the stores survived, and some new national chains moved into town. The Commons formally opened in 1975 and was an instant success. As a response to the enclosed suburban mall, Ithaca had constructed an outdoor pedestrian mall that, despite the region's four to five months of winter, kept the downtown alive and active. It was an exemplary response to intense new competition from the suburban mall.

**Figure 1.1** State Street in Ithaca, New York, ca. 1950. Photo courtesy of the History Center of Tompkins County.

**Figure 1.2** State Street, now the Ithaca Commons Pedestrian Mall, ca. 1975. Photo by Jon Reis.

CHAPTER 2

# CLUG

## A Lesson in City Planning

The period 1971–75 was a watershed in other ways as well. While Thys Van Cort was designing and building the Commons, I had returned to my hometown of Ithaca and was purchasing and renovating a few run-down old houses. After graduate school and working as an actor in five seasons of summer stock theater, I had moved with my wife and two small children to New York City to "make it" there as an actor. I had failed, and was now divorced, broke, and living on half of an $8,000 instructor's salary teaching film production at Ithaca College—the other half went to the children and my former wife, who was pursuing her PhD in Georgia.

One option was selling shoes on Saturdays to augment my meager income. Something had to be done. Selling shoes held no appeal. Maybe finding a property in Ithaca? In New York City for a couple of years I had net-leased a vacant Manhattan brownstone on West Eighty-Second Street, cleaned it up, leased out five small apartments, and lived rent-free in an eight-room apartment on two floors in what friends then called "the armpit of Manhattan." With additional income from freelancing as a filmmaker and driving a cab, there was just enough to live on. Maybe that could be done in Ithaca. It was all about survival. Getting by—make enough to pay bills and live rent-free. At twenty-eight years old, with a crayon, I had written on the wall of my study in NYC: "*Nothing ventured, nothing gained.*"

With no money and no banking history, I found that income properties in Ithaca weren't easy to come by, but at last one appeared. With no money down, and after a quick renovation changing a single-family house to a two-family, there was $100 a month free and clear in my bank account. A refinancing using the first house to raise money for a down payment enabled the purchase of a second property—a two-family that would also clear about $100 a month. Looking ahead, perhaps there was enough money to be made between the rental properties and the job at Ithaca College to continue to send money to my family every month and have enough to live on myself. It was a focused, small circle in which I lived. Life went on around me. The small city of then approximately twenty-five thousand people was there. I hardly knew it. Expanding personal income was the goal. Never mind the city and how it worked. Never mind anyone else. Income, and sending money for the care of the children. That was my world.

One afternoon a call came from Thys. As the city planner, Thys was always available to explain things during the acquisition and renovation process of my first two properties. He explained what zoning and building codes meant; whether it was legal to add a bedroom; how many people could live there—those sorts of issues. He was an important and valuable resource. He was smart, he knew the political system, and he was a likable, easygoing guy.

Thys was calling now to invite me to Cornell's architecture school to play CLUG. "What the hell is CLUG?" I asked him.

"CLUG stands for the Community Land Use Game," he said. "It was invented by a Cornell professor, Allan Feldt. A small number of us are going to play it over the next three evenings at the architecture school. We divide up into teams and play a conceptual game figuring out a city—any city: how it works and fits together, how rental property, public infrastructure, and industry all relate. In general, the dynamics of what makes a city. Come give it a try." This was his invitation.

That night I showed up at the Cornell architecture school—the College of Architecture, Art, and Planning. It was in an old building—Sibley Hall it was called. My father had studied engineering there from 1936 to 1940. Being a student again felt a little strange—in a classroom, shy, uncertain, a bit skeptical, but ready to learn.

"The Community Land Use Game." The professor stood at the blackboard. A dozen students—politicians, the city planner, and a landlord or two—sat around a circular table. The group played. There were no computers then. It was chalk on the blackboard. The professor asked us to choose a town. "Ithaca?" I suggested—self-serving, but it was here everyone in the room lived, and suddenly it became important to know how this city worked. How could one make more money? We divided ourselves up into teams representing the city council, owners of industry, property developers, and rental housing.

To play the game, each team had to meet certain conditions. The professor laid it out. You couldn't just go out and build rental units. First there had to be streets and sewers and public utilities. There couldn't be streets and sewers and public utilities until there was a tax base to support their construction. There couldn't be a tax base until there were jobs and income to produce a tax base. There couldn't be jobs and income until the workers had a place to live. It was a circular dilemma that we had to solve. It immediately became clear: I was not living in a vacuum. No one in the game could live independently; we were all totally *interdependent.*

In order for "Ithaca" to be successful, there was going to have to be some negotiation among the teams. Someone would have to build factories, but first someone else would have to build streets and sewers: Before that, someone else had to build the housing to hold the workers to work in the factories, but first someone would have to build the factories for the workers to work in so they could pay the taxes to build the roads and sewers, and so on. Who would go first? Who would take the risk? The teams had to talk about this. All parties had to agree on a formula that would work. Over the next three nights the group played "Ithaca." It seems every generation has to relearn this process. To construct our chosen Ithaca, based on the parameters of the game, everyone needed to negotiate. Everyone needed to cooperate. It was going to take more than just one guy buying and renovating a few run-down houses to build this city. The community needed to work together, even if it was just around a blackboard.

In retrospect, playing CLUG was an elementary lesson in city planning. Living in a closed circle of survival, of trying to make enough income to pay bills and support an absent family, it was as though a light bulb turned on. The streets and sewers, the water supply, and the electricity had all just been there. Didn't they just exist for all to use? The rental market was there. Everyone needed a place to live. To have a place to live, there had to be jobs, and to have jobs there had to be a place for people to work, and to have a place to work, there had to be infrastructure, and taxes, and so it went. It was elementary. It was a Catch-22. It was the way all cities are structured; all of us are indeed part of a community. A window was opening for each of us in the room through which to view modern civic society.

It was then that the negotiations began. The professor guided us through the process. The teams began to broker agreements. "We'll build the industrial facility if you'll build the housing and the infrastructure for the community." "We'll build the housing if you'll build the jobs and the streets and the sewers." "We'll build the streets and sewers, the public utilities, if you'll house the workers and you'll create the jobs . . ." We were all in this together. The professor set the guidelines: "It takes fifteen hundred jobs to create the tax base needed for enough sewers and streets to take care of them. It takes an investment of $60 million to create the factories and the industry to create the fifteen hundred jobs. It takes $15 million to build the housing for the people to work in the jobs."

The exact ratios and numbers may have varied, but it was the interrelationship, the dynamic, that was important. Who would take the first step? Who would take the risk of building their piece of the puzzle in the hope that the rest of the puzzle would take shape, that no one would go broke "building Ithaca"?

Several things happened over the course of those three evenings at the Cornell architecture school: each of our teams became part of a virtual community; each of us became part of constructing "Ithaca" in our dreams; and, as the dreams of the group expanded, our individual horizons kept pace. It was possible to add zeros—000,000,000s—to housing numbers with impunity in the classroom playing CLUG. No longer did an individual need to be limited to buying and renovating single-family houses. The community needed more. No longer was it just one man owning a few income properties. Our city needed hundreds of units to house the workers who would work at the jobs that would support the factories that would pay the tax base to create streets and sewers that would service the housing to support the workers—etc., etc., etc.—to create "Ithaca."

It was elementary, and it was fascinating. Many years later, Thys and I would look back on those exciting nights at Cornell. Since then, both of us had helped "build our city." Thys had spearheaded the Commons development, our pedestrian mall, in the early '70s, and dozens of other projects over the next thirty-five years. I had built and renovated dozens of my own projects over the same period. Thys had retired on a city pension and had become an unpaid occasional consultant to my son and son-in-law, who continued our development business under the name Travis Hyde Properties. They carried forward a real estate portfolio that housed hundreds of people, leased to scores of offices and retailers, and supported many dozens of workers and their families.

Of course, generations before us had grown Ithaca organically from the swamps at the base of Cayuga Lake. Ezra Cornell purchased and cultivated the East Hill site for his farm, which became Cornell University. Hundreds—thousands—of men and women were the farmers, shopkeepers, city council members, firefighters, entrepreneurs, visionaries, and real estate developers who shaped Ithaca over two centuries. Ithaca, like every city, was a continuum; many people contributed and would continue to contribute to its past, present, and future.

Completing our evening seminars together those few evenings at the Cornell architecture school, Thys and I had become colleagues and friends. On every future project, I would first run the idea by Thys for his opinion as to its viability.

CHAPTER 3

# THE STRATEGY (1973–92)

## Quality Housing

From its earliest beginnings in 1865, Cornell University housed nearly half its students in private housing within the Ithaca community. Later, dormitories were built, but as Cornell enrollment expanded over the years, many of the once-elegant houses surrounding the university were divided up into funky student apartments—"with character," one might say. The parents bringing their son or daughter to campus might have called them "slums." Over the years, the owners, many of whom were absentee landlords, charged ever-higher rents to students who had little choice other than to rent apartments with ever-lower standards. The housing stock in Ithaca was in a pathetic situation in the early 1970s.

My first houses were purchased as a matter of expediency. They were downtown, several blocks from the university and Ithaca College. They were negotiated for purchase with little or no cash. Each one could produce more income by adding a bedroom or dividing a single-family house into a two-family unit. The demand for housing was phenomenal. Virtually anything would rent. Ithaca's vacancy rate was under 1 percent. One could make money just from owning and managing real estate. Things were looking up.

But as strong as the rental market was, it is probably human nature to figure out how to position oneself to the best advantage—how to lower one's risk and improve one's chances of having success and of making money. If students, and the general public, were being offered junk housing, would it not make sense to adopt an approach of providing "quality housing" for rent? The suburbs had nice housing, but little for rent to students. Besides, students preferred to live within walking distance of their schools. They were captive, so to speak, in a housing market whose quality was declining. If one were to find older, junk properties close to Cornell and close to Ithaca College, and if one were to renovate them into high-quality housing, would the students not flock to them? Would quality properties not have a strong competitive edge? Of course they would. And of course, over time, they did.

I started my new company, Ithaca Rentals & Renovations, based on the following strategy: buy houses as close to the schools as possible. Buy houses that are in a state of disrepair. Improve them and turn them into highly desirable apartments at rents competitive with the junk being offered in the student market. In other words, buy problem properties that could be turned into *quality housing*—for it was in the solving of their problems that value could be created quickly. Problem properties could be bought low and, once improved, fit directly into the intense competition of the student rental market. One could augment one's meager college income and make a living. CLUG had shown that it was simply a matter of adding zeros—000,000,000s—and as long as the bankers went along with the idea, it would work.

And the strategy did work. Collegetown is Ithaca's "second city"—an area of not more than ten blocks adjacent to the university and home to hundreds of Cornell students who rent apartments in the area. I bought my first Collegetown house—a large burned-out shell on Eddy Street, a block from Cornell—with no cash. The owner negotiated, took back a mortgage and subordinated his mortgage for the sale price, to a bank mortgage that financed the renovations. Thus, with a seller's subordinated mortgage and a first mortgage from the bank, I was able to change a burned-out shell into high-quality student housing. The first banker: George Gesslein at Citizens Savings Bank, who over time on that deal became a good friend, a mentor, and a supporter. The system: running the crews in the morning before going to work at Ithaca College; coming back at lunch hour to monitor the progress; returning after work at the end of the day to check on what had been accomplished.

Thys, now firmly ensconced in his job as city planner, helped with the concepts and cheered the project on. Thus, the gutted shell of a three-family row house morphed into several five-bedroom town houses, a two-bedroom unit, a one-bedroom, and a studio. Students stopped by to watch the work—they could see the progress, and they loved the location. Every single unit rented for the next school year even before the sheetrock was hung on the walls. The apartments were rented while the crews were still framing out the units and with no advertising—nothing more than a "picture and a promise." "Quality housing" was indeed going to be a successful approach.

At this point, with this strategy, the goal of *creating an independent income in real estate* seemed like a genuine possibility. Another owner called and offered a second burned-out shell on Quarry Street, three blocks from

**Figure 3.1** The Eddy Street house was a burned-out shell before this reconstruction in 1977. Photo by author.

Cornell, on similar terms. The process was repeated. The lessons learned playing CLUG provided a strong underpinning. The confidence in adding zeros was real. The necessity of fitting into a community with city planners and city building departments and zoning and taxes and roads and sewers was a given. It wasn't that difficult to negotiate. Personal financial survival was still the goal, but in the process, almost by default, one became a member of the community.

Certainly luck played a role—finding and acquiring properties with no cash down, properties where the seller would hold a second mortgage and allow refinancing at the bank with a first mortgage to do the construction, was working. The banks allowed the second mortgage from the seller to serve as the equity in the deal, they would lend 80 percent or even more of the "as-built" value, and the seller would provide the rest. The question was how to grow the business.

Having developed some twenty units in five buildings since 1974, I thought perhaps it would be possible to find a site even closer to the university—perhaps the university itself would have land for sale. It was mid-July 1980. A phone call to the head of Cornell Real Estate, Jim Yarnell, proved fruitful. In our first meeting Jim said the university never sold anything. A few days later he called back. The university did have a three-acre parcel down the hill and across the street from the main campus. They would consider selling that. We met again.

The price, he said, was $125,000. "Is the price negotiable?" I asked. "No." "Would the university finance the acquisition?" "No." "Let me think about it, and I'll call you back."

The first stop was Jim Kerrigan, my attorney. Jim had handled all the previous real estate work and was by now an indispensable sounding board. "They'll sell the land, but they won't negotiate the price at all," I told him. Jim paused, looked across his desk, and said, "What do you care how much it costs? It's three acres across the street from Cornell University!" He was right. What did it matter how much it cost, except I had hardly any cash and the seller wouldn't finance it.

My father had lent me $5,000 as the down payment on the acquisition of an earlier property. The loan was set up as an arm's-length transaction complete with a note written up by Jim Kerrigan. Every single payment had been made on time. Some years later, my father said that he had never expected to get paid back. I had paid him back fully! My "credit was good." He was looking forward to retirement from his engineering business in Nashville. Lending money and becoming a partner in a real estate project run by his son in a town that he and Mother had loved since college could become a source of income for him in the years ahead. Provided the financial pro forma proved successful and the bank would approve financing, he and Mother agreed to lend the $125,000 to purchase the three acres across the street from Cornell.

Kerrigan drew up the purchase offer and submitted it to Jim Yarnell. He took it to the Cornell Board of Trustees for approval. My then accountant, Andy Sciarabba, suggested David Taube of HOLT Architects, who had recently designed a new four-story office building Andy had developed on the former site of the YMCA, which had burned down several years before. The team was in place—Jim, Andy, and David—attorney, accountant, and architect. This team was to be a huge asset for many years to come.

Jim Yarnell called. The Cornell trustees had accepted the purchase offer. My father joined a new limited partnership, Travis and Travis, which on closing would become the owner of a three-acre site across the street from the Cornell campus. It was then that I learned the steps to ground-up real estate development.

David Taube and I worked at his architectural office over a long weekend to design the full concept. The new project could accommodate forty units with parking on the three-acre site. I knew the rental market and what could be expected for rents and operating expenses. David knew the construction process, how to estimate costs for site work, foundations, framing, electrical, plumbing, and finishes. Together we built a financial pro forma with a few sketches of the buildings—a twenty-page business plan, enough to take to the bank for a preliminary look, and enough to satisfy the other partner in Travis and Travis LLC, my dad. Once approved, there would be a project.

The banker, now a friend and supporter, George Gesslein at Citizens Savings Bank, agreed that the $125,000 paid for the land would suffice as the equity down payment on the mortgage. Within a matter of weeks HOLT Architects had developed a full schematic design and construction estimates, and George gave preliminary bank approval. My father's close friend and engineering class of '40 classmate from Cornell, Ray McElwee, had worked as a contractor, constructing scores of buildings in Ithaca over the past forty years. Like my father, Ray was close to retirement. He agreed to join the team as a construction consultant. Compared with building a forty-unit building from the ground up, the proposed general contractor (GC)—me—had only the limited experience of simple renovations.

With Ray looking over my shoulder, my father and the bank agreed I could serve as GC for the project. And although he recused himself from the vote, it didn't hurt that Ray served on the board of directors for Citizens Savings Bank. With the accounting, legal, and design team in place, and now with an experienced contractor providing oversight to the inexperienced GC, our project had instant credibility.

Could the project proceed? Ray checked the architect's preliminary construction estimates. He did his own materials takeoff, making many suggestions and changes. We all waited anxiously for his determination as to the financial viability of the project. David Taube suggested it could be done by fast-tracking the development process, which meant the first building would be designed, permitted, and under construction while HOLT completed the design for each of the other buildings in sequence. The idea of fast-tracking was brilliant—this would save months of time waiting for the design and approval of the entire project before starting construction. It was important that the new project open the following August in time for the new school year.

Ray finally completed the construction budget and agreed that the project was viable. The bank agreed to the financing, and Travis and Travis closed on the land with Cornell. Again, with Ray's help, we selected and obtained bids from the subcontractors and began construction in late September. In less than two months the land had been secured, financing was in place, working drawings for the first phase of construction were completed, the building permit was issued, and our subcontractor was excavating and pouring the footers. Construction work on Travis and Travis's first major real estate development had begun.

The construction was completed in less than a year, and the ribbon was cut on the forty-unit complex, which we named Ravenwood. The university was pleased. Ravenwood became the first new housing development designed specifically for students outside of the dorms on Cornell's campus.

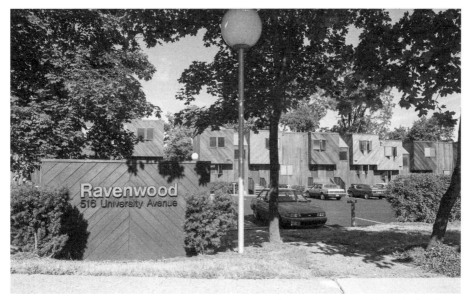

**Figure 3.2**  Ravenwood, home to 140 students, opened fully leased in 1981. Photo by Jon Reis.

**Figure 3.3**  Forty apartments, one block from Cornell University. Photo by Jon Reis.

It accommodated 140 students, and once again the project was fully leased for the following fall semester from a "picture and a promise" even before the sheetrock was on the walls. Quality housing was paying off again.

Shortly before completing construction on Ravenwood, another opportunity appeared. Stu Lewis, a wealthy retailer who owned a building in Collegetown, called. He had a four-story tenement-style building at 407 College Avenue with two retail shops on the ground floor and three floors of apartments above. The building, located less than half a block from the main entrance to the Cornell campus, was nearly a century old. It needed major renovation, and Stu wanted to sell. We met at the property. He agreed to finance the purchase and again subordinate his mortgage on the property to the first money mortgage that would be required for renovation. George Gesslein again agreed to lend the money for a total renovation. Thys again guided the project through the zoning and construction codes. Within another year, 407 College Avenue was gutted and redesigned, and new housing for fifty more Cornell students was completed. The strategy of providing quality housing was now a well-tested formula.

Number 407 was basically a tenement-style house with porches across the front and long railroad apartments running the east–west length of either side of the building. The strategy was to divide the building midway north and south by building a stair tower on each side of the building, thereby picking up the use of the interior former stair and ventilation space for kitchens and bathrooms. Three eight-bedroom units would be built across the front, and two three-bedroom units on either side across the back half of the building.

The large apartments were a huge hit with the students. Once again, they were leased before construction even started.

These real estate deals had appeared serendipitously and fully in the open. It never occurred to me that in some cities it takes under-the-table money to make things happen. Thys's only motivation was to make the city of Ithaca a better, stronger place. The banker, the contractors, the city inspectors—all were aboveboard. In my forty years of developing real estate in Ithaca, not a single palm was ever greased.

Before the end of the 407 construction in 1982, David Taube of HOLT Architects called to say the city had announced plans to issue an RFP (request for proposal) for a developer to take the lead on a major Collegetown redevelopment project. The city of Ithaca and Cornell University would provide the site—a vacant parking lot bordering the campus. A US Department of Housing and Urban Development (HUD) grant to the city would be made available to the chosen developer as a loan at 1 percent interest to assist with secondary financing. All that was needed was a developer

**Figure 3.4** Construction under way at 407 College Avenue, 1982. Photo by Jon Reis.

to work with the city and Cornell to create a project that would provide jobs in order to qualify for the 1 percent HUD loan and hopefully inspire others to begin work on this blighted, neglected, yet extremely popular area bordering the university.

Although there had been plenty of risk involved in each of my projects to date, and although this one appeared to be a long shot—finding

**Figure 3.5** After an eighty-seven-day total gut and renovation, 407 College Avenue housed fifty-six students. Photo by Jon Reis.

the funding, working with so many parties within the community—it made sense to give it a try. There was nothing to lose by submitting the application. Meetings with the city and Cornell were required as part of the application process. Two major developers (one local and one from New York City) were the competition. My team made its presentation to the selection committee, and I was dumbstruck when we were selected over the two very substantial developers. Thys told me that the selection committee liked the work we had done with student housing at Raven-wood and 407. They liked the initial design approach we had laid out in the application. They liked our local team. And they probably liked the idea that I was thirty-eight, young, and pliable. Cornell and city officials probably felt I would follow their suggestions and their vision for what should be built.

All that said, we were selected. It took five years, four different conceptual designs, and unbelievable patience working with the city planning department, the city council, and the university administration to complete this project. Two local businessmen joined us as partners. My family sank our savings into the quarter million dollars in soft costs to cover feasibility studies and design, closing HUD and bond financing before we could even break ground. By taking that risk up front, we were able to construct and finally, in 1987, cut the ribbon on Eddygate—eight stories, sixty-four units, and seven stores in the heart of Collegetown. Eddygate was surrounded by a new city parking garage, the new $26 million Schwartz Center for the Performing Arts, and two newly renovated Cornell dorms—all built more or less at the same time.

The strategy of building quality housing had dovetailed nicely with the city's and university's desire to improve the housing stock at the entrance to the Cornell campus. With a lot of support and assistance from both entities, Eddygate became the pioneer project in the redevelopment of Collegetown. As planned, the idea caught on, and other developers began constructing building after building in Collegetown. At last Cornell had an entrance to the university that they could be proud of; the city had an increased tax base; and at Eddygate, 180 students now had a better place

**Figure 3.6** The Eddygate building in 1987. Sixty-four apartments and seven retail tenants. It took five years to permit and build Eddygate, which opened fully rented. The two Cornell dormitories and the Schwartz Center for the Performing Arts are in the background. Photo by Jon Reis.

to live—with several new restaurants, an optician, a stuffed animal store, and a copy center.

Later, Thys told me that his motivation for the effort in Collegetown and for the government support for a private-sector construction project was to prove the market for new, quality student-housing construction in College-town. The investment repaid the city handsomely. In the thirty-five years that started with Eddygate, city property tax revenues from Collegetown have grown far beyond expectations. In addition to the parking garage and as part of the overall project, the city made a substantial investment in the public infrastructure in Collegetown. Streets and sidewalks were recon-structed, and small open spaces and street amenities, including benches, improved lighting, and plantings, were designed and constructed.

With a lot of support and assistance from the city and the community, from business partners and family members, the project was successful. The concepts from CLUG were making more sense now than ever. A developer does become part of the community, and quality housing is indeed the key to success in real estate.

While working on Eddygate, I acquired two additional brick apartment complexes on the north side of Cornell—Westview and Lakeland Apart-ments, close to a hundred units in total. It was 1984, and in the midst of all these new acquisitions and development projects, I remarried.

Continuing to expand the real estate portfolio into downtown Ithaca, in 1988 my wife Carol and I bought a set of three-story row houses built

**Figure 3.7** Westview Apartments. Fifty-six units, purchased in 1985. Photo by Jon Reis.

exactly a century earlier, in 1888, across the street from the Tompkins County Courthouse. Constructed of brick, the three row houses had bay windows and three lovely arched entrances across the street front, two of which had been bricked in when the buildings were turned into a single dorm for Ithaca College in 1929. Inside, the floors were out of level and slanted from wall to wall. Carol did some research in the archives at Ithaca College and found its historic name to be Westminster Hall.

As the crews gutted the building, they found the rear wall was basically a stack of bricks with the interior supporting studs rotted out and turned to powder from decades of water dripping down inside the wall. The crews repaired the roof and the gutters; they went to the basement and poured new footers; they added a steel supporting structure up through the building; they rebuilt the teetering back wall and entirely repointed the brick exterior with fresh mortar. They totally rebuilt the building inside and out. It opened in 1989, with nine apartments on the top two floors, and offices for Ithaca Rentals & Renovations and Travis & Travis Real Estate Development on the ground floor. This was our first historic renovation.

For the next project, in 1990, together with our two Eddygate partners, Cayuga Apartments, LLC was set up to purchase a handsome, neo-Georgian brick apartment building that was six stories high, had twenty-six units, and was located on a main street corner across from DeWitt Park in downtown Ithaca. Our business strategy was evolving from simply providing quality housing for students as close as possible to the university to expanding into any properties we could find at the right price and terms, and that had potential for income growth. Our approach in offering quality housing was continuing to pay off.

**Figure 3.8**  Westminster Hall, built in 1888, purchased and renovated in 1988. Photo by Jon Reis.

**Figure 3.9** Cayuga Apartments. Twenty-six units, built in 1933, purchased in 1990. Photo by Jon Reis.

**Figure 3.10** The River House. Seventy-two units in Binghamton, New York, acquired out of bankruptcy in 1992, 27 percent vacant. We renovated it and had it filled within a year. Photo by Jon Reis.

Although we were focusing on quality housing in Ithaca, I couldn't pass up the opportunity when a bankruptcy trustee called me one afternoon and asked if I would like to look at his portfolio of foreclosed properties. A couple of days later he came to my office with a folder three inches thick filled with photos and specs of property after property that his bank had repossessed in upstate New York—Watertown, Newburgh, Poughkeepsie—traditional two-and-a-half-story garden apartments built in the 1960s and '70s, let go by their owners, grass growing up through the parking lots. This was not Ithaca. Then he turned the page to a seven-story brick building in Binghamton— the River House, right on the Chenango River. This was it! Seventy-two units, built in 1963, 27 percent vacant, foreclosed for $2.9 million; the bank was asking $1.9. I said I was interested and would talk it over with Carol. We'd be back to him on Monday. That Sunday we drove to Binghamton to take a look. The building was locked—a good sign. We pressed a buzzer for the top floor. An elderly woman answered, and I told her my wife and I were down from Ithaca and looking to rent an apartment. Would she be so kind as to show us hers? Of course she would, she said. And what an apartment—hardwood floors, two and a half bathrooms, a balcony looking over the city, and three huge bedrooms. On Monday I wrote an offer to the foreclosure trustee for $1 million.

It took the better part of a year to negotiate the deal, but eventually the bank sold it to us for $1.1 million and lent us another $450,000 to put into redecorating and upgrading hallways, kitchens, and baths. Our problem property was in excellent condition, and within six months the River House was 100 percent rented. I found out later that the owner lived in the Bronx, had built the building in 1963, and had been very successful with it. He refinanced it after twenty-some years for the $2.9 million, installed a half million in new windows, and then seemed to lose interest. By now he was elderly. The trustee said his new manager and her husband were alcoholics and had been purchasing carpet and materials on the building account, reselling them to other parties, and pocketing the money themselves—hence the eventual foreclosure. Not all problems with properties stem from being run down. Management and attention to detail are key. Whatever the problem, I was more convinced than ever that turning a problem property into quality housing was a sure way to success.

# CHAPTER 4

# CENTER ITHACA (1980–94)

## A Financial Failure

Shortly after construction of the Ithaca Commons in 1974, the city planner, Thys Van Cort, actively sought and obtained a HUD grant for development of a vacant urban renewal site directly on the Commons. The
historic Rothschild's Department Store had been torn down in the '60s,
and the site had been vacant ever since, used at various times as a skating
rink, as home to the farmers market, as the site of the first Ithaca Festival,
and, sadly, as a trash dump in the very heart of downtown.

A local development team consisting of Stanley Goldberg and Scott
McRobb, working with the city and utilizing below-market Urban

**Figure 4.1** Vacant urban renewal site, a huge "missing tooth" in our downtown smile.
Photo by Jon Reis.

Development Action Grant (UDAG) financing, designed and began construction on Center Ithaca, a 144,000-square-foot mixed-use building with
sixty-two apartments, a public atrium, a dozen stores, and twenty offices
adjoining the new city parking garage. Its facade, designed by internationally
known architect Werner Seligmann, appeared on the cover of the magazine
*Progressive Architecture* (*PA*). Thys tells the story that Seligmann once said
to him during the design of Center Ithaca: "I am not designing this building for Ithaca. I'm designing it for the cover of *Progressive Architecture*."
It turns out that he was the guest editor of *PA* for the edition that featured
Center Ithaca on the cover. Center Ithaca was completed and opened. It
was a financial failure from the start.

**Figure 4.2** In 1980 construction began on Center Ithaca, the 144,000-square-
foot building adjoining the new Green Street parking garage. Photo by Jon Reis.

**Figure 4.3** Construction under way on Center Ithaca (1980). Photo by
Jon Reis.

**Figure 4.4** The new facade of Center Ithaca with the retail storefronts designed by HOLT Architects. Photo by Jon Reis.

Originally, Seligmann designed the food court to be in the basement, and retail was to be conducted from rolling kiosks at street level. One entered through the garage-like doors built across the front facade. Seligmann had modeled it after Faneuil Hall in Boston, a city with several million people. However, this was downtown Ithaca, New York, with a population of only thirty thousand on a good day. The project was conceptually flawed considering our much smaller Ithaca market.

The developers were enterprising. Within two years they convinced bankers and investors to do a second, new public offering and raised an additional $4 million to renovate the unsuccessful two-year-old potential anchor building for downtown. The local firm of HOLT Architects was selected to redesign the building. They moved the food shops from the basement to the first-floor atrium, removed the garage doors and the kiosks, and built out real storefronts on the Commons. Occupancy improved slightly, but the vacancy rate hovered around 20 percent.

Thys tells another Seligmann story. Bob O'Brien, one of the principals of HOLT Architects, was at an American Institute of Architects accreditation dinner sitting next to Werner Seligmann. Seligmann drank a little too much and soon was bragging about his achievements. He told Bob that he never listened to the client, and said to Bob that HOLT Architects would never be anything but hacks because they did. Bob finally had enough; he turned to Werner and said, "Maybe that's why we are redesigning your building."

With the failed start-up and the additional debt load, when the building went bankrupt in 1994, it went under owing $21 million. In fourteen years it had never paid a dime of debt service. The investors lost all their original investment, plus they had tax recapture on the write-off they had claimed for fourteen years. They were not happy. The original $8 million loan was 85 percent guaranteed by the Farmers Home Administration, so at least our local banks didn't get hurt too badly. They began looking for a buyer. This was my first experience of having a bank contact me about a deal.

I had two moneyed partners that had joined in on Eddygate. I had a management firm. There was concern in the business community and at city hall that Jason Fane, a landlord known for his extremely aggressive rents and large numbers of vacant stores on the Commons, would buy the building. He had already made an offer surpassing the amount Stan Goldberg and Scott McRobb had offered in their attempt to do a "cram down" with the banks on the first mortgage—their idea was to retain ownership by offering the bank a severely discounted buyout of the first mortgage. When the trustee for the foreclosure heard the offer from Jason, he decided the property should be put up for auction and sold to the highest bidder. Andy Sciarabba invited me to his office, where he laid out the proposed deal from the banks.

One of my two partners was already an investor in Center Ithaca. Andy told me that if the three of us made an offer and we won the auction for the property, the banks would agree to finance it with only 10 percent equity in the property. My partners and I discussed it. It was important to the city that the public restrooms and use of the atrium be kept as public amenities. This had been one of the conditions of the initial HUD grant for the property. It was a quasi-public-private partnership. The public side of it could have disappeared with foreclosure to an unsympathetic buyer, but we agreed that should we be successful in winning the auction for the property, the public restrooms and the use of the atrium as a public space in the heart of downtown would remain.

The bank commissioned a Member Appraisal Institute (MAI) appraisal on the property—one of the highest standard appraisals available. The valuation came in at $3.25 million. The three of us agreed to go in on the deal as equal general partners and offer the MAI appraised value at the auction, but no higher. I would be the managing partner responsible for turning the building around. We had the mortgage papers drawn up at the lead bank and left early one morning with our attorney, Peter Walsh, for the four-hour drive to Albany.

There were hundreds of people in the courtroom. Many projects were being offered one by one to the highest bidder. Our turn came. We had been looking around for Jason. Surely he was going to bid on it. The judge asked if there were any bids on the "Ithaca Center" property. We waited. No sign of Jason. The judge asked again for bids. Peter spoke up and said his client was

**Figure 4.5** The Center Ithaca atrium and food court—a quasi-public space. Photo by Jon Reis.

prepared to offer $3.25 million. We looked around for Jason to raise our bid. If he was there, he wasn't raising his hand. The judge asked our attorney if this offer was a fair price. He told the judge it was the MAI appraised value. The judge seemed satisfied. "Going once; going twice . . ." We looked again— no Jason. The judge pounded down his gavel. "Sold to the highest bidder."

Nearly $17 million had gone up in smoke. It was 1994, and my partners and I now owned the largest building in downtown Ithaca.

Seeing Jason on the Commons some months later, I told him we had been quite surprised that he was not at the auction. Jason smiled easily and said, "Enjoy your new building." I was grateful for that response. I thought later, it must not have fit into his strategy for downtown acquisitions. He could easily have outbid us had he chosen to.

My partners and I met regularly. We agreed to a restructuring of the rents, and renovations on sections of the building. Within a year, it was turned around from 20 percent vacant to 100 percent leased. We were now completely invested in the success of downtown.

CHAPTER 5

# THE BID (1993–95)

## A Business Improvement District

Later in 1994, we got a call from Ken Walker, one of the partners in our accounting firm Sciarabba Walker & Co. He said, "We need you to join the steering committee to help form a business improvement district—a BID."

"No thanks, Ken. I appreciate your thinking of me, but I don't have time for the civic stuff. I'm too busy running my own business" was my response.

A week later Ken called again. I gave the same answer. A week later he called a third time. He'd obviously been charged by the mayor with forming this committee, and he was twisting my arm, and hard. Given his perseverance and his partnership with Andy Sciarabba—my accountant and one of my principal advisers—I decided to listen.

"OK, so what's a BID?" I asked. "What's involved?"

Ken described a business improvement district as a set of enabling legislation at a state level that allowed a municipality to form the boundaries of an "assessment district" to raise money for an operating budget by assessing property owners up to 20 percent of the city taxes. The members within the BID would form a board of directors comprised of property owners, merchants, tenants, and city council members. With input from the BID membership, the board of directors would set the priorities of what they expected the BID to accomplish.

More taxes? More government involvement? Yes, but it sounded like this could be an opportunity to have a direct hand in establishing the priorities for the area within a BID district. It would very probably include some of our downtown properties, and very probably would improve the market, as well as positively affect the rental market. With the purchase of Cayuga Apartments, the Westminster building, and now Center Ithaca, Carol and I were becoming heavily invested. That part sounded interesting.

Ken concluded, "The mayor has directed the city planning department to establish a steering committee in order to determine whether this could be a useful tool for downtown Ithaca. You were recommended to become a member." I agreed to attend the first meeting of the steering committee.

Ithaca is a small town. The census for 1990 showed a population of just under 29,500 within the city limits, including the students at Cornell and Ithaca College who resided in the city. There were roughly fifty thousand in the urbanized area and about a hundred thousand in the county.

While Ithaca is a very pleasant small city, the downtown was deteriorating. The vacancy rate in the downtown retail stores was over 20 percent. Maintenance costs on our pedestrian mall—the Commons, now almost twenty years old—were appalling. Police presence was spotty. The center of downtown had devolved from a strong retail center with national stores such as the Gap, CVS, Rite Aid, and B. Dalton Bookseller, to a run-down, problematic center for the homeless and all that they brought with them. Ithaca was not unlike most small towns across the upstate area, except that it had the saving grace of our parklike (although by now decrepit) pedestrian mall as the center of its downtown.

The city had intervened in Collegetown adjacent to Cornell over a decade earlier when we were chosen as the preferred developer. Our public-private endeavor there had stimulated significant development in the area and improved the major entrance to Cornell University.

While most of our property holdings were concentrated up the hill close to the university, Carol and I were becoming more involved in downtown real estate. It might make sense to see what this "BID" could do, if anything, to improve downtown and thereby protect our investment there.

Over the years, I had watched in city meetings as irate property owners confronted the zoning board, planning board, or Common Council with loud and often unreasonable demands only to come away disappointed and bitter. Eddygate had been a lesson in the democratic process. Since, as preferred developer, I was applying through the city for a HUD grant, every decision on the Eddygate project had to be considered, debated, discussed, and voted on by the Common Council. It was tedious. It was often frustrating.

I was an entrepreneur, used to making my own considered decisions and putting them into action. An important lesson I had learned from Eddygate was that no one person, no matter how good their ideas, could ride roughshod over the rest of us. And that included me. I could make all the considered decisions I wanted, but they could not be put into action until they had been approved by the planning board, the Common Council, and the Ithaca Urban Renewal Agency. I learned to be patient and follow the process—the democratic process.

I found that a conciliatory approach was more effective—*asking* if a plan would work, *asking* what changes the city recommended—and then

listening and adapting. This required getting to know the players in each
city department, learning the name of each building inspector in charge
of code inspections, working with them, and including them in the early
planning stages of each project. I had taken the approach that the city of
Ithaca administration was an ally in each and every project. And they were.
Our city planner, Thys, was always a supporter of my projects, and a good
friend at a professional level. Most of the city staff were knowledgeable and
helpful in their fields. Most of the committee members for planning and
zoning were volunteers, people doing their civic duty, and all were interested in creating the most desirable Ithaca they could conceive of.

The first meeting of the BID steering committee was convened in Ken
Walker's conference room. There were over fifteen of us assembled, including
major property owners and their managers; tenants, merchants, architects;
the deputy director of planning and development, Herman Sieverding; and
a representative from Common Council. Herman told us that in July 1990,
then mayor Ben Nichols had formed the Downtown Vision Task Force
(DVTF) to address issues and problems facing downtown such as increasing retail vacancies and an exodus of professional and service businesses
to Lansing, northeast of Ithaca. Downtown didn't have enough parking.
There was increased competition from the suburban Pyramid Mall, from
catalog shopping, and from discount stores. The DVTF had commissioned
Halcyon, a Washington, DC–based consultant, to survey downtown Ithaca
and develop strategies for improving retail sales and business retention.

In their report to the city in January 1991, Halcyon had presented nine
strategies for downtown revitalization. They recommended formation of
a business improvement district to implement them, and that is why we
were gathered here. In February 1991, the DVTF issued a report based on
the Halcyon findings in which they stated,

> Revitalization of the downtown area, taking advantage of its many strengths,
> is a primary goal of the Ithaca community. The downtown should continue
> to serve as the center of the county's economic, social, and cultural life. . . .
> Strong support is required from . . . City and . . . County Government . . . ,
> from businesses . . . developers, arts organizations, Cornell and Ithaca Col-
> lege, and—above all—from all citizens of the Ithaca area.

The report went on with a list of recommended approaches:

- **Architecture and land use**: "Development should enhance the
  unique character and scale of our small city. . . . Land use regulations
  should be modified as required."

- **Retail environment**: "Specialty shops . . . should be strengthened. . . . A higher level of coordinated marketing should be achieved. . . . Restaurants and cafés . . . should offer . . . diverse experiences, including outdoor ambiance."
- **Commercial and office environment**: "The County government should be encouraged to concentrate its offices in the downtown area. . . . Downtown should continue to be the financial center of the county. . . . Retention of government, financial, and other professional businesses . . . upgrading of existing office space and construction of some new Class A space . . . is a key factor."
- **Culture and the arts**: "Integration of studios, . . . performing locations, art exhibit areas, schools and galleries into the fabric of the city should be encouraged. . . . In addition, a center of arts activity located downtown would be an important component."
- **Transportation and parking**: "Maximize public access . . . [with] creation of additional . . . parking, and the development of programs that reduce the need for single-occupancy automobile trips. . . . The parking system as a whole needs to be managed in an organized and understandable manner which would support retail and office activities."
- **Marketing**: "Downtown Ithaca should be the primary focus of the County's tourism effort. . . . Visitors are crucial to the success of the downtown. . . . [Consider] development of additional conference or small convention business, probably in conjunction with Cornell."
- **Arts center and conference center**: "The development of a facility . . . for an Arts Center or Conference Center could have an important impact on the community."
- **Housing**: "Should be abundant for all income levels, and should provide a variety of ownership or rental options."
- **Linkages**: "Downtown Ithaca . . . should seek innovative ways to increase its connections with the broader community."

This was comprehensive. It was going to be a lot of work: housing, arts, transportation, parking, marketing, office, retail, land use . . .

Herman laid out the basic legislation. He told the steering committee that BIDs are tools for community and economic development. Whereas special districts are created for a whole host of *single purposes* (sidewalks, libraries, parks, water, schools, lighting, and so on), BIDs can be used for *multiple purposes* relating to the betterment of the district. They essentially are special districts with a twist. He told us BIDs had become a primary tool in downtown revitalization and management and were prevalent across North America and indeed worldwide. (There are BIDs in nearly one thousand cities nationwide—at least one in every state. New York City alone has sixty-seven BIDs; Albany, the state capital, has a BID comprised of fifty square blocks. It is charged with *restoring, promoting, and maintaining the character and vitality of downtown Albany.*) Herman told us that BIDs were a proven method for redevelopment and revitalization of a downtown area. He said the mayor felt that downtown Ithaca would benefit from the formation of a local BID, and we, as the steering committee, were charged with its formation.

We learned that to form a BID, the steering committee must first determine the boundaries of the BID district. It must hold town meetings and survey the owners, residents, and merchants within the district to determine their major concerns. The resulting *district BID plan* would then lay out the structure of the BID—what its staffing and budget would look like—and what its major activities would be. Would the BID charge the maximum 20 percent of the city tax rate permitted, or a lower amount? In other words, if a property owner pays $5,000 in city taxes on their property annually, will the district BID plan, once adopted, set their BID assessment at $1,000 per year (20 percent annually) or less? We could set the assessment percentage at any amount up to 20 percent. The only catch was that 51 percent of the property owners within the defined district had to approve the plan, but once they did, every property owner in the district could be assessed—the democratic process.

With the funds raised from the assessment, Herman explained, the BID could hire an executive director and support staff. It could undertake whatever projects its membership directed it to undertake—including expanding maintenance, hiring security, and conducting outreach and marketing programs to help fill vacant stores. Some BIDs in the country even took over management of the parking garages, security, and trash pickup within their boundaries. Some became developers in their own right through formation of an LDC—a Local Development Council. The opportunities were limited only by the collective imaginations of the membership and the board of directors that would be formed to oversee the BID.

We questioned Herman. Were we not taxed enough? Was the city not just sneaking in double taxation by forming the BID to take over what should be basic city services? Was this not a sly way to get more money out of the property owners? Would not property owners be up in arms about this additional *tax*—this "assessment" of up to 20 percent of their annual city tax? Herman said these were legitimate concerns the property owners would have, but the legislation spelled out that any services performed by the BID should be *in addition to current services offered by the municipality.* The city could not cut back on police services, maintenance crews, or trash collection because now they were being supplemented by the BID. The city could not lower their existing level of service within the BID boundaries once the BID administration took over whatever services it determined needed improvement. In fact, the legislation directed that a *memorandum of understanding* (MOU) be enacted between the city and the BID—an agreement that would spell out the current level of services that the city provides, and the city would acknowledge that the BID budget would be used toward additional selected areas of improvement as determined by the BID board of directors.

The initial task of the steering committee was to lay out the proposed boundaries for the business improvement district. Next, the committee would design a survey for the membership, and then, utilizing the survey, it would hold half a dozen public meetings, at different locations within the area, to determine the concerns of the people. It would then reconvene and develop a district BID plan that would lay out the proposed priorities for the BID, the percentage amount of the assessment up to 20 percent, the budget, and the basic plans for establishing this new structure.

By now I was fully committed to this civic endeavor. It took several meetings over a period of a few months to come to agreement on the boundaries. The committee members grew more and more enthusiastic about the entire process as we proceeded. Here was an opportunity to take matters into our own hands, bypassing the sometimes cumbersome and unresponsive bureaucracy of city hall and the department of public works. The committee agreed on the boundaries recommended by Halcyon, which covered a wide area of downtown, including over 140 blocks radiating out from the central Ithaca Commons.

The chosen area was diverse. The boundaries encompassed two major retail centers, with lots of rental and private residences in between, a host of county and city offices, and dozens of attorneys' offices. If Ithaca was going to create a BID, the committee wanted it to be as strong and diverse as we could possibly make it. We had learned we could not just include the retail and commercial areas without including all the intervening residential area. The enabling legislation required that BID boundaries be contiguous.

The mayor had charged the steering committee with beginning this process of establishing a BID. The committee was comprised of local merchants, property owners, and city representatives, with Ken Walker, the president of Sciarabba Walker, a major accounting firm in downtown Ithaca, as the head. The steering committee organized and prepared a draft of the district BID plan and designed the survey. As the survey results came in, the committee members were so enthusiastic about what we heard in the public meetings that in our naïveté we stated publicly that if we didn't get at least 75 percent of the property owners within the district voting in favor of the district BID plan, we would scrap the idea.

The required public meetings were held throughout the proposed BID district. With the BID, property owners, merchants, and tenants would have a structure that would allow them to improve this area themselves, semi-independent from the city. What did residents and property owners want? What were the concerns of the potential members within the proposed district? They responded: "Fill the vacancies. Clean up the area. Repair the potholes. Keep us safe from crime. Bring in national stores again to our downtown."

Utilizing the input from these public meetings, Herman wrote up several drafts for approval by the committee. He distributed the final draft to the proposed membership area in preparation for the vote. The committee members all felt that the BID was too good an idea not to pass with 75 percent of the vote, and we stated again that we would not proceed without that majority. How could anyone not like the idea of improving cleanliness, safety, parking, and filling the stores? The downtown would be vibrant and active once again. How could anyone with any sense vote against it?

A local attorney on the proposed northern border of the BID district led the charge against the plan. "A 20 percent assessment?!" (The committee had proposed only a 17.5 percent increase in the city taxes, not 20 percent, but the idea of increasing taxes on the outskirts of the BID for the benefit of the central core of downtown, the retail district, was more controversial than we realized.) Didn't everyone accept the steering committee's view that a more economically viable and aesthetically pleasing downtown was in everyone's interests? Apparently not. The plan garnered over half the vote, but that was not enough. The committee had publicly stated that it would not enact the plan unless 75 percent of the property owners in the district voted in favor of it—52 percent or 53 percent wouldn't do.

The original effort to establish a BID had lasted two years. The steering committee's time had been wasted. The mayor was not happy. The committee was not happy. We dropped the idea, dissolved the committee, and went on with our lives. We had learned what a business improvement district could do. We had learned how to set one up, but to no avail. I went back to focusing on my real estate development and management activities. It was 1995.

# CHAPTER 6

# A SECOND ATTEMPT (1996–98)
## Success

It had been two years since Ken Walker first convened the steering committee meeting for the BID. It had been a year since the committee gave up on its first attempt to establish the BID. The mayor still thought it was a good idea. After the purchase of Center Ithaca, my partners and I were even more committed to seeing downtown revitalized. Herman Sieverding, Thys's deputy director of planning and development, reconvened the BID steering committee.

At the first meeting, the committee agreed that this time they would abide by the "democratic process." Anything over 50 percent of the vote would suffice to establish the BID. However, this time the group would do what they could do to ensure that they succeeded in passing the BID legislation for downtown Ithaca. They shrank the BID district. We all agreed the first boundaries had been too large, too diverse. The decision was made to cut back the boundaries to the two blocks surrounding the Commons. The new boundaries encompassed only twenty-two blocks on the four sides around the Commons, far less than the 144 blocks originally proposed. This eliminated most of the single-family residences. It eliminated the antagonistic attorneys who didn't see the advantage of paying the assessment to improve the services in our downtown area. It focused the BID on the central core of downtown.

The state-mandated survey was repeated. Again, the committee held the public meetings. The concerns were the same—cleanliness, safety, more parking, fewer vacancies. The district BID plan was rewritten with the revised boundaries, and this time it passed with 52 percent of the vote. It was smaller than originally planned, but we had established the Downtown Ithaca Business Improvement District in the central core of downtown Ithaca.

The district BID plan had called for a committee structure that would address the concerns of the membership: business retention and development, events and marketing, government relations, as well as the usual finance and executive committees. The board of directors would have a member appointed by the city council, several merchants, several property owners who were also merchants, one residential tenant, and several additional property owners, including representatives from a local bank that owned their own building downtown. Initially, there were about a dozen members on our board. M&T Bank provided their conference room. We met weekly for the next six months—long, four- or five-hour meetings—to organize, build a budget, and implement a nationwide search for an executive director.

The search attracted several applicants, and we hired a young director, Doug Pessefall, who had run a BID in Piqua, Ohio, for three years. Doug arrived in town, rented an office, hired staff, and began the business of the BID. He held a public competition to choose a name, and out of fifty suggestions, the board chose "Ithaca Downtown Partnership" (IDP). Our tagline: *It Works!* The BID would be known as the IDP, and it would work. The executive director negotiated with the city to take over downtown events, such as summer concerts, holiday decorations, and celebrations. The board completed a memorandum of understanding with the city to ensure that city services would not be reduced, and that in the case of the events, if the BID took them over, it would be paid to do so by the city.

During the initial period of establishing the BID, the steering committee appointed by the mayor had been charged with performing a survey to see what the public's concerns were for the proposed BID area. What were the problems? What did the property owners, the merchants, the residential tenants, and the city administration want to see happen in their new business improvement district?

Of the scores of surveys returned, some emphasized parking, some cleanliness, some more security and police presence downtown, but invariably, every survey returned included the statement: "Fill the vacancies!" Fill the vacant storefronts. Bring new life back to the Commons, our pedestrian mall.

In the public meetings, my response to the idea of filling the vacancies had been: *You don't just go out and fill vacancies.* That's rather like saying, *Be happy.* No one can force you to be happy. They can create an environment that causes you to feel good and be happy, but they cannot force you to *be happy.* Neither can a new business improvement district force potential store owners to fill vacancies. We have to create the environment that will attract them, that will attract shoppers to their stores. We have to charm them into their decision to locate in our downtown. We can't just make them relocate in downtown Ithaca and be happy.

There were steps to go through in this "happiness business." While our storefronts weren't yet boarded up, we had to create a renewed and attractive environment so people would want to shop downtown. With new shoppers would come new owners to fill the vacant storefronts. To create a renewed environment downtown, the BID had to move on all fronts at once. It wasn't enough to plant more flowers in the planter beds on the Commons. It wasn't enough to see that the streets were cleaned regularly and the sidewalks and tree grates kept in a better state of repair. It wasn't enough to have a policeman on every corner, as there had been in the old days. It wasn't enough to have more parking and free parking, concerts, and events—all these things alone just weren't enough. Santa Claus arriving every Christmas. Decorations and banners on the light poles. Freshly painted benches. New buildings, hotels, offices, housing, publicity, and marketing for downtown—none of it by itself would be enough. We needed all of it! And we needed it all to happen at once!

One person, one leader, one developer, cannot be expected to do everything needed to cover all aspects of downtown revitalization. Committees provided opportunities for people to join in, to participate and share in the decisions that were forming our downtown. There is strength in numbers. The original structure of the BID in the district BID plan had set forth a committee structure. We were, after all, the Ithaca Downtown *Partnership*. We had four hundred member businesses and property owners in the district. Each committee of the BID was formed with from six to twelve volunteer members from the membership. The chair of each committee was a member of our board of directors. Our committees addressed each area of concern that our membership had expressed for downtown:

The *government relations committee* was charged with working with city government to improve police presence downtown, parking management, cleanliness, trash pickup, and signage . . . anything relating to city government.

The *marketing and events committee* was charged with planning and publicizing events such as our concerts, sidewalk-sale days, holiday decorations, and craft fairs. It was charged with creating a complete marketing plan for downtown. They were the BID's publicists.

The *business retention and development committee* was charged with retaining existing businesses within the district and bringing in new ones. It would work with developers on their new buildings and recruit new store owners through trips to neighboring cities. It would develop a database of vacancies and publicity to place on the BID website. The activity of this committee relied heavily on the activities of the other committees to create the attractive, "be happy" environment. Its primary job was to bring in new businesses.

The *finance committee*, working with the executive director, developed an annual budget and performed monthly reviews and oversight of BID income and expenses.

The *executive committee* assisted the executive director in setting the focus and priorities of the organization. It also functioned as the personnel committee, setting policy for BID employees and developing a personnel handbook for BID staff.

The BID board of directors expanded. The board gradually added a representative each from the county, Cornell, the chamber of commerce, and Ithaca College. Over time, the BID board of directors grew to nineteen members. The committees learned their roles. We proved we could operate the BID for the betterment of downtown—and the executive director oversaw it all.

Doug, as our new ED, began meeting the membership and scouring the countryside and surrounding towns for new retail prospects to fill the 20 percent vacant stores within the district. The board meetings calmed down to one a month instead of one a week. He found and furnished an office for the organization, and the committees began their work on promotions and events, establishing outdoor dining on the Commons, developing the website, holding breakfast roundtables with business owners, volunteers, and the mayor. We hired a marketing director. The police satellite office was established on the Commons in Center Ithaca—in a space that my partners and I donated to the City of Ithaca Police Department.

Doug had the idea for, and set up, an open house for retailers. The BID would advertise regionally for people interested in starting new businesses to come to Ithaca in the spring. They would meet in a large vacant store, hear a few retailers and board members speak about the advantages of doing business in Ithaca, and then take a tour of the vacancies. It seemed like a great idea. The board fully endorsed it. Advertising was placed. The board members set up chairs in one of the vacant stores on the Commons and prepared refreshments. The members were pleased and surprised when forty people showed up on a Saturday morning to hear about the downtown and tour the vacant storefronts.

"Downtown Ithaca is a neighborhood," began one of the retailers who was presenting. "We know each other. We help each other to succeed. We share market data. We lobby the city for improved police presence, cleaner streets, and free parking. It is a strong market. It is a wonderful place to live and raise a family." All of this was true. Forty members of the audience along with our full BID board were listening. Chosen board members gave tours of the downtown stores. The open house was a success. Afterward, the ED made follow-up calls from the list of attendees.

The BID's 1998 annual report stated our accomplishments for the first year:

- The Great Race vintage car race came to town on June 12.
- The Art Walk, Back-to-School, and Apple Harvest Festival were among the dozen events we hosted.
- Expanded outdoor dining.
- Hosted a chamber of commerce after-hours event in cooperation with Center Ithaca.
- Worked with Leadership Tompkins to develop a recommendation for uniform store hours downtown.
- Hosted a downtown showcase with forty potential new tenants. This event generated twelve leads.
- The IDP supported the relocation of the library into the then-vacant Woolworth building. We lobbied the county for and obtained additional financial support.
- The mayor established the Commons Design Review Committee to plan for the future of the Commons—pedestrian mall or road?
- We expanded the vision statement beyond "more attractive and economically viable downtown" to the following: "Downtown Ithaca is the economic, social, and cultural heart of Tompkins County. The Ithaca Downtown Partnership will strive to preserve and develop the central downtown core as the region's center for banking and finance, business and professional offices, government and community services, downtown residences, and as a retail destination highlighted by specialty shops, restaurants, arts, and entertainment. Downtown serves people who live and work downtown, city and county residents, university and college communities, area visitors and tourists."

I was invited to speak to the Ithaca Board of Realtors about the BID and what it had accomplished in its first year of operation. I prepared notes to speak to a full room of thirty-five of the top real estate agents in the Ithaca area:

Our Ithaca Downtown Partnership committees have taken over all the functions of the former Downtown Ithaca Merchants Association. We've hired staff, rented an office in the First National Bank building. We carried out the summer concert services and held a back-to-school block party. We held the Apple Harvest Festival, organized an art walk and a quilt walk, and carried on the Downtown Dollars gift certificate program.

We established outdoor dining on the Commons from May through September; we planned and implemented the Ithaca Festival Craft Fair and distributed downtown Ithaca tourism brochures with a $10,000 grant from the Tourism Council. There are 80,000 of these on the New York State Thruway and in tourist centers around the state.

The partnership lobbied the city and obtained two-hour free parking from November 29 through January 9, and we lobbied the city and obtained a police satellite office on the Commons.

This week our drug dog, Odin, began working—when you arrive from New York City on the bus, Odin will inspect your bags and welcome you to Ithaca. He will also walk the Commons. One wag suggested we call him our "welcome dog."

The partnership lobbied for the creation of the Commons Design Review Committee, which is now into their sixth meeting this week. We received a $20,000 grant and together with the Center for Governmental Research designed and implemented a marketing survey of the downtown. What do people want to see downtown? What stores? What future for the Commons? And we established a database of empty space with rents, square footage, and contacts available at the partnership office.

We held an informational forum with the building commissioner about upper-story development and found that elevators are no longer a requirement in most of our buildings. Under five units does not require ADA accessibility.

We published a sales brochure with updated demographics designed to attract business to locate in downtown Ithaca—"Where your business prospers!"

I distributed "Downtown Ithaca Welcome Packets" full of merchant coupons to the real estate agents and urged them to use them with their prospects, both residential and retail. I explained that Doug was an impartial rep for brokers, landlords, and prospects looking for rental space downtown. "He's there to help you. He's there to help potential business owners. He's on the road himself scouring the region for businesses to relocate or expand to downtown Ithaca." I continued:

I asked Doug the other day what he had done in the way of press releases. He looked a little hurt. The next day he hand delivered a two-inch stack of paper—press releases all of them. And I realized that every time there is an article on something good downtown, it is a result of one of Doug's press releases.

We are establishing an associate members program to include a community advisory board and Friends of Downtown Ithaca. Carl Haynes and

Peggy Williams, presidents of TC3 (Tompkins Cortland Community College) and Ithaca College, have both agreed to join.

We are lobbying the city to expand the shuttle bus service to the university and Ithaca College. It currently runs 10 a.m. to 2 p.m. five days a week every ten minutes to Cornell and downtown. Cornell and IC are two of our greatest assets for downtown and for the entire community. We need to reach out even more to the students, staff, and faculty.

And this year in addition, there will be a spring craft fair. The summer concert series, Thursday evenings at 7 p.m., will be expanded from ten weeks to fourteen and sponsored by the *Ithaca Times*. We are, by the way, looking for an additional corporate sponsor.

The Partnership and restaurants on Aurora Street will be adding entertainment Tuesday and Wednesday evenings during the summer—street musicians (buskers), jugglers, and bands.

Free parking has been expanded to four hours with up to four coupons from downtown merchants. Make a purchase and ask for their parking coupons—each one is an hour free. And of course parking is free after 6:30 p.m. daily and all weekend.

TC3's civic training course—Leadership Tompkins—has taken on a project with the business retention and development committee. A group has designed a survey of merchants to see what interest there would be in expanding store hours, if their neighbors would agree as well. Now, more and more, shopping takes place on evenings and weekends.

And I told the board of Realtors that these are only some of the things going on downtown as a result of the activities of the Ithaca Downtown Partnership committees and staff. They appeared impressed and pleased at the positive effect the BID was having in improving downtown. All the positives going on downtown could only improve the real estate market in Ithaca.

Another six months passed, and our young executive director surprised the board by saying he had decided to leave Ithaca and return to Ohio to attend law school. Doug had been in Ithaca eighteen months. He had been successful. During the second year of the BID, he attracted a few new businesses and had five major expansions in downtown. He was young and energetic, and he was leaving.

The board felt abandoned—we were back to square one. It was some consolation when in the *USA Today* weekend edition for March 10–12, 1999, Ithaca, New York, scored fourth in the nation as the most desirable place to live out of 193 cities rated by the "Small Cities" guide.

We questioned ourselves. What was the purpose of a BID? We were doing well with our summer concerts on the Commons. We were successful setting up the office and the structure. We had an enthusiastic board and committees. We had lobbied the city to provide a stronger police presence on the Commons, but we'd had little success with cleanliness and only a handful of new store rentals. We had the MOU with the city. But now we needed to resume our search for a leader. Our volunteer board could not run the BID on a day-to-day basis. It was too complicated, and we all had jobs.

We met again on a hectic schedule. We wrote up a revised job description expanding the duties of the executive director. We advertised in a national planning magazine and on the Web. Seven candidates applied. Over several meetings spent reviewing the applicants' résumés, we narrowed the group to three. Interviews began. One candidate stood out above the others. His name was Gary Ferguson. He had run five BIDs over the past fifteen years. He currently served as the assistant director of the BID in Dayton, Ohio. His business development plan for Dayton had recently been recognized by the International Downtown Association as the best in the country. The board was impressed. But why was he moving from a city the size of Dayton, with over two hundred thousand people, to Ithaca, with less than thirty thousand? And did he know the salary we were offering?

During his interview, Gary said he was attracted to Ithaca because he and his wife, Lisa, had vacationed in the area a number of times, and they were looking for a community closer to their families in New England. Lisa wanted a place where she could set up a farming opportunity. Gary said he wanted a city that was interested in growth and development and that had an upside potential for its downtown. They both wanted a college community. He saw Ithaca as a place where he could truly make a difference. We asked him if he had read the salary we were offering, and with a cautious pause, he said yes, he had read it.

Thys also interviewed the candidates on behalf of the planning department. He and I met one day walking along the Commons shortly after the interviews. "You will not get anyone with experience to come here for the $40,000 you are offering," he said. (Remember, this was in 1999.) "You need at least $60,000 to be competitive. Gary Ferguson, the one you prefer, has been offered positions in much larger cities. He likes this area, but you are offering to pay a beginner's salary."

"But that's the extent of our budget," I said. "We can't go broke hiring a new executive director, no matter how qualified he is." I had been elected president of our board, and the fiscal responsibility of making it work financially was my primary responsibility. "Let me see what I can do," Thys said.

Thys ended up going to the mayor, Alan Cohen, who went to city council and pushed through an additional $20,000 for the salary of the executive director of the Ithaca Business Improvement District. The BID was now able to offer the job to Gary Ferguson with a salary and benefits comparable to bigger-city offers at the time. Thys had been correct, and Gary accepted.

Over the years, Thys had overseen the building of the Commons and the HUD grant for the building of Center Ithaca. He had assisted with the HUD grant and the building of Eddygate, the formation of the BID, and now he had arranged for the hiring of an experienced executive director—one who was likely to stay for a while. The city and the BID were beginning to take shape.

# CHAPTER 7

# ARRIVAL (1999)

## The Candidate

On a Saturday morning in April of 1999, Carol and I drove to the outskirts of town. A U-Haul truck with an open trailer in tow was just pulling up the driveway to a large house on a hill overlooking Ellis Hollow, an area that was home to many Cornell professors. We followed the U-Haul up the drive. In the trailer, surrounded by hay bales and none too happy, stood two large goats straining at their tethers, obviously ready to end their trip from Ohio and start life in their new home in Ithaca—on the ground.

"They're happier in the open trailer than in an enclosed truck, so we brought them this way," said Lisa, Gary Ferguson's wife. Their two teenage daughters began unloading the truck. "Our eldest daughter is in college in Boston and couldn't join us for the move," Gary told us. Carol and I were there to help, so we pitched in, moving boxes and furniture up the hill into the house. "Nice house," I commented.

"It belongs to a Cornell professor on sabbatical, and we've rented it for a year," Gary said. "It will give us time to look around and get to know the area." It made sense, and based on Gary's credentials, which I knew from the search process, we were ready to have him stay for a long time. The goats, however, were a surprise.

"We had a small organic farm in Dayton," Gary said. "It was a hobby, but we couldn't leave the goats. We're going to look around here for a comparable place." "Great," I thought. "Putting down roots already, and 'organic' certainly fits Ithaca." I was gun-shy after the untimely departure of our first executive director, but now I was more pleased than ever with our pick for his successor. I had a feeling Gary would indeed be with us for a long time.

At his first board meeting with the BID board of directors, Gary laid out his credentials—not in a boastful way, but a factual recounting of what he had accomplished in his fifteen-year career working in a variety of business improvement districts. He and his wife were both graduates of Bates College in Maine. He didn't mention it, but I knew from reading his résumé and talking with him during the selection process that they had both graduated near the top of their class. One of Gary's earlier positions had been with a BID in Haverhill, Massachusetts. During the selection process, I called one of the bankers there who had been on their board. He would, he said, "hire Gary back in a heartbeat!"

After Haverhill, Gary spent five years working as the director of a BID in Grand Junction, Colorado, where he was instrumental in turning the city around with events, retail recruitment, and improved cleanliness and police presence. He had been in his latest job—as assistant director of a BID in Dayton, Ohio—for seven years. His main project there had been to build a baseball stadium in the heart of downtown. It had taken millions of dollars and complete community involvement. He had orchestrated it and pulled it off.

When someone else was chosen over him to replace the executive director, Gary began looking elsewhere. He confirmed what Thys had said—he had looked at positions in larger cities, like Baltimore and Philadelphia, as well as Ithaca. He and Lisa held a family conference, and Ithaca came up as their first choice. It was close to existing family, and central to an area of the country that both parents and their three daughters were drawn to. It had a pristine natural setting on the lake with waterfalls and forests. Two major educational institutions were here—three, counting the local community college, TC3. I was impressed to hear that this had been a family decision. This man would definitely fit the emotional and intellectual climate of Ithaca.

At that first meeting with the board of directors, Gary wanted to hear what had been accomplished to date. He was intimately familiar with the functioning of a BID and its potential for improving a community. Where were we in the process? It was heartening to hear the board as they responded. As disappointed as we had been at being abandoned by our first director, we had in retrospect accomplished many of the tasks of a start-up business. We had established the BID as a legal entity—a 501(c)3. We had approved the district BID plan. We had the committee structures in place and a mission statement to create a more aesthetic and economically viable downtown. We had a fully committed board of directors, a small staff, and after an exhaustive search we had rented an office, with telephones and donated furniture. Our new name was the Ithaca Downtown Partnership, complete with letterhead, logo, and a recruitment packet publicizing Ithaca as one of the best small towns in the country. We handled city events such as concerts and the Apple Harvest Festival.

In addition, the Ithaca Downtown Partnership had conducted a Commons design review. What should the future of the Commons be? After twenty years, should it be turned back into a street or maintained and improved as a pedestrian mall? We told Gary our findings: "A few retailers wanted the street returned, but enough felt that the Commons still gave them an edge on the mall competition that they wanted to retain it. By and large a majority of the public loved it as a park and place for community gatherings and events in the heart of downtown where they didn't have to worry about dodging cars, where they could stop and sit on a bench or walk along and talk to friends." In our report to the mayor, we had recommended that the Commons be kept as a pedestrian mall, and that if anything, it should be expanded and improved. We had rented a few stores, but other than an open house we hadn't yet done much in the way of recruitment. Overall, we had proven our worth. The BID had been well launched as an organization. Gary was inheriting a fully functioning business structure—he wouldn't need to start from scratch. He could focus immediately on filling vacancies or whatever other priorities we as a board, in concert with him, came up with.

He listened, and he outlined his approach. His first step would be to meet the rest of the membership and the merchants. He wanted to hear firsthand what the major concerns for downtown were. The board felt they represented a good cross section of the membership, but Gary wanted to hear for himself the fears and aspirations of the people he would be serving. After that, he said, we would see where we should go.

With his clear thinking and structured approach, Gary immediately established credibility with the BID board of directors.

# CHAPTER 8

# THE STRATEGIC PLAN (1999–2000)

## Headed Up or Headed Down?

Gary moved into his office on the second floor of the Bank of America building on the Commons. He began visiting shop owners, property owners, and businesses. He took on supervision of the staff and assured the board that downtown events would continue as planned: Ithaca Festival, Sidewalk Sale Days, Summer Concerts—fifty-seven events in all were planned for the summer. There was a lot already under way. He wasn't there to scuttle anything.

At the next board meeting he reported on his interviews with merchants and businesses in the downtown. His most dramatic conclusion was on the meeting with Thomas Associates Architects, a firm with a staff of 180 employees located in class A offices that they had designed and built on the upper floor of a converted department store in the heart of downtown—the Rothschild's Building. "I sat with the principals for two hours," he told us. "They want to expand. Their firm has so much work they need to expand. But they don't know whether downtown is headed up or headed down," and he used his arms to indicate the graph of upward success or downward failure. "Is downtown Ithaca a place that warrants further investment, or is it in decline?"

"They have choices," he said. "They can locate in Lansing, five miles out of Ithaca near the mall; they can move downstate to Westchester. They have nine offices across the country; they could relocate to any one of them. Their staff, however, loves living and working in downtown Ithaca. Here they can shop during their lunch hour, and there are dozens of restaurants to choose from."

Gary continued, "When they first moved downtown seven years ago, the city guaranteed the firm a preferred parking plan for their employees in the city garage adjacent to their offices. The principals like their downtown location, because it keeps the staff efficient. They can have their lunch, shop, and be back at their desks all within the sixty minutes allotted. In the office park near the airport in Lansing, they wouldn't have that luxury. They had tried that before from their location several miles from the city center. Hundreds of man-hours were lost to long lunches. But given the vacancies downtown, they don't know whether they should invest in expansion here, or look elsewhere.

"The other owners I met with are concerned about the usual stuff—cleanliness, more police presence, more parking, filling the vacancies—all important issues, but with Thomas Associates we have a potential disaster. Here are 180 employees that could leave. I asked them how long before they needed to make a decision?" he said. "They indicated they had eighteen to twenty-four months. I asked them to give us six months and we would be back to them with a plan. They agreed.

"What we need," Gary said to the board, "is a strategic plan. As a city, we need to think about what we want Ithaca to look like ten years hence. We need to determine what we want—specifics about what we want to see happen downtown. There are basically three things that drive downtown redevelopment: *arts, dining,* and *entertainment.* Once those are established, housing, retail, and commercial offices follow."

We already had the basics in our downtown. We had a very successful seventy-five-seat theater called the Kitchen Theatre. It had been around for fifteen years. Another historic theater—the State, which opened in 1928 as a vaudeville house—had morphed into a movie theater and had recently been purchased by Historic Ithaca, the preservation group, to save it from demolition. This group was planning to turn the sixteen-hundred-seat historic theater into a performing arts center for both local performances and touring Broadway shows. In addition, there were a dozen art galleries and a couple of shops specializing in crafts and gifts, one of which, Handwork, sold sophisticated local artwork. Downtown was at least well covered on the artistic front. Restaurants were strong too, particularly along Aurora Street, the favorite hangout for Ithaca College students. There were seven cafés in the atrium of our newly acquired Center Ithaca building on the Commons. A small three-screen art cinema, Cinemapolis, was located in the basement of Center Ithaca. Based on Gary's "arts, dining, and entertainment" formula, the board felt that Ithaca was well positioned for downtown revitalization.

The central core of downtown had a few hundred units of housing—sixty-two units in Center Ithaca; another forty or so in the converted Montgomery Ward building at the west end of the Commons owned by Jason Fane; and perhaps another hundred or so scattered around the BID area. There were retail stores—clothing, gifts, shoes, sporting goods, children's toys, even a pharmacy. The banks, lawyers, city and county offices, and post office were all located within the BID. Downtown was still the center of commerce. Even with a 20 percent vacancy rate, Ithaca had a fully functioning downtown.

In the mid-1990s Ithaca was the envy of less fortunate small cities in upstate New York. In a period when retail and housing were fleeing downtowns for the suburbs, and industry was fleeing New York State for lower taxes and cheaper labor in the South, it still had Cornell University, with eighteen thousand students, Ithaca College with six thousand, and a downtown extension campus of TC3 with 750. It was a healthy educational center. It had also been able to maintain a small industrial base, including BorgWarner, Emerson Power Transmission, and a budding group of high-tech companies, which were mostly located out near the airport, in an industrial park that had been created by the local development agency, Tompkins County Area Development (TCAD), in cooperation with Cornell University. What else, then, was needed to attract housing, retail, and commercial offices to the central business district?

Gary was in the process of telling us. In order to convince Thomas Associates with their 180 employees to remain downtown, the BID needed to develop a strategic plan that would set forth specifics. How many units of housing need to be added within the business improvement district during the next decade? How many new offices? How much retail square footage? What are the opportunities for growth? For if downtown is not growing, it is standing still, or worse, it is continuing in decline. What are the events and marketing we need to undertake to create the more aesthetically pleasing and economically viable downtown that is the BID's mission?

The board of directors was made up of professionals—merchants, businesspeople, politicians, property owners. They knew how to run stores and businesses and city administration, but here we were getting a lesson in how to take charge and shape the market itself. Each of us was experienced in our own small realm, but now we were being given a lesson in how to shape the central core of the city.

As with any business, goals needed to be set. Vague wishes and abstractions would not do. Gary told us he had used strategic plans in Dayton, Ohio, and in Grand Junction, Colorado. "A strategic plan is basic to the BID's ability to show Thomas Associates Architects, with their 180 employees looking to leave downtown, why they should stay," Gary said. "It is basic to retail recruitment. Why should anyone locate a new business in downtown Ithaca with a 20 percent vacancy and a dirty, declining central core? It is our job to paint the picture. It is our job to tell them why this place is worth investing in. This is why the board needs to develop a strategic plan for the BID."

Gary's plan was reminiscent of my own development strategy—develop a vision with *quality*, get it approved by city hall, work out the budget, rent it on a picture and a promise—only, now our BID was going to apply these principles of development to the entire central core of the city.

Under Gary's leadership, the board developed a schedule for several public meetings over the next few months. They would listen to the membership and the stakeholders who were paying the added assessment to support the BID. They would listen to the city council, the county, and the educational institutions. They would hear from the general public about what it wanted to see the downtown become. And they would hold a final brainstorming session with the board and a number of key people from the community. With all this input our new executive director would compile the suggestions into a document for the board to review.

Gary convinced the board that a housing study was needed to determine the number of units that could be built downtown. He had worked with the Danter Company from Columbus, Ohio, when he was in Dayton. With board approval, Gary contacted Ken Danter, and was quoted a price of $15,000 to perform a housing study for downtown Ithaca. The city agreed to cover $5,000 of the fee, members of the BID board agreed to contribute funds toward another third, and the chamber of commerce agreed to the final third. This would be a collaborative effort. In less than a month the Danter Company arrived in Ithaca and stayed for several days. They studied our demographics; they surveyed property owners, tenants, and employers. Within two months they delivered a written report with their recommendation: downtown Ithaca could support eighty to a hundred units of housing a year for the next four to five years—we could support an additional *three to five hundred housing units* over that period in our downtown!

I was incredulous. I could not believe it. This was my field. I felt I knew the market. How on earth could they predict this huge amount of growth with any degree of accuracy? At Gary's suggestion, I called up Ken Danter to inquire: "Are your recommendations that we can build eighty to one hundred units for all of Ithaca, or just within the twenty-two blocks of the BID district?" I asked.

"Within the twenty-two blocks of the BID district," Ken replied.

"How can you know that?" I asked, still not believing what he said.

"We looked at the vacancy rate for the Ithaca area—under 2 percent. We looked at the absorption rate of new properties built in the area—under six months. We looked at the unemployment rate—under 3 percent—plus a host of other variables. We have done fifteen hundred of these studies across the country, and based on our past experience, we feel confident about our recommendation to you."

I was stunned. Ithaca could build three to five hundred units over the next four to five years and feel fairly confident, based on the Danter study, that they would rent. This was CLUG all over again, only this time it was for real.

Gary continued with the public meetings and the studies. He helped bring James Howard Kunstler to town for a public lecture at the Unitarian church downtown. Kunstler had written a number of books on downtown revitalization and urban sprawl. He spoke about his findings in his book *Home from Nowhere.* Its opening page had a photo of a bright smiley face painted on a water tower high over a sprawling suburban strip—anywhere and everywhere USA.

"They can't charm you with the ugly retail districts that look just like every other sprawling strip mall in the country," Kunstler said, "so they try to make you feel good with this ridiculous smiley face on their water tower." He spoke with some bitterness.

**Figure 8.1** From Kunstler's book, *Home from Nowhere.* Photo by Peter Katz.

Kunstler didn't mince words. Our built environment has become so homogenized that one can't tell the strip malls in Poughkeepsie from the ones in Detroit, Del Ray, or Kansas City. Everywhere you go in our country it looks the same—the chain stores, the strip malls. The heart has been taken out of our downtowns and moved to the malls. *IT ALL LOOKS THE SAME!*

Kunstler's home was in Saratoga Springs, New York. He showed us pictures of the once-magnificent Victorian Grand Union Hotel in the heart of their downtown, which had been torn down to make way for a one-story brick box—their new, consummately ugly Grand Union grocery store. It mirrored the heartbreak that accompanied urban renewal across the country as our architectural icons were torn down and swept away during the '60s and '70s. Kunstler urged us to retain our history in the architecture that made our downtown unique.

**Figure 8.2** The Grand Union Hotel in Saratoga Springs, New York, was demolished in 1953 to make way for a grocery store. Ironically, the name of the supermarket was also "Grand Union," although the name was totally coincidental. Photo used with permission of the Saratoga Springs History Museum.

**Figure 8.3** The strip mall built on the site of the former Grand Union Hotel was anchored by a Grand Union Supermarket similar to the one pictured here. Photo credit to Litefantastic at English Wikipedia.

It had happened in Ithaca. The historical society could sell you a photo of the beautiful, historic Hotel Ithaca, a brick colossus that had been torn down to make way for the two-story brick box that became the Rothschild's Building. The library donated by Ezra Cornell to the city was demolished to make way for a six-story parking garage. And so it went. Even the Center Ithaca site that my partners and I now owned had once been a lovely brick department store. But buildings grew old. It became uneconomical to maintain them, much less modernize them. We still had enough of the old Ithaca architecture to be regarded as historic and quaint. Kunstler was urging us to retain it, restore it, and keep our architectural heritage. This seemed like a wonderful idea—up to a point.

The final version of the 2010 strategic plan was ready for board review and approval in late October. It would be sent to city council for approval at their December meeting. It set specific goals for the decade 2000–2010: in the next decade, downtown Ithaca should build new housing, office, and retail space. The BID should begin a redesign of the Commons, add three new annual events, and promote creation of jobs in the downtown. It should help the newly salvaged State Theatre grow. It should retain the Kitchen Theatre within the BID district, improve the police presence and cleanliness. The plan recommended that the city build a new parking garage downtown, and that a developer be found to build a new hotel—one was already being considered. A list of nearly two dozen recommendations for improvements to the downtown followed. The board, under Gary's guidance, had developed a ten-year plan that called for these specifics:

- 50,000 square feet of new retail space
- 150,000 square feet of new office space
- Fifteen hundred new jobs
- Five hundred new or renovated housing units
- Rehabilitation of the State Theatre
- Construction of a new convention center and hotel
- Construction of a new parking garage
- A refurbished and well-kept Commons
- Improved perception of Ithaca as the region's safest and friendliest commercial district

A host of other items were also part of the plan, including an arts incubator, new signage, and new tourist attractions.

Gary felt it would be important for the Common Council (city council) to review and approve the plan. The BID, while financially independent from the city, still relied on the city's approval for its existence. According to the founding legislation at the state level, the BID could be dissolved at any point by a majority vote of city council. The council members should know what we were doing, Gary reasoned, and they should buy into this plan for the central core of the city. After some consideration and refinement, the council voted to "accept" the plan. This was not "approval." The council did not want to be held accountable for building a new public parking garage without going through the public process that this sort of thing would entail. In general, we took their "acceptance" to signify they were pleased with the direction we were headed.

Armed with the strategic plan, Gary headed back to Thomas Associates, the architecture firm that was considering leaving. This was the direction downtown was headed. The housing, retail, and commercial investment within the BID would total $100 million over the next decade—$100 million! Many people expressed their concern that this bordered on the absurd for our small town, but if one added up all the projects planned for, this was the number. The principals at Thomas Associates were impressed. Our board was impressed. Here was a plan, an ambitious plan, a practical plan for revitalizing our downtown.

Thomas Associates bought into it. They would stay, provided space could be found for their expansion. Gary and I had already been talking.

Center Ithaca was adjacent to the Rothschild's Building, where the Thomas offices were located. Our designer measured the floor differential between their office on the second floor of the Rothschild's Building and the office suites on the second floor of Center Ithaca. It was less than twelve inches. With the proper permits and a design for a steel fire curtain, it would be possible to break through the walls separating the two buildings, and by installing a short ramp between the spaces we could create another 7,500 square feet for their expansion—just what they needed. There was only one small problem: the section of our Center Ithaca office floor that was contiguous to Thomas Associates was occupied by eleven very happy tenants, tenants with leases.

Our building manager began the process of talking with the Center Ithaca tenants. Would they consider relocating? A computer firm and a brokerage house, both with short-term leases, were already planning to relocate to larger cities. Two more were going to close at the end of their lease. As their landlord, and with considerable negotiation, we were able to find homes for the remaining tenants. We paid for their relocation, and after six months we had the space arranged for Thomas Associates to expand. Gary's strategic plan, together with the cooperation of our Center Ithaca management and tenants, would assure that we retained 180 jobs in the downtown.

Here was another advantage of having created a business improvement district for our downtown. Without the vision and the coordination that had just taken place through the BID, without the strategic plan, and without Gary's guidance, downtown Ithaca would have taken yet one more hit, one more blow to its vitality and strength as a functioning, thriving downtown.

All this work had gone on behind the scenes. It had been crucial to the retention of a major business with 180 employees in our downtown, and it had given us a direction for the first decade of the twenty-first century. Downtown Ithaca was headed up!

Meanwhile, in 1998 there was a major fire in our 407 College Avenue building. It was more than 50 percent destroyed, which required that it be demolished. Fortunately we had insurance on the building. The insurance company offered $745,000 as settlement for the fire damage. A public adjuster had contacted me the morning after the fire. He ended up counting every piece of "irreplaceable" chestnut trim and negotiated a settlement with the insurance company for $1.45 million. It was enough to provide the equity to build a completely new building. From this experience, I recommend public adjusters in such a situation.

**Figure 8.4** The new 407 College Avenue. No one was hurt in the fire that destroyed its predecessor. Photo by Jon Reis.

# CHAPTER 9

# CRISIS (2000)

## A Postal Disaster

The timing of the 2010 strategic plan coincided perfectly with the arrival of the new century. The year 2000 brought new vigor, new vision, and a new mayor. The BID knew where it was headed; it had a plan for downtown Ithaca for the coming decade. But the plan for growth depended on selling the vision to developers. It depended on attracting new stores and businesses to downtown. Gary reactivated the dormant retail recruitment program in the BID. The open house from two years ago was about to pay off. A restaurant from nearby Binghamton, one of the attendees at the original open house, purchased a vacant retail building on Cayuga Street and began a two-year renovation to create the Lost Dog Café. Gary worked with them to help obtain building permits and introduce them to local contacts. Downtown Ithaca was after all a "neighborhood." Gary and the BID staff were to become its local "welcome wagon."

However, suddenly the BID had an unforeseen potential disaster on its hands. The local post office announced plans to relocate from their ornate turn-of-the-century Beaux Arts limestone building in downtown to a location out of town.

They intended to consolidate with their main distribution center five miles away near the airport. The consolidation would save them money. They would close the post office in the central business district, and it would be a disaster for downtown. How could a downtown thrive without a post office?

Gary sounded the alarm. He called a meeting of the business retention and development committee. This would be one more disincentive for businesses to locate downtown. The removal of the post office to the suburbs would contribute in no small way to the demise of downtown.

At the next full board meeting, he announced that this simply could not happen. If the United States Post Office moved from downtown, it would

**Figure 9.1** Ithaca's post office, built in 1910. Photo provided by the History Center of Tompkins County.

only confirm the fears of downtown business owners and the public that downtown Ithaca was in decline. He urged board members to take immediate action. Talk with the new mayor. Talk with the postmaster. Let them know the danger of this relocation and its potential effect on downtown. The town of Ithaca was already talking with the post office and had their eye on the building for their new town hall. (Cities in New York State are situated within a township, townships within counties—three layers of government independently incorporated, with a high level of duplication of services and administration, not to mention taxes.) It might be to Ithaca's advantage financially to have a consolidated, much larger town of Ithaca office within the BID district, and moving might save the USPS money, but from our point of view, none of this was worth the cost of losing the downtown Ithaca post office to the suburbs.

The board of the BID responded to Gary's call. Each member began the campaign, speaking with council members and town of Ithaca representatives. Gary spoke with the local postmaster himself. Gradually it became a public issue. Relocation of the post office would not be in the best interests of downtown. The decision, however, was not up to the BID or the city of Ithaca. The United States Post Office took its orders from Washington. A small business improvement district and the city council itself in Ithaca, New York, were powerless.

The local postmaster was sympathetic. In speaking with Gary he mentioned the idea of a postal store. Perhaps the post office could still sell the building to the town and keep a smaller postal retail store in a portion of the building to the side of the main structure. Albeit smaller, the location would be in the same building, and the basic services would be the same from the public's point of view, but the sorting and receiving that took place behind the scenes would be moved to the airport location. Gary was heartened; he thought it might work. The problem was that the entire post office building would have to be gutted for the town to take it over and for a new postal store to be constructed. The process would take more than a year. During that time the post office would have to be closed, and even that was unacceptable. Downtown could not thrive without a continuously operating post office. The postmaster was amenable to staying open, but only if a location could be found for them on a temporary basis.

Serendipity often shapes events in ways we cannot foresee. Across the street from the post office on Buffalo Street was a two-story building that housed the Acrographics copy center. It had been shoehorned between, on the east, the Unitarian church—a Romanesque stone building dating to 1893 and designed by a prominent Ithaca architect, William Henry Miller—and, on the west, the former YMCA building, which burned down in 1978 and had been replaced by a four-story office building developed by Andy Sciarabba and Ken Walker.

Years ago, when I was building Ravenwood and Eddygate, I had met the owner, Jim O'Rourke. He sported a shock of snow-white hair and an equally snow-white, fantastically long, handlebar mustache. For years every architect in town had used Jim to run copies of their design drawings on his then state-of-the-art Xerox equipment. Huge copy machines the width of a car still filled the entire front of his store. Digital technology had long since passed Jim by, and he had closed his business ten years ago. Rumor had it that he lived in the back of the building with no shower, only a toilet and basin, and a small bed in the corner.

Walking back from Center Ithaca to my office across from the courthouse one morning, I had the impulse to turn and walk down the side alley next to Jim's building. At the rear of the building, through a large picture window, I saw Jim hunched over his desk. He gave me a look of recognition and motioned for me to come in through the side door.

It had been years since I had been inside his building, and I had never been in the back behind the counter. It was true. Jim lived there. There was a small bed in the corner, a narrow door into a toilet large enough to hold the basics—no shower—and in front of the counter, a sea of huge dust-covered copy machines neatly spaced between the rear of the store and the glass windows that stretched across the front facing the street.

Jim and I began talking. He opened the door into his garage at the rear of the building and proudly showed off his dusty 1958 cream-colored Mercedes Gullwing sports car. His dream was to restore it and head west. I listened and then asked if he would consider selling his building. I told him why I was interested—the post office needed a temporary location while they renovated the main building into offices for a new town hall and a smaller postal retail store.

Jim listened. He appeared interested and offered to give me a tour of the building. We went upstairs to the never-finished raw concrete-block room that duplicated the floor space below. The first floor would be adequate for the post office relocation. We could probably rearrange the entrance and make a private front stairway for offices upstairs once the post office lease was up.

After some calculating, I returned to Jim a week later with a purchase offer. We negotiated. He thought he could be out within sixty days. If the timing worked for him, this would allow us ninety days over the summer to build out the post office and relocate them to the new location in time for the town to begin their yearlong construction project in the existing post office building. We arrived at a final number, and Jim signed the deal. His only concern was how and where to remove equipment so large it wouldn't even fit through the double glass doors at the front entrance. The facade of the building obviously had been completed once the copy machines had been positioned on the ground floor. I told him that if he could find a place for them, we would see that his machines were moved—and at our expense.

Gary was elated. This might work. After approval from their superiors, the Ithaca post office accepted the location for their temporary store. After we explained the community benefit of the deal, the local Tompkins Trust Company Bank lent Carol and me an unsecured note for $385,000, the full purchase price plus the cost of the renovation into a new post office. We drew up an eighteen-month lease for the post office, contingent on final purchase of the building.

Jim delayed. He couldn't find a home for his equipment. Ideally he wanted to sell it. He had it appraised by Xerox, and they estimated the total value might be $10,000, but they were not interested in buying it. It was outdated. His original outlay of $500,000 twenty years ago was basically worthless, and the clock was ticking. Jim was frozen. He couldn't find a place to store his machines, and his dream of traveling west in his restored Mercedes was basically dead. It turned out his brother-in-law had been lending him money over the past ten years based on the value of his building. His mortgage had finally exceeded the value of his equity in the building, and his brother-in-law would not lend him any more against the property. Jim no longer had a source of funds to live on, or any place to move his equipment; he also needed to clear up the mortgage with his brother-in-law.

Jim didn't give up totally. He found a garage on the outskirts of town where he moved his few personal belongings and his Gullwing—the car was valued by *Hemmings Motor News* at over $300,000, so Jim was not destitute—but his dreams for the trip west were in serious jeopardy. We found a solution for the removal of his equipment, and although not exactly to his liking, given the financial pressure he was facing, he finally agreed.

My wife, Carol, stood by Jim on the sidewalk next to a dumpster the size of a small railroad car positioned in the street. She held his hand and talked softly with him as the riggers removed the glass facade from the building, drove in their forklift truck, backed out with each car-sized Xerox machine, turned, and carefully lifted the machine upward and over the side of the dumpster. They tilted it into the container, where it crashed to the bottom. For the entire time, Carol stood by Jim, talking him through his personal Armageddon. With each crash Jim visibly winced. The check from the dumpster company totaled $212—twenty cents per hundred pounds—at the scrapyard!

Carol and I hired a contractor and built out the temporary post office space to US government specifications. Our local post office moved into

**Figure 9.2** The Acrographics building, shoehorned between the Unitarian church and the Sciarabba Walker office building, became Ithaca's temporary downtown post office. Photo by Jon Reis.

their newly renovated location in Jim's old store. Eighteen months later, once their new postal store was built in the new "Town Hall," they moved out of the temporary home we had provided and into their final home—the brand-new postal retail store. Between the BID calling attention to the problem, the board turning a potential disaster into a public relations event, the postmaster listening, the local bank lending the money, and Carol's and my efforts as developers, we had kept the post office in downtown. If all of us were not shaping a city, we were at least keeping it from slumping into decline.

Jim moved out of town. His brother-in-law got paid. Once the post office lease was up and they were ready to move out of their temporary quarters, a pillar of the community, Dave Cutting, who also happened to be a member of the Unitarian church next door, called me to get together. "The church should own the building," he said. "They need it to expand their Sunday school and their preschool programs. They have contemplated moving out of downtown to get the room they need. You should sell it to them."

If nothing else, Dave Cutting was direct. He had been a civic leader and successful businessman in Ithaca for all his professional life. When he spoke, you listened. You wanted to listen, because he was so well regarded and well respected, so I did listen, and we agreed to sell the building to the Unitarian church. It felt as though we had come full circle—"mission accomplished." The intervention Carol and I had made happened because of Gary's continued attention to the pulse of downtown. All of us on the BID had contributed toward keeping the post office downtown, and we had taken another important step in keeping downtown intact and poised for growth rather than decline. And at the end of it all, the Unitarian church had gotten their Sunday school building, which would make their organization even stronger and more viable as a long-term downtown institution, and they would no longer have a reason to move.

The post office project had not been specifically included in the BID's strategic plan, but keeping it downtown certainly fit the BID's overall mission of creating a more economically viable downtown. Without the BID, and without its executive director, Gary, serving as a catalyst, no one downtown would have realized the potentially negative impact of this pending disaster until it was too late to affect the outcome. The post office would have moved out of town, and that would have been the end of it. The advantages of having formed the structure of a business improvement district for downtown Ithaca were becoming ever more evident.

# CHAPTER 10

# GATEWAY PLAZA (2001)

## Survival, Vision, and Tax Abatements

One of my jobs as president of the BID board of directors was to assist Gary in selling the policies and strategies of the BID, not only to the city, but also to officials and potential donors at the university, the college, the medical center, and local corporations. To maintain our programs and budget, the BID needed buy-in and financial support beyond the basic 17.5 percent of the city tax base we had chosen. We needed to sell potential donors, as well as the city council, on additional support for the BID. We needed the city and developers and institutions to help us implement the ambitious goals as presented in the strategic plan—housing, jobs, retail expansion, a parking garage, and a hotel. It was a question of survival for the downtown merchants and the property owners—indeed a question of survival for all of our city. It was again apparent to me we were playing the Community Land Use Game whether we knew it or not, only this time it was definitely for real.

The strategic plan was the blueprint, our road map, developed with community input. The BID board of directors truly felt that it would direct us toward upward development, not decline. I began using the following points in selling the strategic plan:

Picture downtown boarded up—empty, plywood covering the windows of all the major retail shops, newspapers blowing about the street, dirt, filth. Would you want your incoming students to identify with this image of downtown Ithaca? Would you want the new employees you are trying to recruit to your university, your medical center, your company, to identify downtown Ithaca in this way? Like it or not, when you think of Ithaca, the image that first comes to mind is the downtown—the Commons. It is the emotional heart and soul of Ithaca. It can become boarded up and filthy, or, with your support, we can turn it into the vibrant, beautiful city envisioned in our strategic plan.

Our BID board of directors saw this as a distinct choice. Members of the BID spoke of their concerns throughout the community as they had been voiced originally to Gary by Thomas Associates—was downtown headed up or was it headed down? This was the picture we painted for all who would listen.

Talk is cheap. However, talk is also necessary for creating the vision of what can happen—what *should* happen. But talk is indeed cheap when compared to the risk and financial investment involved in taking the steps necessary to build a project. The strategic plan set forth measurable goals for development. Our goals included fifteen hundred new jobs, 50,000 square feet of new retail, 150,000 square feet of new office space, five hundred new apartments, all within the next ten years. We wanted to see vacancies filled, events held. We wanted a "more aesthetically pleasing and economically viable downtown," as stated in our BID plan. Could we do it? As a community, could we move past the talking stage and really make this happen? There had been only a few isolated projects built in downtown Ithaca in the past thirty years. Now we had a comprehensive development plan. Who would take the first step?

Any development is risky. Downtown infill development is particularly risky. Land assembly can be difficult. Many downtown sites are brownfields. Convincing a bank to lend in a run-down downtown can be difficult and could lead to higher capital cost. The regulatory approval process can seem endless. It had taken us three and a half years to obtain final approval, and another year and a half to build the Eddygate Collegetown project. Just assembling a parcel of land on which to build can be time-consuming and more costly than in undeveloped areas. In many cases it may be necessary to demolish a building before one can even begin construction. Planning departments, which must approve the design of a project, and which are subject to public hearings and public input, can demand more expensive and intricate design for an urban infill project. Because such a project downtown can become a matter of civic pride for the community, cheap construction will not do.

Thys had publicly stated his position on density as a city planner: "As a planner, I have always believed that density was a good thing. If you believe that growth is important, and I do, it either has to go up or out. 'Out' means sprawl into suburbia. 'Up' means density in the core areas. Density is a better option. That is true in Collegetown. That is true in downtown. And it is true along several of the other growth corridors in Ithaca."

Building up rather than out to create density in an urban infill area requires a more expensive type of construction than building a one- or two-story wood-frame building. Buildings over four stories typically require steel and reinforced concrete construction systems. We had faced all of these problems on infill sites in Collegetown, both when we began construction of our Eddygate building in 1986, and again in 1998 when the original 407 rebuild burned down, and we were confronted with the need to construct a completely new building on the site. Urban infill construction is expensive.

With the renewed interest of many people, particularly professionals and the young, there can also be advantages to building in downtown, such as lower infrastructure costs and higher rents. For decades in most communities, the balance has been difficult to achieve, as downtowns became run-down and emptied out. Downtown Ithaca was no different; the same could happen here.

What can a municipality do to stimulate development in its downtown? Thys had the idea and proposed a *tax abatement based on density* to the mayor at the time, Alan Cohen, applicable to the downtown assessment district. Alan liked the idea. Thys called the state assemblyman Marty Luster and asked if he could be of assistance in bringing about a change to state law, either specifically for Ithaca or as a general law that would affect all communities in the state with the exception of New York City. Marty suggested that Thys talk to the head of the tax committee in the assembly, who listened carefully and then advised Thys that "it would be a really, really difficult thing to do either as a special act or as a general act."

He suggested instead that Thys should approach the local industrial development agency—the Tompkins County Industrial Development Agency (TCIDA)—to see if they would be willing to undertake such a program. Thys knew that IDAs could use their authority to hold title and create payments in lieu of taxes (PILOTs) for industrial and commercial properties. He was not aware that this power could be used to assist residential properties.

According to its charter, an IDA has the authority to abate a variety of local and state taxes. It can also serve as a conduit to the tax-exempt bond market for private sector projects. Its authority is guided by federal and state laws, as well as policies established by its board of directors to "maximize the return on investment of scarce community resources."

With his new understanding that IDAs had the authority to abate tax on *residential* properties as well as commercial properties, Thys wrote up a proposed density tax abatement for downtown residential development. He went through a process similar to that which the steering committee had followed to establish the boundaries for the BID. How many properties should be in it? What types of properties should be able to take advantage of the program? How deep should the abatement be? How long should it last?

He developed a chart that would give properties the maximum abatement if developers built their top floor to the maximum allowable within the zone. They would get some lesser abatement if the property were lower or less dense, and no abatement for one- or two-story buildings. He proposed that there be 100 percent abatement on the increased assessment in the first year, with the abatement going down and the new taxes going up 10 percent per year to get to full taxation at the end of the tenth year.

He then wrote a proposal explaining the purpose of the abatement program, which was to stimulate development and create more density in downtown and other included areas, and he explained how the program would work. His next step as the director of planning and development for the city was to sell this idea. He took it to Common Council to get their support.

The council was quick to support it, and with their approval in hand, Thys then went to the board of the IDA. He tried to convince the IDA that they had the authority to grant abatements under the state law and that they didn't really need to go and ask all the other taxing jurisdictions whether they liked the idea. The IDA board, however, insisted that the other jurisdictions, in addition to the city, had to approve the proposal before they would consider it.

With that directive, he next took it to the county board of representatives. At first they balked, but after what Thys called "some pretty spirited discussion," a majority voted in favor.

Next stop was the Ithaca City School District and the Ithaca Board of Education. Thys took the mayor with him on this one. They were tougher than the board of reps, but ultimately they, too, voted in favor of the abatement. Thys then returned to the IDA board and again faced some intense initial opposition from those who felt this was simply a gift to developers. However, he finally swung enough votes to get the program approved.

Thys had intended and designed the program to be formulaic, i.e., if a proposed development met the density requirements and if all three jurisdictions were in favor of supporting it, it should be entitled to the abatements. However, abatements like this should be given only to projects that would not go ahead without the benefit of a tax abatement.

In addition to its primary focus on industrial development, and thanks to Thys's intervention and the continued support of the concept by the mayor and the BID, the IDA did develop both a residential and commercial policy of encouraging development in specially designated urban and community centers, specifically in the central core of downtown.

Both Gary and Thys lobbied strongly to have any tax abatement discussion adhere to the formulaic approach that Thys originally proposed. They did not want every project to become a political football, but with each new project, special committees tried to add layers of additional secondary requirements to it, such as labor standards, energy efficiency conditions, and minority employment. Gary and Thys pointed out that while these may be laudable goals, they were not the goals of the program as originally proposed and as approved. As Thys said, it became very apparent that if the IDA tried to make this a program that everybody could hang their own pet desire on, it would ultimately grow too expensive and cumbersome, and fail to serve the purpose for which it was originally designed.

And this is exactly what happened. Despite Thys's good intentions and despite the way the program was originally envisioned and approved, it very soon became a political football. The notion of a program like this is that it provides enough financial incentive to make an otherwise marginal or financially impossible project doable—hence its value in stimulating downtown development. If every project that comes for abatement is required to add all kinds of expenses such as higher labor costs, environmental add-ons, and similar betterments, the projects soon become financially infeasible. This had been Thys's concern about proposed modifications to this initially fairly simple and straightforward development assistance program.

Meanwhile, as a developer, I had taken the first steps and spoken with an older gentleman, Don Dickinson, who over several decades had assembled a four-acre parcel along Six Mile Creek, right downtown within both the business improvement district and the boundaries of the new tax abatement area. It was only a block from the Ithaca Commons. Since the late 1960s, Don had owned a solid, poured-in-place, concrete, six-story warehouse, originally built in 1924. He and his wife Sue ran it as a Mayflower storage warehouse. They had recently consolidated several neighboring parcels with the idea of doing a major development on the site, but at eighty years old, the more we talked about it, the more Don grew receptive to the idea of selling his warehouse and four acres to a developer who would carry his dream forward. He and Sue could spend more time in Florida playing golf.

I spoke to them of the strategic plan for downtown. I told them about the housing study and the need for eighty to a hundred residential units a year for the next five years, the plans for 50,000 square feet of new retail, and 150,000 square feet of new office space over the next ten years, the plan for fifteen hundred new jobs downtown. Don and Sue appeared intrigued.

After working up a conceptual plan with HOLT Architects, I went back to them and painted a picture of turning the warehouse into 50,000 square feet of class A offices—one-third of the office space called for in our ten-year plan—turning a large part of the site along the creek into a park, complete with a city right-of-way for access to the walking trails farther up the creek, and 140 spaces of landscaped parking. We would call the project Gateway Plaza.

I held out the promise of a second phase, Gateway Commons, tearing down all the old, dilapidated structures on the site and building a six-story luxury apartment building where these structures had been. Don and Sue listened intently, and finally agreed to buy into the vision. They liked us, and they liked our approach. With only a small down payment, they agreed to finance our purchase of the four acres. They would hold a second mortgage for the purchase price and subordinate it to however much financing Carol and I needed to build out this dream project at the eastern end of the twenty-two-block business improvement district.

Ours was an ambitious project based entirely on the vision for downtown as set forth in the strategic plan. The numbers were tight, but with a financing package, again from the local Tompkins Trust Company, and with the newly conceived tax abatement figured in, it could work. Thanks to Don and Sue's cooperation, the belief in our own hype engendered by my involvement in and enthusiasm for the goals of the BID, plus the IDA tax abatement envisioned and negotiated by Thys and Gary, Carol and I were taking the first step.

Once again, similar to our Eddygate development fifteen years earlier in Collegetown, we felt like pioneers setting forth into unknown territory. What was to become our $10 million Gateway Plaza project at the foot of State Street hill was soon designed and financed, and the construction was under way. Our personal financial survival was once again tied to the survival of downtown Ithaca. We had followed the principles I had learned so many years ago at the Cornell school of architecture. Now we were the ones agreeing to jump into the risk equation—providing offices for businesses and their workers, stores for a growing retail sector, and hopefully, in a second phase, luxury housing to increase the number of residents living in downtown. This was like blowing up a huge balloon with hot air—with talk—only this time talk was not to be cheap!

I presented the whole plan to Gary. He was pleased, and I felt like one of the players on his chessboard—very like the CLUG board I had played on thirty years earlier at Cornell.

Initially the IDA was successful with the tax abatement program and its expanded mission to encourage new projects and density in the downtown. Our Gateway office building became the first project to be built with the new tax abatement. Prior to renovating the warehouse in 2001, the property had paid about $30,000 in property tax for the run-down buildings and the four-acre site. Once the renovation was complete and the building fully rented, the abatement program kicked in, and the initial abatement diminished at 10 percent a year. Gateway Plaza, as the entire property is called, began to provide a greater and greater share of taxes to the city, the school district, and the county. Our total property tax bill in the tenth and final year of the abatement was over $225,000. If the IDA and their tax abatement had not been in place, this annual payment in increasingly larger amounts would never have reached the taxing authorities. Without the tax abatement, we could not have undertaken this pivotal project.

Thanks to the cooperative effort of Thys and the department of planning and development, Gary and the Ithaca Downtown Partnership (now called the Downtown Ithaca Alliance), and the board of the Tompkins County Industrial Development Agency, plus the financial support of our local bank, the Tompkins Trust Company, the Gateway Plaza development became a successful public-private partnership. It would become an inspiration to other developers to attempt projects in downtown Ithaca. The renewed vision for downtown was becoming a reality.

**Figure 10.1** Gateway Center during reconstruction, while window openings were being enlarged. Since its poured-in-place construction in 1924, the building had been used as a warehouse. Photo by author.

**Figure 10.2** Note the spread columns and how they are incorporated into the office design, seen in figure 10.3. Photo by author.

**Figure 10.3** Finished office floor. Photo by author.

**Figure 10.4** Gateway Center complete with new windows throughout, sixteen offices, three restaurants, a history museum, and a clock tower topped with a flag—a 52,000-square-foot adaptive reuse project in downtown Ithaca. Photo by Jon Reis.

# CHAPTER 11

# THE HOTEL (2002–5)

## Throwing Down the Gauntlet

Momentum was gathering downtown. Our executive director's role was to oversee all the BID staff and committee activities, as well as bring in new business. Sixty percent of Gary's time was to be devoted to attracting new stores and new development. The board had put that in his job description, and he had his finger on the pulse of virtually every new downtown project.

The Ithaca economy, while not wildly thriving, was stable. Ithaca was listed in five different nationwide surveys as one of the top ten cities in which to live, raise children, retire, or start a new business. The message of *density* as the key to downtown's success was beginning to be driven home. The Gateway project was under way. The new office building would top out at six stories—eighty-five feet—once the clock tower was constructed. The tax abatement was in place and became a huge stimulus for development within the defined area—basically the BID district.

The Lambrou family, together with a successful merchant, Tom Pine, owned a one-story building on the corner of Tioga and Seneca Streets. It housed Beam Travel, a travel agency owned by the Lambrou family, in one half of the building; in the other half were Race Office Equipment, owned by Tom Pine, and Cameras N' Things, a camera shop owned by Tom's tenant. It occupied the busiest street corner in town, directly across the street from the six-story M&T Bank on one corner, a seven-story Bank of America building on another, and a 450-space parking garage on the remaining corner. The Beam Travel/Race building was a one-story, underutilized space on the most active street corner in downtown.

Born in 1931 in Greece, in the midst of the Great Depression, Gus Lambrou had immigrated to New York City in 1956. A short time later he moved to Ithaca to be close to his brother, who was attending Ithaca College, and began working in a friend's Greek restaurant. He saved his money, opened his own small grocery store, and bought a student apartment building. He saved more money and bought another, and another, and another. As supermarkets emerged, Gus saw the writing on the wall for his small Collegetown grocery store and he purchased a travel agency—Beam Travel downtown. It had always been Gus's dream to return to Greece, but he was well into his seventies now and would only return for vacations. He sported a shock of white, wavy hair. Gus always wore a suit and a smile. One day, with a broad grin, he told me he had *$5 million cash* in the bank.

His son, Nick, had taken over management of his dad's real estate empire and the travel business. He had expanded the real estate portfolio, developing several apartment buildings in Collegetown within a block of our Eddygate project.

One day, we began talking about downtown development. Nick was aware of the strategic plan for downtown. He understood the concept of density as the way to maximize economic success in downtown Ithaca. He was aware of our Gateway renovation. We had by then completely gutted and rebuilt our six-story warehouse and turned it into class A office space. We had been successful, very successful, renting it out to sixteen new businesses in less than a year. Our tenants were lawyers, computer specialists, Cornell Alumni Magazine, several accounting firms, and, on the ground floor, three restaurants. Several of these businesses would have relocated to the suburbs had we not offered them new space and on-site parking in the downtown area. Approximately 150 people worked at the Gateway Center building in Gateway Plaza, and we were planning the construction of the next phase of a luxury apartment building—Gateway Commons. Nick knew all of this.

Gary and I, functioning together as part of the Business Retention and Development Committee of the Downtown Ithaca Alliance, talked with Nick one day about his one-story site at the most heavily trafficked corner in downtown. Nick had been thinking about building a hotel there. His dad had capital, and they had other friends within the Greek community who were willing to invest. I told him about my experience building Eddygate and that one of the initial iterations of that project had been a hotel. It had required a feasibility study before a lender would even look at it. Nick was aware of the process he had to go through to verify that a market for a hotel existed. He had made some preliminary financial assumptions and asked us to sit with him to review his numbers.

The three of us sat in Nick's Collegetown office and reviewed his business plan. Nick felt certain he could build at least one hundred rooms in his new hotel. He had talked with several franchises and thought a Hilton Garden Inn might work. His numbers looked reasonable. I told him of my experience with Gateway. Downtown was alive and well. We had rented our new offices in less than a year. Nick's idea of a hotel two blocks away from Gateway fit perfectly into the strategic plan for downtown.

Real estate development, while driven by numbers and market assumptions, is, in the final analysis, an emotional decision. At least on the level at which an individual or a family may be risking all they have, it is an emotional and often gut-wrenching decision. At some point you have to look inside and say to yourself, "Yes, I'm confident I can do this."

Nick listened to our upbeat vision for downtown Ithaca. He knew he could raise the money. He had the development experience, having built several apartment buildings from the ground up, and he had his father behind him. Finally he turned to me, slapped his thigh, and with the exuberance that must be part of being Greek, said, "If you can do it, I can do it too! If you can build Gateway, I can build my hotel!" Nick had made his decision. He had thrown down the gauntlet for himself. If one person could develop a major project successfully in downtown, he could do it as well.

There are some basic rules to real estate development. The first one is *site control*. Until you control the site on which you want to build, you are still just playing with dreams, or as I said to Nick, "You are just a handsome guy in a nice suit." The next rule is, it takes *money*. Somehow, someway, you have to find the money to build your project. The third rule, particularly as it relates to developing a hotel, is you need *experience*. Nick fell short on all three of these requirements.

First of all, he did not own the entire site. He owned half of it. Tom Pine owned the other half, and while Nick had spoken with Tom and thought he had an agreement to purchase his half of the building, nothing had been put in writing. It turned out Tom was toying with the idea but was not fully committed, not yet.

Second, while he had investors and family money, his group still needed to borrow $10 million for the project as conceived at this point.

Finally, Nick found that no lender was interested in financing a hotel project without an experienced manager. Running a hotel that has to be booked 365 days a year is a totally different business from apartments that have to be rented once a year. While they agreed the market was probably there, no lender would finance the project without an experienced manager running the hotel, and preferably the manager should own a percentage of the deal.

As a developer, when confronted with the seemingly insurmountable, it sometimes helps to step back and take a second look at what you are trying to achieve. It also can help to get another opinion. By now, Gary had been executive director of the BID for over three years. He knew the Ithaca players. He knew the dynamics for development, and he saw the possibilities for an expanded project. But there were a host of issues that would have to be resolved for it to happen. Nick and Gary conferred and thought it might be a good idea if Gary met alone with Tom, the co-owner of the building.

Gary met with him, and he was open to the idea of selling his interest in the building, but he didn't particularly want to participate in the hotel project. Tom ran an office supply and copy business. He knew nothing about hotels. Cornell University was one of his biggest clients. If he sold his share of the building, he would need a new location from which to run his business, service his clients—primarily walk-in customers—and make deliveries. Nick had offered him space in the new building once it was erected on their site, but Tom could not afford the downtime with his business. His tenant, the Cameras N' Things shop owner, had a lease and did not want to leave. And price was an issue. What was his share worth? He and Nick had not arrived at a price.

To interest a lender in the project, Nick realized he needed a hotel management company—perhaps as a partner. He began looking. Meanwhile Gary and the mayor, Alan Cohen, began talking. One of the important goals of the strategic plan was to expand jobs downtown—and a hotel might add thirty or forty jobs. Why not expand the project somehow and create more jobs? If Tom would relocate, and if Nick would accept a partner, why not go to the university and see if they would get involved?

Alan had attended Cornell, class of '86. After graduating, he purchased a small bar and restaurant downtown called Simeon's and turned it into one of the most successful food and beverage operations in all downtown. In 1995, he ran as an independent candidate for mayor and won. At the age of thirty-two, Alan became mayor of a town of thirty thousand with an annual budget of $45 million. Alan was an entrepreneur. Nick needed a partner. Alan and Gary began talking. Both of them knew Hunter Rawlings, the president of Cornell. Alan, in his role as mayor, spoke with Hunter about the possibility of joining the Lambrous in their hotel project. And in addition, he suggested, why not bring some Cornell employees downtown? The Lambrou project could become both an office building and a hotel—expand the vision!

At our business retention and development committee meeting, Gary laid out an additional idea that might make all this happen. The local CVS pharmacy had announced it was leaving the Commons to move out to "big-box row" at the south end of town. The 7,000-square-foot building would soon become vacant. The owner, local stockbroker Dave Barr, was anxious to find a new tenant. Maybe Tom Pine would relocate into the CVS space on the Commons?

Gary mentioned this to Tom, who liked the CVS location but didn't want to be a tenant; he wanted to own. Gary met with Dave Barr. They discussed a price. Gary returned to Tom. He was interested. However, word of Cornell's possible involvement in the project had gotten out. And now realizing the potential value of the location, Tom wasn't sure he wanted to sell at the price he and Nick had been discussing.

Gary kept our business retention and development committee informed as the project evolved. President Rawlings agreed, subject to trustee approval, that Cornell would move its development office from out near the airport to downtown—380 employees. They liked the downtown location, but they were concerned about Nick's ability to pull it off. He was young, and inexperienced in a project of this magnitude. Would he accept a partner? Cornell issued an RFP (request for proposals) from local and regional developers with whom they had previously collaborated. Gary served on the selection committee whose responsibility was to select a developer who they were sure had the capability to complete the project, and also propose a multiuse project that would leverage Cornell's office presence together with the hotel.

Cornell had worked on other projects with a company from Buffalo, Ciminelli Construction, which had built and managed numerous hotels and office buildings across upstate New York. They responded to the RFP and were selected as developer for this landmark project, teaming up with Nick and his group to propose a venture that would deliver 70,000 square feet of office space; the 105-room Hilton Garden Inn, for which Nick had already secured the franchise; and a ground floor of retail. Then there was the question of parking. If Cornell were to come downtown, the city would have to build a new parking garage. There was no question about it, and some of it would have to be dedicated to Cornell employees. Additionally, there was the issue of hotel parking. How would that be solved?

There were many balls in the air by this point—hotel, offices, Tom Pine, Cornell, CVS, a parking garage . . . Gary was juggling mightily. Alan was steady ahead. Hunter Rawlings was committed. Ciminelli was in, and Nick was amenable to whatever it took to get his hotel built.

Gary put Tom Pine together with Dave Barr, the owner of the CVS building. They worked out a deal, and Tom agreed to buy the CVS building and move his office supply company there, subject to arriving at an acceptable price for the sale of his share of the Beam Travel/Race property to the Lambrou family. Unfortunately for Nick, the closer they got to an agreement with Cornell and Ciminelli, the larger this price grew. Tom was no dummy. Once he saw the possibility of a nine-story building on the site of their one-story building, the more valuable it became in his mind. He wanted to share in that added value.

Nick told me that in retrospect he had truly made a big mistake by not obtaining an agreement in writing from Tom prior to embarking on the project. *Site control*—rule number one. But Nick had a vision, and it was expanding. He continued to work with Cornell and Ciminelli. He had already secured a height variance and the agreement with Hilton Garden Inn. After Mayor Cohen arranged a meeting with the heads of Cornell Real Estate, Nick agreed to let Ciminelli take over as lead developer for the project, and with this decision came Cornell's agreement to participate. Shortly thereafter, Ciminelli found a lender in M&T Bank, with whom they did business throughout the state. Nick and his investors would become partners with Ciminelli and retain an ownership position of a much larger project than originally conceived. What was to have been a four- or five-story hotel grew in concept to a nine-story building.

Plans were drawn. Thys oversaw the writing of the zoning change for the planning department and developed the arguments for the board of zoning appeals (BZA) that would be needed to build a nine-story building on the site. The planning department also wrote the environmental review. The tax abatement was negotiated with the IDA. Ciminelli asked the mayor to consider eminent domain as a last resort for acquiring the property. The two small business owners were holding up a project that would create hundreds of jobs in downtown, bring in thousands of tourists every year, and ultimately yield millions of dollars of tax revenue to the city. Although it was highly controversial, Mayor Cohen agreed and helped set in motion a process that would ultimately end in condemnation. Fortunately, the owner of Cameras N' Things agreed to terminate his lease, and Tom Pine finally agreed on a price that all parties could live with. *Site control* (with adequate zoning), *experience*, and *financing*—all three components were now in place.

Parking, however, was still a major hurdle to be overcome. Our city planner, mayor, and council had years earlier conceived of a parking garage and development plan on an urban renewal site adjacent to the old Woolworth building. Now the time had come to make it happen.

After months of discussion, under Alan and Thys's guidance, Ithaca's city council agreed to construct a state-of-the-art, $14 million, 750-space parking garage with retail on the ground floor two blocks from the new project! They worked out an agreement with Cornell in which their employees would park only in this new Cayuga parking structure. They would not be allowed to buy permits for the Green Street or Seneca Street garages, because the City did not want the parking garages close to the hotel to be flooded with 380 Cornell employees. They would have a place to park, but not get any special price or deal on the permits.

Ciminelli was a very experienced developer. In order to agree to build a hotel in downtown Ithaca, the company insisted not only that the city follow through on the new 750-space Cayuga Street garage but that they be allowed to lease one hundred parking spaces in the existing Seneca Street garage directly across the street from the hotel. As Thys describes it, "Providing parking for the hotel guests was a huge struggle. First of all there are some pretty strict laws governing how the city treats people who rent facilities like parking spaces from them. Essentially, no entity can be given a special right to those spaces, so the first thing we had to do was get around that. With the assistance of the urban development council, we created a Rube Goldberg financial structure that would issue debt backstopped by the city's full faith and credit, and that debt would be sold, resulting in a very low interest rate. In addition, it would not go against the city's debt limit. So actually the new parking garage was NOT financed with city debt."

Another even more contentious issue for Thys was Ciminelli's proposal to provide the hundred best spaces in the Seneca garage to the hotel patrons. Thys went head to head with the mayor on this point, taking the position that they could get the deal done by agreeing to provide spaces in the garage with no preferential treatment for the hotel guests. For some reason, Alan was absolutely convinced that the city should make the first hundred spaces on entering the garage available exclusively to hotel patrons.

As Thys said, "This came to a head at one meeting where Alan invited David Chiazza, Ciminelli's project manager, and asked him if he really needed the first spaces. To my shock and amazement, he insisted that he did. Alan said: 'See, it's essential to the project's success.' Alan got his way, and to this day all the people coming to downtown grumble as they drive past the empty spaces in the Seneca garage to find space on a higher floor." Thys had lost this one!

As part of the package of coming downtown, Cornell agreed with the city that up to 250 parking permits at the city's soon-to-be-built Cayuga Street garage would be made available to Cornell, and that the Cornell employees would be encouraged to park at the new Cayuga garage. Part of the city's reasoning was to encourage the employees to walk through the Commons, thus increasing pedestrian volume, liveliness, and potential sales there.

In addition, after a long and particularly heated public discussion—(why should city parking be preferentially allotted to a privately owned hotel?)—it was agreed that 104 parking spaces would be provided for the hotel on the lower floors in the Seneca Street garage across the street from the new building. It was decided that forty employees in the hotel, 380 employees from Cornell, and another thirty with the brokerage firm Smith Barney, which had leased the top floor of offices—a total of 450 new employees in downtown, plus the hundreds of visitors that would come to the hotel—justified the use of the Seneca Street public garage for hotel parking, particularly since a new garage nearly twice the size was going to be built a couple of blocks away. In addition, while the tax abatements for the Seneca Place hotel would be worth about $3.9 million to Ciminelli and the Lambrous, the project would add close to $30 million to the assessment rolls, which, over time, as the specially negotiated tax abatement diminished by 5 percent a year for twenty years, would produce significant additional tax revenue for the city, county, and school district.

All the pieces were in place. In late August of 2004, the groundbreaking was held for Seneca Place—a 185,000-square-foot mixed-use complex located in the heart of downtown Ithaca, at the corner of Tioga and East Seneca Streets. It would become a 105-room Hilton Garden Inn built atop a five-story office complex. The total reconfigured nine-story facility would be home to 93,000 square feet of class A office space, with Cornell University as the anchor tenant. It would house not only 380 employees from the Cornell Development Office, but also the brokerage firm Smith Barney and, on the ground floor, the hotel lobby, restaurant, and meeting rooms. In late August 2005 the building opened fully leased.

**Figure 11.1** Seneca Place: a four-story Hilton Garden Inn atop five floors of offices. Photo by Jon Reis.

The strategic plan included the goal of getting the three educational institutions—Cornell University, Ithaca College, and Tompkins Cortland Community College (TC3)—more involved in downtown. The community college was secure and growing, located ten miles out of downtown Ithaca in the village of Dryden. President Carl Haynes had already established a strong presence in downtown Ithaca, initially by renting office and classroom space for an extension campus on the first floor of the former Rothschild's Department Store on the Commons. In the long term, however, in order to provide more convenient access to their students, Carl envisioned that the college should own its own building for a permanent extension center in downtown Ithaca. Networking was to provide the solution.

As one of his civic duties, Carl served on the board of the Cayuga Medical Center, Ithaca's local hospital. Bob Abrams also served on this board. Bob was a former New York City property developer who came back to his alma mater and was instrumental in establishing the Cornell graduate-level Program in Real Estate. Carl spoke with Bob about his desire to find a site in downtown Ithaca for the college.

Bob had been involved in finding and working with Ciminelli Construction when Cornell had gotten involved in the downtown project by relocating their development offices in the new Seneca Place building. He knew Ciminelli was still looking for tenants, so Bob suggested to Carl that perhaps the TC3 Foundation could *purchase* a couple of floors of the new Seneca Place building rather than renting them from Ciminelli.

At Bob's suggestion, Carl called David Chiazza, the project manager for Ciminelli. Instead of renting, would they be willing to sell the TC3 Foundation two floors of the new Seneca Place building on a condominium basis as a home for the TC3 campus in Ithaca? David told him they were not set up to do a condominium offering and that it would not be possible from a financing standpoint.

Carl, in addition to heading TC3 as president, has used his skills as an entrepreneur to cast a wider net. He has the temperament for business. Networking through Bob had opened the door, but he knew that if you don't put your vision and ideas out there, nothing happens. If you do keep your vision and are willing to take the risk, then sometimes things work out. Carl had told me in one of our many conversations that "you have to have faith. Serendipity plays a big part in being entrepreneurial." He was rejected but not discouraged.

Ten minutes later, the phone rang. David at Ciminelli was calling him back. "If you're looking for a place for the college, why don't you consider buying the M&T Bank building across the street from Seneca Place?"

"I had no idea you owned it," Carl said.

"We had to buy it when M&T sold us their bank drive-through. We didn't need it, but it was part of the deal with the bank to secure the entire site we needed for the Seneca Place project."

David and Carl agreed to get together to discuss the possibility. Carl had never previously used donor money for real estate purchases, though he had made several for the college through the TC3 Foundation. Ciminelli did not need the bank property. They were willing to sell it to the TC3 Foundation for the amount they had paid for it—$1.8 million. David laid out the deal, and Carl listened.

Carl approached the TC3 Foundation board, which authorized him to obtain an independent appraisal of the property, which came in at $2.4 million. This made the purchase price of $1.8 million a good business decision. The foundation board then authorized him to pursue finding a mortgage. Carl obtained a mortgage from the local community bank, Tompkins Trust Company, for 75 percent of the appraised value—$1.8 million. This provided the cash to purchase the property from Ciminelli and in turn provided Ciminelli with a $600,000 donation credit for donating their equity in the building as part of the $2.4 million purchase established by the appraisal. Carl and Ciminelli had arranged the purchase of the entire building with no cash required from TC3.

The building was six stories high. David told Carl that the bank wanted to stay on as a tenant on the first floor; they just didn't want the hassle of actually owning the real estate. The college would rent floors five and six from the TC3 Foundation for its extension campus—floors two, three, and four were already rented to several professional tenants, so Tompkins Cortland Community College could take the top two floors as their permanent campus in downtown and rent out the rest, thus providing the college with an ongoing stream of income.

The deal was done, and now the college would pay market-rate rent to the TC3 Foundation, 50 percent of which would be reimbursed by the state since the college was using it for instructional purposes.

Carl had his downtown campus. He had a brass plaque installed crediting the donation that Ciminelli Construction had made to the project. TC3 and Cornell were now both major presences in downtown Ithaca, fulfilling one of the primary goals of the BID's strategic plan.

The Gateway office building had retained 150 jobs downtown in its new building. Between the hotel, Cornell's development employees, and the Smith Barney brokerage firm, Seneca Place would add another 450 jobs. We now had a permanent home for our community college, a new parking garage, a new hotel, and a new restaurant. Alan orchestrated a redo of the central part of the Commons with new light fixtures, brick paving, and a new fountain in preparation for the hotel opening.

**Figure 11.2** The M&T Bank building, new home of Tompkins Cortland Community College—a no-cash transaction! Photo by Jon Reis.

The Lambrous were pleased: Nick had picked up the gauntlet and met the challenge. Tom Pine was pleased: he was able to purchase his own building in the heart of the Commons. Carl Haynes was pleased: Tompkins Cortland Community College now *owned* their new extension center—with no financial outlay—and Cornell was pleased to be recognized for strengthening the "town-gown" relationship and finding new modern office space for their development office.

In addition, Gary and the BID members and the city planning department were pleased to have participated in creating the tremendous synergy that had taken place due to their behind-the-scenes efforts, first in helping create the vision for downtown, and second in helping make the many deals with all the interested parties work out smoothly.

# CHAPTER 12

# BEHIND THE SCENES

## Growing the Market

Working with the BID, landlords on the board of directors gained a heightened sense of the balance and synergy required for a community to continue to develop. Property values depend on the rents that can be paid for a particular space, and these rent values depend on retail sales. Retail sales depend on creating an inviting environment and attracting the public to an area with stores, restaurants, and entertainment that complement each other to serve the public with what they want and need. In spite of the attraction of the Commons, downtown had lost nearly every large regional and national retailer.

Greater Ithaca was in the crosshairs of the major national players. Our downtown pharmacies, Rite Aid and CVS, were moving out toward the malls. The part of town known as the Southwest had one aging strip mall and another small mall mainly occupied by local stores, a Staples, Kmart, plus a few other national brands, while the remaining area along Route 13, the old city fairgrounds, was essentially vacant land. In typical Ithaca fashion, when Walmart proposed their first store for Ithaca, it was shot down. In key public meetings the opposition came out in droves to oppose construction based on the proposed Walmart development and the withering effect it would have on local retailers. It was attacked on the grounds that the massive building and parking lot would have a negative impact on the views from Buttermilk Falls State Park. Never mind the increased tax base and the new jobs it would create, Walmart was not welcome.

Wegmans, the super grocery store, came to town. They were welcome. After much negotiation with Thys and the planning and development board over landscaping, sidewalks, and down lighting to control light pollution in the night sky, they located out on the old fairgrounds in the Southwest. Benderson Development, one of the largest developers in the country, with over seven hundred properties in thirty-eight states, had found Ithaca—a tertiary market, but one that was gradually being recognized as a development target worthy of the attention of national chains. Benderson wanted to purchase significant acreage in the city's Southwest and bring dozens of major chain stores to Ithaca.

Our mayor, Alan Cohen, was pro-development. He had overseen the development of the new Cayuga Street garage, and the new Seneca Place hotel and office building had also been constructed on his watch. He had repaved the part of State Street leading up to the Commons with brick pavers, and had installed new classic streetlights there, to match the design of the rest of the Commons. He had the aging and broken fountain on the Commons removed and a simple but working one put in its place. He had even introduced for public debate the question of reopening State Street for automobiles. Whatever it took, his goal was to make downtown as successful as possible.

But downtown was not his only area of focus. Alan welcomed any interest in development in Ithaca overall. The BID members were extremely concerned over the possibility of increased competition. The original Commons, constructed twenty years ago, had somewhat counteracted competition from the new Pyramid Mall up the hill in Lansing, which had continued to develop with office complexes and a variety of strip malls as well as new garden apartments. The focus of major retail had already shifted to the northeast of town. What could we do in downtown to offset development in the Southwest?

The question was whether to welcome the new development or to watch it go—along with its tremendous potential to increase the tax base for the city of Ithaca—over the city's borders into Lansing, where it would be welcomed with open arms. Much of the land in the Southwest area was owned by a few real estate developers. The city could not directly interfere with the sale of private property, but they could control the use of the land through zoning, hence affecting the value and the probable outcome of its sale.

Since his arrival, Gary had been invited to attend a standing meeting with the city administration once a week in Thys's office, when the mayor, the director of planning and development (still Thys), and other planning and development staff, including the economic development director, met to discuss projects and concerns affecting the entire city. The mayor made it known that he felt the need to have the support of the Downtown Ithaca Alliance (DIA) in order to change the zoning to allow mall development in the Southwest. It was not mandatory that the BID board weigh in on it, but it would be politically useful, because many members of the public would be concerned about the economic fate of downtown if dozens of national chains opened in the Southwest. Would the BID publicly give its support to development there?

Gary brought this dilemma to the next board meeting of the DIA. What should their position be regarding support for the Benderson project? Members of the BID, including retailers, property owners, tenants, and businesspeople in the offices downtown, had to decide. Were they going to watch what was left of downtown wither as more and more competition dragged the stores and offices away from it?

The idea of attracting national brand retail to the heart of downtown had been tried over the years. Stan Goldberg had attempted it at his Center Ithaca in the '80s and was initially successful in attracting B. Dalton Bookseller. There were several major department stores in Ithaca—Rothschild's, Iszard's, McCurdy's—but they had all succumbed to competition from the malls. The Woolworth Five and Ten Cent Store opened its first Ithaca branch on State Street as early as 1910. In 1967 developer Dave Abbott lured them to the vacant urban renewal site a block away by building a 70,000-square-foot store for them. In 2008 Woolworth, a successful firm since its founding by F. W. Woolworth from Rodman, New York, in 1878, was closing all of their stores internationally.

Knowing Woolworth's lease would be up and closure was likely imminent, Dave reported that he had made repeated attempts over the previous two years to re-lease this 70,000-square-foot monolith. He said he had been to New York City many times to present his downtown Ithaca location to big-box stores like Target and Walmart and had contacted most of the major chains; none of them wanted a downtown location today—not in what they termed a "tertiary market." They wanted "the strip"—the malls in larger cities. Furthermore, they told Dave, there was simply not enough population in downtown Ithaca to support their numbers. There wasn't enough parking downtown to fit their typical format, and if there were, the city was certainly not offering it for free. They could relocate outside of downtown in malls in a stronger suburban market and have free parking. Never mind that Dave could show them sales figures from his Woolworth store that verified their Ithaca location was one of their top performing stores in the country. Today's demographics did not support big-box development in downtowns. Dave had finally concluded that his efforts to attract big-box retail to downtown were futile and had given up that approach.

How much more difficult it was going to be to attract national chains to the downtown Ithaca pedestrian mall. It wasn't going to happen even with the most intense marketing. Small-city downtowns no longer fit the paradigm of big-box stores.

The BID members were faced with the dilemma of supporting the big-box development in the Southwest at the expense of downtown vitality, or not supporting it and watching the corresponding tax revenue go up the hill and out of town to Lansing, where it was welcome. The last attempt at a full-blown department store had been McCurdy's in the old Roth-schild's Building adjacent to Center Ithaca. It had closed in 1994, and Andy Sciarabba and Stu Lewis, as Comex Associates, converted the second floor to offices for Thomas Associates, with two restaurants on the first-floor street front, classrooms for the downtown branch of the local Tompkins Cortland Community College behind, and bank offices in the basement for Tompkins Trust Company—Ithaca's only truly local bank, which had been in business since 1836.

Downtown was filling up with crafts stores, tattoo parlors, restaurants, and head shops. There didn't appear to be much hope. As a planning spe-cialist, Thys knew that renting to offices along the street front, particularly on a pedestrian mall, would kill the retail continuity. In an effort to pro-tect the retail we did have downtown, Thys prepared a zoning amendment to present to Common Council prohibiting offices on the ground floor in areas zoned for retail, but the council was unwilling to adopt it.

The BID had no power to control small stores moving out of downtown and renting in the proposed development in the Southwest. Why should we then support Mayor Cohen's rezoning of the Southwest? Gary had the idea that perhaps the BID could suggest to the city that they limit the size of retail stores that could locate there to nothing under 5,000 square feet. That would discourage most downtown retail tenants from moving out of downtown to newly developed space in the Southwest. This made sense, but would the city do it? Since none of the new space was built, and since zoning was a legal and effective way for a municipality to control develop-ment use, there was a distinct possibility the BID could at least try to exert its influence in order to protect the retail market downtown.

Property owners downtown were already in the position of renting to small retail shops on the Commons and in the surrounding areas. There were few stores larger than 2,500 square feet. If we accepted our enforced limitation of no national big-box chains downtown, which was already now apparent by default, perhaps we could focus and promote the BID as the area for *specialty retail*—clothing, gifts, crafts, books, sportswear, and of course the restaurants that were already prevalent downtown.

The board of directors discussed this at length and came up with a reso-lution in support of development in the Southwest *provided* the city would enact zoning prohibiting retail stores under 5,000 square feet. This was done with the tacit understanding that the city would increase financial support for the BID area in relation to the increased income it would receive from the enhanced tax base.

Gary took this idea back to his weekly planning and development meeting in Thys's office. The mayor liked it. Thys liked it. When the time came for the city planning board to consider the Southwest development zoning proposal, they could do so knowing they had the support of the Downtown Ithaca Alliance.

# CHAPTER 13

# GATEWAY COMMONS (2005–6)

## The Pride Project

CLUG had played an important role in my early development and helped expand my vision of what was possible. In addition to Center Ithaca, my wife and I now owned a four-acre site in downtown. We had successfully renovated the six-story office warehouse there into an office building, Gateway Center. It was fully rented to sixteen businesses with a total of 150 employees. The Seneca Place hotel project was under construction. The new city parking garage would soon be built. Our pedestrian mall, the Ithaca Commons, only a block from our four-acre site, was undergoing minor renovation. Based on the Danter housing study, we felt it was time to move on to phase 2 of our Gateway project. It was time to build luxury apartment housing in Ithaca.

The Danter housing study, commissioned as part of the strategic plan, had called for eighty to a hundred units a year to be built within the BID district over a four- to five-year period. It had broken down the types of units that the market could absorb: 50 percent should be in the "affordable" range, 40 percent should be in the "market rate" range, and 10 percent could be built in the "high end," or luxury, range. No new units had been built so far. This was a stretch. According to my calculations, one simply could not afford to build "affordable" units without some kind of major subsidy. With construction costs for any type of housing in Ithaca hovering around $200 per square foot, there was no way to pay for a project by renting to tenants who could pay 30 percent of the area's median income—$600 or $700 per month for an apartment wouldn't begin to cover the operating expenses, much less the debt service for new construction.

Provided the new building was at least six stories high, the project would be eligible for the maximum tax abatement program. This would help. Although the project was eligible, and we had received a tax abatement on phase 1 of the Gateway site (the office building), this abatement application proved contentious at the IDA. One of the county legislators said he didn't want to give tax abatements to "build condos for yuppies." Thys went to bat for us and argued that no project had been built in downtown since 1960 without some sort of subsidy. Gary and members of the BID board spoke in favor and eventually the project passed.

HOLT Architects took on the design. However, there was a problem. There were two buildings on the site near the street, both of which had previously been gas stations. Red alert! Storage tanks and the possibility of fuel spills. A study of the old Sanborn maps of the site showed only two tanks. Test borings on the site indicated no leakage of fuel into the shale. We were extremely lucky, because just about every site in the central business district has some sort of contamination problem.

HOLT put their best designer, Anton Christiansen, on the job. He made a casual reference to "green construction." I let it slide, with no idea really what he meant. We began negotiating with the city and with the state, because the project would need approved access for the ingress and egress to the new building onto Route 79, a state highway that runs through the heart of downtown. A traffic study had to be conducted, and a complete phase 1 and phase 2 environmental study of the site had to be performed. A usual member of our development team, Trowbridge and Wolf, landscape designers, got to work on the site plan.

**Figure 13.1** Oil storage tanks—but no leaks! Photo by author.

With the initial designs, the layout was for twenty-six luxury units, which ranged in size from 850 square feet for a one-bedroom to 1,200 square feet for a two-bedroom and over 1,700 square feet for a three-bedroom—larger than any units in the downtown Ithaca market. The Danter study called for a total of eighty to one hundred rental units a year to be built, with 10 percent of them at the high end of the market, which is where our rents would have to be for these apartments. Twenty-six units would be a start. Besides, that was all we could fit on the site, within the maximum zoning envelope of six stories.

My son, Frost, had gone through the Cornell Baker Program in Real Estate, graduating with a master's degree in 2000. He had been exposed to sustainable design—"environmentally friendly development," or "green" design. As he went into detail about what it meant, and the added costs, I held up my crossed index fingers and informed him that I had no desire to add costs to the project. We would build our projects in a conventional manner: luxury, yes, but as economically as possible—no green design.

My sister in Greensboro, North Carolina, had been reading a book called *Green Capitalism*. She sent me a copy, which proved to be an inspiration. As a result, Bill Petrillose, our facilities manager, and I signed up for an Urban Land Institute conference in Washington, DC. We flew there and spent three days listening to lectures and presentations on green design—earthen roofs, recycled gray-water systems, superinsulation, low-e triple-pane windows, natural and recycled carpets. We learned that contrary to building specifications then in effect, all plywood used on the site had to be formaldehyde-free—this included kitchen cabinets and the elevator cabs, which would have to be specially manufactured. We heard of the health benefits, and the addition of 2–3 percent in construction costs, as well as the cost payback in health and marketing. To achieve the highest designation, the building had to be left vacant in order to be aired out with high-performance "MERV" filters for two weeks at the end of construction. These were massive requirements, but when they showed us photos of the polar ice cap, which had suffered a 40 percent reduction in size over the past twenty years, and the 10.4 acre Ford Motor Company roof in Detroit planted in grass and flowers complete with nesting curlews, I was sold. So was Bill, who would be in charge of managing the facility on completion.

A luxury building in today's market must be *green*! HOLT Architects was right; Frost was right. I came home and instructed the architects to change direction. We would build a green building—the first green apartment building, as it turned out, in upstate New York. Its name would be Gateway Commons, and it would include manufactured bamboo flooring, wool-blend carpets, a highly efficient air-conditioning and heating system, exterior walls up to eighteen inches thick, solid maple cabinets, an elevator cab with "no form-aldehyde," and we would use low-VOC (volatile organic compound) paint. The building would have a white membrane roof. It would be aired out 24-7 with the super thick MERV filters for two weeks before occupancy, thereby removing any residual toxins. For this it would achieve a LEED (Leadership in Energy and Environmental Design) silver designation—not gold, not platinum, as it didn't have the recycled gray water or an earthen roof, but this was what we could afford. And it would be built to a standard that would assure that the building was as healthy as possible for its residents. It opened with no new-carpet or new-paint smell—no headaches, no allergic reactions. It was healthy, and the apartments leased quickly. Gateway Commons was one-third rented in the spring of 2006 when it opened, and fully rented by the end of July. Not only was green construction healthy for the residents; it was also a great marketing tool. Thys later told me that he was enormously impressed with my willingness to take on this project. The market for green, high-end rental apartments was truly untested in downtown, or for that matter anywhere in Tompkins or surrounding counties. Thys told me that I had put on wings and jumped off a building to see if I could fly. We were both thankful I could!

However, there was another consideration. The two outbuildings that were originally gas stations had years ago been converted to restaurants—Napoli Pizzeria had been in business on the site for nearly thirty years, and Sticky Rice, a small but fine Thai restaurant, shared the other building with Domino's Pizza, which had been there for fifteen years. It was a difficult situation. Their leases were up. They had no legal right to remain,

**Figure 13.2** Gateway Commons, concrete basement foundations and walls under construction. Photo by Jon Reis.

**Figure 13.3** "Flying in" a concrete plank that forms both ceiling and floor—the entire building system is called "block and plank" construction. It is extremely sturdy and soundproof. Photo by Jon Reis.

**Figure 13.4** Gateway Commons—six stories and twenty-six luxury apartments. Photo by Jon Reis.

**Figure 13.5** Aerial view of Gateway Center and Gateway Commons. Photo by Jon Reis.

**Figure 13.6** The ribbon cutting at Gateway Center: (left to right) Mack Travis, Bill Petrillose (facilities manager), Mayor Carolyn Peterson, Carol Travis, Anton Christensen (architect). Photo by Jon Reis.

**Figure 13.7** The LEED (Leadership in Energy and Environmental Design) plaque hangs in the lobby. Photo by author.

but it was not in our job description to put people out of business. Our job, particularly as it related to the goals of the BID, for which I still served as president, was to endeavor to retain current businesses and to develop new ones. Yet we needed the entire site to build our new building and to accommodate the parking we had planned.

In the early phase of design we worked out an agreement with each of the three tenants to relocate them to the unused ground floor of the neighboring Gateway Center. We would build out three new restaurants. They would pay a portion of the costs over a time frame that would work for their cash flow. Construction would be coordinated so their new restaurants were completed prior to the demolition of the old gas stations. They would be able to transfer their entire operations to the new spaces over a weekend. We chose to do it this way. My wife and I felt that it would simply be "bad karma" to end people's livelihoods in order to achieve our dream of a new building.

At the opening party, catered by our relocated restaurants, we congratulated the BID and Gary for the vision they had provided for new housing downtown. We congratulated HOLT Architects, Northeast Construction, and the workers for an award-winning design and its successful execution. We congratulated the city for its role with the tax abatement and the financing, and my son for awakening me to the need for green construction. It was an untried concept—luxury, green housing in downtown Ithaca. We were lucky that the building rented so quickly, and as I also said at the opening—at the *highest rents in New York State outside of Manhattan!*

It was true. The units were expensive, but they were larger than anything available for rent in Ithaca other than perhaps a single-family house. They offered assigned parking and full-time maintenance. They also came with a terrace overlooking both Six Mile Creek and the downtown. It was a natural environment within a block of the Commons. Furthermore, to provide a link between downtown Ithaca and the incredibly beautiful Six Mile Creek Nature Preserve, Carol and I had donated an easement to the city for a Creek Walk through the entire 2,500 feet we owned along the creek. We built out the first 1,000 feet of the stone-dust walkway along the creek with railings and lighting, and the city promised that they would eventually extend the trail all the way to the preserve.

Gateway Plaza with its office building and new apartments was magnificent! It had landscaped parking and hundreds of shrubs and trees. We had created a park downtown, as well as a walkway along the creek. What had been an industrial brownfield had been turned into a showpiece for downtown. Our rental success, however, had not been by accident. A former advertising executive, David Plaine, spent a year working with us during construction, creating public awareness of our new project. There was a story to tell—Gateway Commons was LEED certified, the first apartment building in upstate New York to apply for the LEED designation.

Stories about the architecture and features to be included in the building were great publicity for the project. David arranged for several front-page articles in the local newspaper. We produced a twenty-minute promotional video, which was unusual for our little town, but it aired nationwide and calls of interest came in from as far away as Mexico and Alaska—with many more from Washington, DC., and New York City. Cornell University has an international draw, and our approach was to tap into the market of retirees wanting to return to their alma mater for their final years. In fact, the first resident was an eighty-year-old woman who had grown up in Ithaca, attended Cornell, and wanted to move back to Ithaca from Westchester, farther downstate near New York City. Never underestimate the value of marketing and publicity.

It had been costly, however—very costly. In an effort to pay all the bills, I contacted Thys. A year or so earlier Carol and I had repaid the original $1.3 million HUD loan from the city to build Eddygate in 1986. After eighteen years of making every payment on time, we had refinanced and repaid the remaining balance of close to $800,000 to the city. Would they consider relending those funds to us to complete the Gateway project? Thys said he would talk to Mayor Cohen. After much deliberation, with a vote by the Ithaca Urban Renewal Agency and final approval by council, the city agreed.

The city had their easement through the Gateway site for a public walkway connecting downtown with eight miles of trails in the Six Mile Creek gorge. Downtown had a new housing project, another step in the goals set forth in the strategic plan. The BID board of directors and Gary shared our pride in the project. Carol and I had a ton of debt—manageable, but lots of it.

Debt aside, we were immensely proud of our new project. Thanks to the original BID vision, thanks to the Dickinsons' faith in the project and in us, thanks to the banks and the city, thanks to our designers and hundreds of workers, Gateway Commons had become a reality. Our residents were pleased. We had a bank president and university professors among our tenants; we had lawyers and computer experts—a group of professional people and retirees who had never before considered the possibility of living in downtown Ithaca. We gave a ribbon-cutting party at the end of the project that was attended by over three hundred people.

When everything settled down, our accountant, Andy Sciarabba, reviewed our numbers. Sitting across the table from me in his office, he pushed aside his review of the financial spreadsheets, shook his head, looked up at me seriously, then grinned and said, *"This was your Pride Project."* And he added, *"You only get one of these in your life!"*

To raise the cash to complete the job, not only did we borrow HUD funds from the city, we also refinanced a large part of our real estate portfolio—but Gateway was built. Other than a few small buildings, it was the first major downtown redevelopment project in decades. It fulfilled a major portion of the vision of the 2010 strategic plan, and best of all, although we still had a vacant ground-floor retail space, all twenty-six apartments were fully rented.

# CHAPTER 14

# THE RIPPLE EFFECT

## Do You Believe?

None of us work in a vacuum. Playing CLUG made that very apparent to me, and I had experienced it again and again, developing various projects in and around Ithaca for the past thirty years. Thanks to the stability brought by Cornell, Ithaca College, BorgWarner, and a growing high-tech sector, Ithaca maintains a strong economic base. In the late 1970s city leaders had formed the Downtown Vision Task Force to set a course for the future. Years of studies, of envisioning what Ithaca could become, were paying off—first in Collegetown, and now downtown. The process of reinventing a city never stops. A trip to the photo archives of the History Center of Tompkins County gives one a sense of how the city used to look. The BID's strategic plan had generated a renewed confidence in the downtown. It had become an idea, a large stone thrown in the water, spreading ripples throughout the community.

In the early 1990s the county was making plans to relocate the public library. It had outgrown the 1967 downtown building, and they decided to conduct a feasibility study on where to relocate. The current building was situated downtown across from the Presbyterian church and the lovely DeWitt Park; it was over forty years old and in need of a major overhaul. The library board formed a subcommittee to survey potential building sites. They searched on the outskirts of town where property was cheap. They surveyed sites far out into the county where it was even cheaper. In our minds, as local merchants, property owners, and politicians, just as with the post office, it was imperative that the library stay downtown. The mayor knew it. The BID board at the time knew it and lobbied strongly for the library to remain downtown. The director of the library said they preferred to remain downtown, but where could they locate?

Dave Abbott was in his eighties and a full generation ahead of most of us; he was a pillar of the Ithaca community. A marine in World War II, he had returned to Ithaca to start his business by transforming an old bowling alley into a women's lingerie factory and sold his products nationwide through J. C. Penney. When the factory closed, he rented the space to a sheltered workshop, Challenge Industries, across the street from our soon-to-be-converted Gateway warehouse at the foot of State Street hill. For twenty-five years, Challenge employed hundreds of special-needs clients. Dave was also one of the first to build affordable housing in Ithaca. In the 1970s, utilizing the major subsidy of below-market HUD financing and tax credits, he had built West Village—350 units on the west side of town—and Maplewood apartments, 394 units on East Hill.

Most real estate transactions take place behind the scenes. The public is never even aware of them until they are announced. This one was no exception. Dave, the ever-enterprising owner of the Woolworth building downtown, made a deal between the county and a friend and major benefactor, Dorothy "Dottie" Park, widow of Ithaca's richest resident, and Forbes 400 communications magnate, Roy Hampton Park. Through her Park Foundation, controlled by herself and her daughter, Dottie would purchase the Woolworth building from Dave for $2 million. She would donate it through the foundation to the county as the site for the new Tompkins County Public Library.

As you help to build your city, never underestimate the largess and potential generosity of civic-minded wealthy citizens. Renovations began in the fall of 1999, and the library opened in its new space in November of 2000.

Although the new project would not directly replace the retail traffic generated by Woolworth, it would retain over five hundred thousand library trips a year coming to the downtown, trips that might otherwise have gone somewhere else. The county agreed to accept the generous donation from the Park Foundation, and the library agreed to move three blocks south to the corner of Cayuga and Green Streets. Between a public fund-raising effort and support from the county, the library secured several million dollars to renovate this vacant, basic box into an incredibly lovely new Tompkins County Public Library, unrecognizable from its original incarnation as a five-and-dime store.

Thomas Associates' decision to keep their 180 employees downtown, the success in keeping the post office downtown, the Gateway Plaza project, the successful retention of the library, the construction and leasing of Gateway Commons, and the tax abatement had spread the ripple effect created by the BID strategic plan. Public belief in the downtown as a viable place for new businesses, offices, and housing was catching on. Downtown was worthy of investment, and momentum was gathering.

Meanwhile, the Department of Planning and Development under Thys's leadership had been working on a plan to expand the remainder of the vacant site next to the new library into housing and retail. It had been cleared of its buildings twenty-five years earlier as urban renewal roared through town, and it had been used as a paid city parking lot ever since. With the new library, and with the newly planned-for housing and retail on the site, it would be necessary to replace the parking lot. A new parking garage would have to be built.

When he arrived in 1999, Gary brought fifteen years of experience to his position as executive director of our business improvement district. He had consultant contacts all across the country, and at one point, he invited a consulting team from Toronto to Ithaca to have them assess our retail possibilities. In addition to telling us we could build another 100,000 square feet of retail in downtown, they pointed out that the typical configuration of the dying downtowns across the United States comprised a mostly vacant central core surrounded by a moat of parking lots, in turn surrounded by the suburbs and shopping malls. They marveled that Ithaca had escaped that fate because it had the foresight to build two large parking garages in downtown—the Seneca Street garage in 1973, and the Green Street garage in 1974, at the same time as the Commons and Rothschild's Department Store were developed. So, due to the fact that parking had been accommodated in multistory garages rather than on vacant downtown sites, our downtown had been left mostly intact and mostly still usable, despite the questionable destruction inherited from urban renewal. Thys, supported by the foresight of our mayors and our Common Councils at the time, had been responsible for building the two garages. It was time now, with the new project at Seneca Place, to build a third.

At Thys's suggestion, the city put out an RFP to attract developers to the project. They had several responses. They twice selected a developer and worked with them through the preliminary conceptual phase, only to decide that neither developer would work out for this project. Finally Gary suggested a third company, a firm owned by Ken Schon and Steve Bloomfield out of Cincinnati. Thys called Steve Bloomfield and convinced him to come take a look at Ithaca. They were selected, and the city announced Bloomfield/Schon as the preferred developer for the library site.

It's interesting how circumstances and serendipity often intervene. Thys's daughter had attended the University of Colorado Boulder. While visiting Boulder on a family weekend, Thys noticed the downtown parking garage. The historic norm for a parking garage, including the two built in Ithaca, has been to tear down a city block and build however many stories necessary to accommodate the required parking. With a parking garage fronting on the sidewalk, the block was, for all intents and purposes, "dead." As important as parking is for a downtown, the municipality would unwittingly create a huge gap in the urban retail fabric of their downtown.

Thys observed that the Boulder garage was different. He found that Boulder architect Chris Shears of Shears Adkins Rockmore Architects had designed *space for retail* on the first floor, with parking above. He researched the firm and found that Chris Shears had designed projects in downtown Denver and along the Pearl Street pedestrian mall in Boulder. He also found out that the firm was known across the country for their urban design projects, and he invited Chris to Ithaca. The city council was impressed. Teamed up with local architects Highland Associates, SA+R Architects was hired to design the new 750-space parking garage planned for Ithaca. This new garage would include retail facades along the street.

Soon, Schon and Bloomfield would begin the process of designing and building the Cayuga Green project in the same block as the new garage, adjacent to the library. Thys would work hand in hand with them through the development of their Green Street apartments, as well as on the master leases for the commercial spaces that would occupy the street frontage in the new Cayuga Street garage. There was no question about the viability of downtown—by then we all believed!

CHAPTER 15

# THE OUT-OF-TOWN DEVELOPERS (2003–15)

## A Study in Perseverance

So far we had a new post office and town hall, two new office buildings, a new hotel, a new library, one new apartment building, and now a new out-of-town developer selected by the city to develop the site adjacent to the library into housing and retail. We had a partially renovated Commons, and we now had new events: the Downtown Ithaca Chili Cook-Off in the middle of February, which brought ten thousand visitors to the Commons at the coldest time of year, and a new summer event called Art in the Heart for showcasing sculpture by both local and national artists downtown on the Commons. We already had the Apple Harvest Festival in October—events were becoming more ambitious and more successful. We had increased rental occupancy downtown, up from 80 percent to over 98 percent. Ithaca was on the map as a very desirable place to live, work, and play. Making improvements had to be an ongoing process. We could never say our work was complete. Businesses still came and went; nothing is ever fixed or static. Police presence and trash pickup could always be improved. But overall the BID was having a very positive impact on downtown Ithaca.

The site adjacent to the library was the most ambitious project to date, or at least it rivaled the Seneca Place hotel and office building in complexity. Steve Bloomfield and Ken Schon from Cincinnati were the third in a line of developers who had been interviewed by the city for development of this highly visible site half a block from our Gateway project, through the block from our Center Ithaca building, and across the street from city hall.

After being formally selected in 2003, Steve and Ken spent about two years working with the city to come up with a viable plan for the project. One of the considerations was to build sheltered housing to serve the mental health group next door on Green Street. They worked with Gary on the idea of a commercial movie theater underneath the garage. The published scope of the project was to have the developers build new housing and ground-floor retail. The city would build the new parking garage on Cayuga Street, and the developer would master-lease and manage the ground-floor retail along the street under the garage. In addition they would master-lease and manage the ground-floor retail under the Green Street garage, the central section of which would be rebuilt. This space could possibly include a new movie theater. Gary and the Downtown Ithaca Alliance (DIA) had been pushing for a multiscreen commercial movie theater with as many as ten screens to be located downtown. This was anticipated to be a large draw for students and the general public—"arts, dining, and entertainment"!

In order to make way for the new housing project, the three-story helix that provided circular access over Green Street and into the Green Street garage would have to be demolished. The center section of the Green Street garage would be rebuilt with ramps to allow for access to the upper levels. Under the new ramps there would be enough room to create a small movie theater complex, not the ten screens, but at least five.

However, when the idea for a new first-run multiplex movie theater downtown was announced, the Regal Cinema in the outlying mall went ballistic. Within a week, they announced their intent to build a fourteen-screen

**Figure 15.1** Green Street parking garage. The helix (lower right) would have to be demolished to allow for development of the Cayuga Green project. Interior ramps in the rebuilt center one-third of the garage would allow access. Photo by Jon Reis.

theater with stadium seating. The war was on. Movies are a complex business. The rule of thumb with major movie theaters is that they should be no closer than fifteen miles of one another. The mall was only 4.9 miles from the downtown location. Gary's idea for a multiscreen commercial theater complex was obviously a nonstarter. In addition, distributors play the controlling role in who gets what movies. The idea of a new downtown commercial cinema simply would not fly once Regal had announced their intent to build the multiscreen theater complete with stadium seating. Major distributors would ignore us in favor of the national Regal chain.

There was an alternative. Ithaca already had an art-house movie theater—Cinemapolis—which had three very small screens and was one of our tenants located in the basement of Center Ithaca, adjacent to the parking garage. After much public discussion it was agreed that Schon/Bloomfield would build a new five-screen movie theater on the ground floor underneath the rebuilt Green Street parking garage. They would serve as landlord for Cinemapolis, which would relocate from our Center Ithaca building into the new space. It was not strictly a commercial theater, and it was not as large as the multiscreen commercial theater we had hoped for, but it fit the goals of Cinemapolis, now known as the Seventh Art Corporation of Ithaca, a 501(c)3, and it fit the goals of the DIA strategic plan to create an entertainment center downtown.

The Schon/Bloomfield project as originally conceived would include sixty-eight new apartments, forty-eight condos attached to the Cayuga Street garage, and management of two retail centers leased from the city on the ground floor of both the Cayuga Street and Green Street garages. They had figured out financing through the New Market Tax Credit Program—their specialty—with a bank from Cincinnati for the first mortgage and the tax abatement from our local industrial development agency (IDA).

Steve Bloomfield and Ken Schon were very likable guys. The BID was not actively involved in the development process, but Gary would orchestrate a number of us to speak in favor of the project at Common Council. Members of the BID board spoke in favor of it when the tax abatement came up for consideration at the IDA. Gary was concerned about the county. Both buildings of the Gateway project—the hotel and Seneca Place—had been recipients of the tax abatement. Gary pointed out to the IDA that neither of these downtown projects would have been built without the tax abatement. But a number of IDA board members were feeling that too much attention was being paid to downtown. The county's largess should be spread more widely through the rest of the population. We felt it was our job at the BID to ensure that Steve and Ken received their tax abatement for the new project.

As far as I knew, no one from Ithaca had looked at any of their other projects in Cincinnati. Bloomfield and Schon had gone through the competitive process with the RFP. After having two other prior choices not pan out, the city planning department and the mayor had been satisfied enough to select them, but were they "for real"? In addition, I had to deal personally with the fact that not only were they taking one of our prime tenants (the movie theater) but also the idea of a competitive project being built less than a block from two of my major housing projects—Gateway Commons and Center Ithaca. From the standpoint of the BID, it was important that we continue to develop housing and retail downtown. Was there really an adequate market to allow more housing? Our personal projects might suffer, but were we going to grow the community or not? And were these the guys to take us to the next step? I made the decision to go to Cincinnati to look at their operations firsthand.

I took a tour through the South—visiting my sister in Greensboro, my daughter and grandchildren near Atlanta—and then headed north to Cincinnati to visit Bloomfield/Schon, real estate developers. My GPS delivered me to their door in an industrial part of downtown Cincinnati. On the first floor of their building in an open atrium on full display stood a bright, shiny, black Model T Ford in mint condition, and according to the plaque on the wall, it had never been restored. It was in its original condition, and it had been built in the very building it now occupied. Steve and Ken had bought the original Cincinnati manufacturing plant for the Ford Motor Company that opened in 1915. I was fascinated. They did what I did. They renovated old buildings and turned them into useful structures for the modern world. Only they did it on a scale far beyond what I had attempted in Ithaca.

Steve and Ken had renovated a building of well over 100,000 square feet on four floors into not only their own offices with a dozen employees, but also other architectural offices, offices for a medical insurance company and many other businesses, plus covered parking for several hundred vehicles. It was impressive. They introduced me to their in-house architect, José Garcia.

We looked at his plans for the Ithaca project. They drove me around town and showed me a four-story, 40,000-square-foot medical office building designed by José—it was modern, clean, crisp, not unlike the modern buildings Carol and I had seen on a recent trip to South America. We drove to an attractive residential part of town where they showed me two dilapidated mansions they had purchased. They had plans drawn to tear them down and build thirteen condos on the site in this urban setting. We went to lunch at a fancy downtown restaurant where they were obviously well-known, and they then drove me to their crowning glory—if a vacant concrete building five stories in height, the size of a half-dozen airplane hangars, with broken-out steel windows, and sitting on an asphalt parking lot of ten acres could be called a crowning glory.

Steve and Ken had purchased the American Can Company Building. It was four times the size of our Gateway warehouse conversion, more like the National Cash Register site on South Hill in Ithaca. At 180,000 square feet on ten acres, it was huge! Since they had announced the purchase over a year before, property values in the vicinity had soared. Many of the small houses, probably the original homes of the American Can workers, had been purchased, renovated, and painted bright colors. Stores and shops had opened. The run-down, long-vacant neighborhood surrounding the original factory complex was coming back to life. It would take them five, six, maybe even ten years, they estimated, to design, obtain permitting, and complete this project of housing, shops, parks, and parking. However, because these well-known local developers had taken it over, already a new confidence was sweeping through the area. I learned that Steve and Ken were themselves both trained as architects. These were guys that really knew how to *shape a city*. Excellence in design was obviously paramount in all their projects.

I returned to Ithaca determined to work with them. It would be the best thing for downtown, never mind my concerns about competition. I would take it as it comes. Their project was complex. The political process for all the approvals required in a public-private partnership in Ithaca was enough to discourage the hardiest of developers. They were obviously very experienced, and it was important to keep them involved and enthusiastic about this site so far from their home location.

Members of the BID spoke in favor of their projects with the city council and the IDA. In an effort to favorably influence the upcoming vote by the IDA on a tax abatement for the project, I wrote the following article in support. It was published in the *Ithaca Journal* on November 13, 2005.

### An Investment in Change

As individuals, we are born, mature, grow old, and eventually die. As families, we marry, have children, and can indeed continue for dozens, if not hundreds of generations. As a city, we are founded, endure eras of prosperity, eras of decline, and subsequent rebirth and revitalization. One force common to our lives as individuals, families, and cities is change. Nothing in the life of an individual, family, or a city remains static. It is our choices that will determine in great part how that change unfolds.

The Brookings Institution, a prominent Washington think tank, recently published a research brief written by C. B. Leinberger entitled "Turning Around Downtown: Twelve Steps to Revitalization." It begins, "Over the past 15 years, there has been an amazing renaissance in downtowns across America." Sampling 45 cities across the country, a Brookings study cited by Leinberger found that the number of people living in downtowns has increased by 14 percent over the past decade "in spite of zoning laws supporting suburban sprawl." He calls this "a testament to the emotional commitment to our urban heritage and the pent-up consumer demand for walkable, vibrant places in which to live and work."

In Ithaca, we have shared this commitment to our urban heritage, remembering the vibrancy of our downtown as a shopping district with major department stores, theatres, services of all kinds. We have created an historic district in our downtown. We have embarked on our own process of revitalization of downtown as a place to live, work, play—our own vision of downtown Ithaca as the center of arts, dining, entertainment—a financial, governmental, and professional office center—the Commons as the major tourist attraction in the area with its specialty retail stores, its festivals and concerts.

The first six steps of "Turning Around Downtown" as outlined in the Brookings Study are ones we have engaged in as a community since Mayor Nichols established the Downtown Vision Task Force in 1990, and Common Council chartered our Business Improvement District in 1997. As a City, we have adopted a *"Common Vision"* formed with input from merchants, property owners, civic leaders, and the public. We have developed a *"Strategic Plan"* for downtown setting forth specific goals for job creation, parking, hotels, new living units, and an entertainment district. We have forged healthy *"Private/Public Partnerships"* with the Seneca Place office building, Hilton Garden Inn, the Cayuga Street parking garage, the Gateway office building, and the Cayuga Green project. We have taken the steps to *"Make the Right Thing Easy"* by changing the zoning ordinance to allow for more density downtown and assisting downtown projects that meet the density requirements, with the IDA-sponsored tax abatements. We have created a *"Business Improvement District,"* which is taking a leadership role in managing implementation of the strategy for downtown redevelopment. In an operational role, the BID is improving the image of downtown by increasing safety and cleanliness. It is increasing the excitement of downtown by organizing festivals and events. And the sixth step is the creation of a *"Catalytic Development Company,"* which, as Leinberger states, will serve as the "pioneer . . . in developing initial projects that demonstrate to the rest of the development community and their investors that downtown development can make economic sense." And this we have done in part through the Cornell/Ciminelli/Lambrou coalition that built the new Seneca Place project, and through the City's active role in developing the Cayuga Street parking garage and attracting Bloomfield Associates as preferred developer for the Cayuga Green project.

Ithaca has scored well in the implementation of the first six steps for downtown revitalization as stated in the Brookings Institution research brief. The brief continues . . . "Once the stage for downtown development is set . . . the private real estate market begins to emerge . . . critical mass is usually achieved . . . in six to ten years." We are on track, but there is more to do.

Steps seven through twelve outline the remaining strategies required to be in place for downtown revitalization: "*Create an Urban Entertainment District* . . . Performing Arts Centers, Movie Theatres, Restaurants, Specialty Retail, Festivals, Arts, Night Clubs . . . 'get feet on the street' . . . crowded sidewalks recommend downtown, signaling a safe environment, and providing an excitement and spectacle that draws people to the area." This we are doing through the revitalization of the State Theatre, the formation of Seventh Art [Cinemapolis Movie Theater], and the proposed Cayuga Green Movie Theatre, as well as our strategy of attracting specialty retail to downtown and holding numerous festivals and concerts on the Commons. "*Develop a Rental Housing Market* . . ." City View, Gateway Commons, Cayuga Green, and other projects soon to come in upper-story development on the Commons, will supplement the housing provided by Commons West, Center Ithaca, and the Park Building. "*Pioneer an Affordability Strategy.*" The Brookings Brief recommends a combination of mandates and grants to achieve affordability so necessary to achieving balance in the downtown housing market. "*Focus on For-Sale Housing* . . . Having an established for-sale housing market is the ultimate test of whether the downtown has achieved critical mass . . . Bringing the middle and upper-middle housing to downtown will provide the tax base so sorely needed by most cities, and members of these households will demand a level of service that will continue the upward spiral." It would appear that as downtown Ithaca strengthens, condos will be part of our future. "*Develop a Local-Serving Retail Strategy.*" We have a strong group of specialty retail stores in our downtown, and as we achieve critical mass it is more likely that we can once again attract basic services such as a grocery store and pharmacy. The twelfth step is to "*Recreate a Strong Office Market* . . . As upper-middle-income for-sale housing is built in downtown, there will gradually be a return of a healthy office market and the employment it houses." We have been fortunate to have retained a strong office market in downtown Ithaca, in spite of the sprawl to the suburbs. Seneca Place, Gateway Plaza, and the Cayuga Green project have, or will add, significantly to the attractiveness of downtown Ithaca as a place to locate professional offices of all types.

Leinberger sums up his research on these twelve steps to downtown revitalization: It is "one of the most complex, challenging undertakings anyone can embark on . . . Yet seeing a . . . downtown come to life is a great reward for any community—and worth investing time, energy, and emotion."

As pointed out again in an *Ithaca Journal* article citing the 2004 edition of "Cities Rated and Ranked: More than 400 Metropolitan Areas Evaluated in the U.S. and Canada," *Ithaca is the "No. 1 emerging city" in America.* Change will happen in Ithaca. Thanks to the foresight of our civic leaders we have been following an effective process for directing the course of that change.

With the upcoming IDA vote on the Cayuga Green project, Ithaca has an important choice to make. We can choose to follow the old way and continue to force change out to our surrounding countryside, or we can invest in change as a community both private and public, and direct development to our downtown as outlined in the twelve steps of the Brookings Institution study. Ithaca is on track in this twelve-step process of "Turning Around Downtown." Until we have achieved critical mass, the IDA Density Policy and Tax Abatement will remain a vital component to downtown revitalization. Let us retain the political will to proceed.

Eventually all the designs for "Cayuga Place" were approved by the city and the IDA. The Schon/Bloomfield project as originally conceived was to have included sixty-eight new apartments and forty-eight condos. In exchange for the proposed tax abatement, the IDA held Steve and Ken up in negotiations by forcing an agreement on them to limit the rents that could be charged for the apartments. As a result, and out of concern for the market risk with that many condos, they decided to reduce the number by half to twenty-four. Ken told me they were prepared that it would take a year or more to rent all of the new apartments, and that if all went well, they would build the remaining condos as phase 2 of the project "in a year or two." As it turned out, it would take them another eight years to complete the build-out of the entire site.

Steve credits the National Development Council (NDC) with getting the Cayuga garage built and arranging the new market tax credits for them. He said it was only by chance that they got the infusion of equity into Cayuga Green. The NDC had a project go bad after they had struck a deal with KeyBank. They had to place the money somewhere, and he and Ken were about ready to go.

He later commented that "Ithaca, despite studies to the contrary, is not seen as a big enough or strong enough market to interest large banks or investors. Nor are Ken and I seen as big-enough players. The new market tax credits helped a great deal to get us going. Then we hit the recession of 2007–8, and our commercial leasing slowed way down. At the end of the seven-year compliance period, KeyBank was unsympathetic and difficult to work with and called our loan. It was difficult to make everyone whole, but we did! The project was doing well and Ithaca's central business district was flourishing. A regional bank, First Niagara [which was also our bank at Gateway Commons] stepped in and took out the National Development Council and KeyBank."

Sometimes in real estate development, the stars align, and for Steve and Ken, this was obviously one of those times. They had persevered and built a full city block of successful projects in downtown Ithaca.

Competition is healthy. It spurs us on to perform and produce at our best. In my experience, cooperation and collaboration can be equally healthy forces, for they spur us on even while we are doing our best, to make sure that all around us are able to do their best, and are getting their fair share. As we all succeed, the overall market can only be strengthened. Many years ago I had tried to expound this philosophy of doing business to Joe "Sonny" Cosentini, who for decades had owned a shoe store in our downtown. "Sonny," I said, "as part of growing the downtown we should see if we can attract another shoe store to the Commons. There is plenty of business to go around." "Don't you believe it!" he said. "Another shoe store on the Commons will put me out of business!"

At that time, Sonny was probably right. We did not have our business improvement district. We had not formulated our overall strategic plan for growing all aspects of downtown to attract more workers, more residents, more tourists and shoppers. If I took a bigger piece of the pie, that would leave less for you. If I built an apartment building next to yours, that would mean fewer tenants for you. Being old-school, and having run a successful business for years, Sonny could not see beyond what he knew, to what he or his business might become.

Having been exposed to the dynamics of successful cities, having worked on the BID with Gary, and having played CLUG, I understood that while we can have too many shoe stores, too many apartments, too many offices for our limited market, we can also embark on a sales campaign that will attract more workers to the area, more people living downtown, that will make our restaurants and our shoe stores even more attractive, more competitive. Rather than carving up the proverbial pie—we can make it bigger! Thys's argument was always that the more stores we have in downtown, the better we would do in our competition with the outlying malls. No matter how many stores we added in downtown, it would still be a drop in the bucket in terms of the entire retail picture in the county.

We can adopt an outlook of growth—that if you build a new apartment building next to mine, we will in turn attract more residents to the area. Of course, there has to be lucrative work in the area so people can afford to move to the downtown—it is all interrelated and requires a continual balancing of supply and demand, demand and supply—and we had it in Ithaca. With Cornell University, Ithaca College, BorgWarner, the many high-tech businesses locating here—we had a labor demand; we could supply more shoes, more offices, more apartments, theaters, and restaurants. When we started the development and construction of Gateway, you could count on one hand the major real estate projects in Ithaca since forty years before, when urban renewal had torn down a great part of our downtown.

I gulped when I first heard that Thys had negotiated with the Cincinnati developers to attract them to Ithaca to build new apartments, offices, and retail across Green Street from our 144,000-square-foot Center Ithaca building, which already had sixty-two apartments, six restaurants, a dozen stores, and twenty office tenants. Could we handle the competition? I realized I had to look at it this way: Steve and Ken would be developing their new project in a torn-down, vacant parking lot that had been nonproductive for decades. They were going to build another hundred apartments or more. They were going to add retail—a pharmacy, a national clothing store. If I believed in growth for our community, I had to cooperate. I felt the conviction that I had to aid and assist the competition.

On their next visit to Ithaca I took it upon myself to share my local Gateway experience with them. I toured them through the new apartments and talked to them about LEED and sustainability. I shared our rent roll, construction and operational numbers—giving them a complete budget for Gateway. I shared with them what I knew about the downtown Ithaca housing market and showed them the Center Ithaca apartments. These units were over twenty years old, but they were priced accordingly and very successful in the market. I had adopted Gary's belief that the activities of the BID, while perhaps detrimental here and there to existing businesses, would eventually "float all boats." If a new project were built downtown, it would add to the synergy of success for us all. I aided the competition, but in the bigger picture, I did it out of my own self-interest.

Working with the BID, one could not help but be repeatedly exposed to the idea that downtowns are an underutilized resource in our country. They have been allowed to go dormant while the life and business activity moved out to the malls. Every inner city has a huge infrastructure just waiting to be developed and utilized, with roads, sewers, utilities, and bus lines. It was important to help our downtown move forward. I felt it was important to cooperate with other developers so their projects would be as successful as they could possibly be. This approach led to an interesting phenomenon.

I had begun cooperating extensively with Steve and Ken; however, as their building evolved and grew to its six-story height across the street from Center Ithaca, I began worrying. Perhaps I had been foolish to give them so much assistance? I had even supported their leasing to our movie theater tenant, Cinemapolis, who would be moving from Center Ithaca to the new theater they planned for the first floor underneath the Green Street parking garage. I had allowed the movie theater to break their lease with us. Was I nuts?

The move would enable them to grow from a small, cramped three-screen theater in the basement of Center Ithaca into a spacious, brand-new, five-screen art cinema in the heart of downtown. A new movie theater was part of our strategic plan. How could I follow my convictions about the growth of downtown "floating all boats" if I were to be selfish and unsupportive of their leaving our building? Carol and I donated $25,000 to their new venture.

Yet how would we handle the apartment competition? The revised design was for forty-eight brand-new apartments in the first phase of their Green Street apartment building. They would slaughter us at Center Ithaca. We braced for the vacancy impact. We held our rents steady for a year—no increases. We offered free gym membership to our Center Ithaca apartment tenants at the Finger Lakes Fitness Center in the basement of Center Ithaca—$100/month per apartment tenant. We did what we could do to minimize the impact of the new competition.

Typically, ever since Carol and I, with our partners, had purchased Center Ithaca out of foreclosure in 1994, we had entered the summer with half of our sixty-two apartments left to rent for the following year. Each year they rented up fully, at least by the first of September. When you own income property, this is the major risk. Will the apartments rent? Will the stores and offices rent? I felt a little like Sonny Cosentini in his shoe store. Was there enough to go around? I remembered he had said, "Don't you believe it!"

Steve and Ken had shared with me that they projected it would take up to two years to fully rent their forty-eight new units. Their new Green Street building was completed in the summer and opened in July 2008 *fully leased*.

It was amazing. The market was stronger than any of us had thought. Center Ithaca leased as well, but as usual it took until September to rent the last remaining units. The following year would tell the story. Would the competition from their project put us out of business?

To my surprise, our rental agent told us on June 1 the following year that we had leased 100 percent. And the year after that we were full by May 1, and the year after that by April 1. These were all leases for the coming year. We always had about one-third of our residents renew, and that did not change, but we filled the remaining units earlier and earlier after the Green Street project was built. The conclusion to be drawn from this was that the new building and the added units at Cayuga Green only made downtown more attractive to a greater number of people. We had expanded the pie. Ken and Steve's marketing helped Center Ithaca, and our marketing helped them. We even recommended their building to prospective tenants who, for whatever reason, did not rent with us. We truly experienced that this new project, this additional attention on downtown, had transformed the central core of Ithaca into a more desirable place to live—it was indeed floating all boats.

I cheered Steve and Ken on to their second phase by telling them it had taken five years for me to pull off the Eddygate project in the 1980s—my first experience with a public-private partnership—but it had certainly been worth it. The Gateway project was another public-private partnership. In both cases, the city had played a large role in facilitating the approval process.

The entire development had extended over five years. Bloomfield and Schon were committed. By now they had survived a three-year political process in Ithaca for all their approvals. They were experienced developers and understood the public-private dynamic—Steve and Ken were indeed a study in perseverance.

**Figure 15.2** Cayuga Green. Forty-eight apartments and retail. Note the new pharmacy. Photo by author.

**Figure 15.3** Cinemapolis. The movie theater was built under the Green Street parking ramp, across the street from the Cayuga Green apartments, and became a tenant of Bloomfield/Schon. Photo by author.

**Figure 15.4** Bloomfield/Schon's Lofts@SixMileCreek later came to be called "Cayuga Place" and was completed twelve years after Steve and Ken were selected as developers by the city. Left to right: former mayor Carolyn Peterson, Mayor Svante Myrick, retired city planner Thys Van Cort, city planner JoAnn Cornish, Steve Bloomfield at the podium, and Gary Ferguson, executive director of the Downtown Ithaca Alliance. Photo by author.

Thys doesn't like to blow his own horn, but the Commons, Center Ithaca, the tax abatement, the Cayuga Street garage, and now the Bloomfield/Schon project absolutely would not have happened were it not for his role as city planner in each project. The same could be said for Gary in his role as executive director of the Downtown Ithaca Alliance, our BID.

The following article by Karen Gadiel appeared in the *Ithaca Times* on January 11, 2006.

"We're very optimistic about 2006," said Steven Bloomfield, of Bloomfield, Schon and Partners, architects and developers of the Cayuga Green project. He said they're anticipating a ground breaking in late spring.

"I think the Seneca Place is very successful; the work that Mack Travis is doing [Gateway] is going to help bring people downtown," Bloomfield said. "Ithaca is following a sort of national trend of repositioning itself in the marketplace to be competitive with suburban malls and suburban sprawl. This is a very important project for us. Obviously we hope to do well, but we also hope to do some good for the community."

Putting things in historical perspective, City of Ithaca Director of Planning and Development Thys Van Cort noted, "Some people have characterized this as a huge amount of growth and in the great sweep of things, it is not that much. There was extremely little growth downtown other than through public sector investment over the past 35 years, with a few notable exceptions." These are the County Mental Health Building, the Social Services Building and the Tompkins County Public Library, built entirely through private funding.

Every other new structure was built with urban renewal help or tax abatements, necessary because building inside a city is both more complicated as well as financially risky.

When asked about abatements, [Michael] Stamm [the president of Tompkins County Area Development (TCAD)] explained, "It's always more expensive to build a project in an urban setting than suburban setting. Construction in a tight urban core is difficult—things have to go up rather than out. And it's difficult to construct when there's a lot of activity around, so the costs are estimated 20 to 30 percent higher. There's a perceived element of higher risk with historically so many failed urban projects. Incentives are important to encourage that kind of development." And if this momentum continues, Ithaca just might be on a roll. "Our goal isn't to create a massive new skyline but to make intelligent use of the space we have," Ferguson said.

# CHAPTER 16

# OTHER FORCES AT WORK

## IURA, TCAD, Historic Ithaca, ILPC, and IDA

Since the mid-1800s, the four-acre Gateway parcel along Six Mile Creek, which Carol and I purchased from Don and Sue Dickinson, had been the site for a variety of mills, a lumberyard, a bus garage for Ithaca College, a printing company for Wilcox Press, and the six-story Mayflower Warehouse, as well as Esso, Mobil, and Texaco service stations.

History is an important force at work in any city. As business owners and real estate developers, even in a small town like Ithaca, we should be aware of our history as we focus on the details of the project we are working on at the moment. We have to live in the present to make a project happen, to handle the thousands of details that are necessary for any real estate development to succeed—from site control to design, financing, construction, and leasing. This becomes our world. We are the ones shaping a city now. It is our projects, our turn . . . but in reality we are only building on what has gone before us.

According to a small history book titled *Ithaca and Its Past*, written in 1982 by Daniel Snodderly, "Ithaca's first non-Indian settlers . . . arrived in 1780. . . . In 1790, Ithaca had about 30 residents, most of them grouped at the foot of East Hill." The book goes on to tell us that industrial centers developed along the various creeks. In 1795 the first road was built between Dryden and Ithaca, and a turnpike was constructed from Owego to Geneva in 1811. The first steamboat, the *Enterprise*, was launched on Cayuga Lake in 1820, and by 1821, when the town of Ithaca was formed, its population was about one thousand. In 1825 the Erie Canal was completed, along with a canal connecting to Cayuga Lake. This opened up trade routes to Chicago and New York City. In 1834 the Ithaca and Owego Railroad was opened.

"By 1850," Snodderly continues, "Ezra Cornell, having made his fortune in the telegraph business [with Samuel Morse], returned to Ithaca to establish a model farm and pursue 'scientific' agriculture. Cornell became

**Figure 16.1** The site of our new Gateway project as it was in the early 1950s. Photo courtesy of the History Center of Tompkins County.

active in local affairs and was elected to the state legislature, where he met a young professor of history named Andrew D. White. Cornell and White worked together to secure the proceeds of the Morrill Land Grant Act for a new university. In addition, Cornell gave $500,000 and 200 acres of his East Hill Farm. Cornell University was chartered in 1865 and opened its doors in 1868." Andrew Dickson White was its first president.

"Another major educational institution, Ithaca College, was founded in 1892, as the Ithaca Conservatory of Music . . . other successful businesses were founded—the Ithaca Gun Company in 1883, and the Morse Chain Company in 1898." By 1900, in a little over a hundred years, Ithaca had grown to a city of over thirteen thousand.

After World War II, the Housing Act of 1949 established the "urban renewal" program nationwide, which provided federal funding to cities for the purchase of areas perceived to be "slums." The municipality could then make these sites available to developers to construct new, modern designed buildings. Under the Ithaca Urban Renewal Agency (IURA) in the 1950s, '60s, and '70s, many historic buildings were torn down in the center of town to make way for a new plan that ultimately failed. How does one account for that?

In a brief history of Ithaca's urban renewal written in 2015 for the online newspaper the *Ithaca Voice*, Brian Crandall cites figures from between 1954 and 1960, when forty-eight offices and retail stores closed or moved out of downtown Ithaca, a drop of 18 percent, and "the city councilmen were concerned."

The concept and policies of urban renewal were adopted by city leaders across the country, in the hope that by tearing down the old building
stock in the city center and replacing it with new modern structures, people
would be lured back from the burgeoning malls and suburbs that were sapping the life out of city centers.

Urban renewal efforts were undertaken in the hope that new buildings
would bring new retail, new jobs, and new residents back to the city. In
Ithaca, even Cornell University supported the urban renewal effort, believing that it would attract more industry and research organizations to the
heart of downtown.

Ithaca City Council also supported the efforts of urban renewal, and in
the 1960s and 1970s, the IURA appropriated land and demolished entire
blocks of older downtown buildings, with the plan that developers would
undertake the construction of new projects. In the process, the city of Ithaca
lost much of its one- and two-story wood-frame housing and shops, several of what today would be considered precious historical buildings—the
old city hall, the Ezra Cornell Library, and Rothschild's Department Store.

As part of this sweeping change, the city proposed and offered its support for these new construction projects:

- a hotel
- a bank
- a bus terminal
- a professional building
- expansion of downtown parking
- relocation of city hall and the fire station
- underground parking
- a supermarket

These plans for downtown development projects from urban renewal
decades ago sound very similar to what we were planning forty years later
with our BID strategic plan. At that time however, few developers responded
to the city's call for sweeping change, and initially only two of the proposed
urban renewal projects in Ithaca were built—a new hotel (the Ramada Inn),
and a new parking garage on Seneca Street were completed—and the city
hall and fire station were relocated.

Today we are building on the vestiges of urban renewal—both the sites
and the concepts. Comparatively, what happened, and why have things gone
so well for us in Ithaca in terms of redeveloping downtown over the past
fifteen or so years? As was the thinking in those earlier times, we have been
*planning*. Our economy has improved. The BID—with its all-encompassing

approach to business recruitment, events, the city/BID MOU emphasizing clean and safe, the objective housing feasibility study, and the emphasis on arts, dining, and entertainment—has made a crucial difference. We know today that the suburbs and the malls are here to stay, and we must work strategically to charm retail, offices, and residents back to the downtown.

Four of the major urban projects that Carol and I completed over the years have benefited from urban renewal. Eddygate in Collegetown, which we developed through long negotiations with the city from 1982 until its opening in 1987, was built on a former urban renewal site. The old buildings there had been demolished. It just took a few decades for new construction to happen, but when it did, it was city bonds and a $1.3 million 1 percent HUD second mortgage, awarded and administered through the IURA that made our project financially viable. In exchange for the low incentive interest rate of 1 percent was the requirement that the project have 20 percent HUD-certified low-income housing units in the overall sixty-four-unit project.

The Center Ithaca building, which we purchased out of foreclosure in 1994, was built on the historic site of the demolished Rothschild's Department Store, built in 1913 and demolished by urban renewal in 1975.

Figure 16.2 Rothschild Bros. Department Store at the corner of State and Tioga Streets ca. 1910. Photo courtesy of the History Center of Tompkins County.

Both Gateway projects at the foot of State Street hill benefited from an urban renewal loan made with the funds we had paid back from the original Eddygate subsidy, and which were held in the Community Development Block Grant fund controlled by the IURA. The Housing and Community Development Act of 1974 established the Community Development Block Grant program (CDBG), which focused on redevelopment of existing neighborhoods and properties, not necessarily in depressed areas.

As much as we have hindsight concerning what some consider the misguided and overzealous destruction of our architectural history wrought by urban renewal across the country, we need to remember that the city councils of their day were doing the best they could to plan and revive their often decrepit cities, which were being further devastated by the flight of business and housing to the malls and suburbs. Prior to the formation of Historic Ithaca in response to the wholesale destruction envisioned by urban renewal, a few of Ithaca's lovely historic buildings fell victim.

Today that is changing, even though urban renewal continues to play a major role in the financial viability of many downtown projects. Ithaca has also preserved many of its historic buildings. Downtown has once again become a trendy place to live and work—without a car required for every trip, one can walk to the store, and one can walk to work. There is a move toward sustainability and walkable communities, and the realization that arts, dining, and entertainment (as well as good jobs and good schools) have made downtowns more attractive, in contrast to the shopping malls and suburbs that many of today's young professionals have grown up with.

In the 1950s, fire officials determined that the 1866 Cornell Public Library was no longer safe to occupy and condemned it. In 1960 it was razed.

The cost of renovating the old city hall, which was built in 1844, was considered prohibitive, and it was torn down in 1965 to make way for the Green Street parking garage.

Soon after, the demolition of the Hotel Ithaca, regarded by many as a historic icon, became the trigger point for a group of residents (many from Cornell) to form an organized resistance to the continuation of this trend.

In an article titled "Historic Ithaca" from the May 1974 issue of the *Cornell Alumni News*, the editor wrote, "Not until landmark buildings began disappearing from the center of Ithaca in the 1960s did the community think much about its architectural heritage. But since then, acting singly and in groups, its residents have won a series of battles to save and adapt to new uses a significant number of old structures well-known to generations of

**Figure 16.3** Cornell Public Library ca. 1957. Photo courtesy of Historic Society of Tompkins County.

**Figure 16.4** The old city hall. Photo courtesy of Historic Ithaca.

**Figure 16.5** Hotel Ithaca, built in 1872, was demolished by urban renewal in 1967. Photo courtesy of the History Center.

Ithacans and Cornellians. . . . At Historic Ithaca's organizational meeting in 1966, a speaker from the National Trust for Historic Preservation . . . urged Ithacans to consider their fine old buildings an important part of the community's heritage, and suggested they make an inventory of important and savable buildings. At one point she made a distinction [that still goes on today] between historical and 'hysterical' preservation."

The four buildings identified as being in greatest danger at that time were the Clinton House, Dewitt High School, Boardman House, and the Tompkins County Courthouse. Each of these buildings had been allowed to deteriorate badly and was being considered for sale, demolition, or both. All four were saved from being torn down by Historic Ithaca's efforts. Historic Ithaca has continued to be the voice of historic preservation in Tompkins County and the Finger Lakes region.

In 1971, the city of Ithaca passed the Landmarks Preservation Ordinance establishing the Ithaca Landmarks Preservation Commission (ILPC). The ILPC "preserves and protects physical reminders of Ithaca's history—those

**Figure 16.6** Top left: Dewitt High School, built in 1915. Top right: The Clinton House, built in 1828. Bottom left: Tompkins County Courthouse, built in 1854. Bottom right: The Boardman House (far right), built in 1867. Photos courtesy of the History Center of Tompkins County.

visual characteristics that make the city unique, identifiable, and familiar to both residents and visitors." Today the ILPC is affectionately known by Ithaca developers as the "History Police." Try to change one window in a building designated as "historic" (as I in my ignorance tried to do with our 1888 Westminster building, which we renovated in 1988), and the ILPC is all over it! I quickly learned that it is better to cooperate and have them as your friend, for they truly do fulfill an important function in the preservation of Ithaca's historic buildings.

The ILPC is administered through the planning and development department. The board is made up of seven members of the community, with backgrounds in architecture, historic preservation, construction, engineering, the arts, and business. They are volunteers appointed by the mayor and confirmed by Common Council. There are seven historic districts, two in downtown—DeWitt Park district and the Clinton Block district—plus numerous individual landmarks.

The goal of the Landmarks Preservation Ordinance is to ensure that exterior changes to locally designated historic properties are compatible with the character of the individual property itself and, if the property is located within a historic district, to that of the district as a whole.

Another major force at work both in downtown Ithaca and through-out the entire region is Tompkins County Area Development. Its mission: "Building a thriving and sustainable economy that improves the quality of life in Tompkins County by fostering the growth of business and employ-ment." TCAD's five-year plan established for the 2014–18 campaign period calls for the creation of 750 new jobs, $45 million in new annual payroll, and $450 million in new capital investment. In the first two years of the campaign period, TCAD successfully influenced the creation of 501 new jobs, $31.4 million in new development, and $449 million in new capital investment.

It is a truism to say that we need jobs to support the development of our city and our region. TCAD cites statistics showing that private sector jobs in Tompkins County have grown steadily from about seventeen thousand in 1960 to fifty-three thousand in 2005. This growth certainly accounts for much of the success of the BID's strategic plan for downtown Ithaca today. There are simply many more people working here to support the redevelopment of downtown and the entire TCAD region.

Tompkins County Industrial Development Agency, better known as the IDA, is another key organization promoting job growth. The IDA's core mission is "to offer economic incentives to Tompkins County businesses in order to create and retain quality employment opportunities and strengthen the local tax base." They primarily target the industrial sector.

In addition to its primary focus on industrial development, the IDA has developed a policy of encouraging both commercial and residential devel-opment in specially designated urban and community centers in the core of downtown through its tax abatement program. Both the Gateway office building and the Gateway luxury apartments, along with the Hilton Garden Inn and offices at Seneca Place, were the first projects to take advantage of this new tax abatement policy of the IDA for downtown Ithaca. Both Gary and Thys had lobbied strongly to have this addition to the IDA's mission to encourage new projects and urban density.

By following its mission, the IDA is indeed strengthening the tax base and the quality of life in Tompkins County by offering economic incen-tives. And while it is often still a struggle politically to convince the legis-lators that tax abatements are a viable form of public-private partnership, primarily because of Gary and the DIA membership's commitment to the development of downtown projects, we have been successful.

# CHAPTER 17

# "CHANGING PEOPLE'S LIVES"

## Ithaca Neighborhood Housing Services

In the 1960s and '70s, Ithaca was not unlike many urban areas across the country. It faced a depressed economy, deteriorating housing, and an exodus of homeowners to the suburbs. Most of the houses in Ithaca's downtown were over a hundred years old. Few owners had the skills or the financial resources to get bank loans either to repair what they had or to move out into new housing.

In 1977, downtown Ithaca neighborhoods were in poor condition. Nationally, urban renewal was designed to get rid of slums, and its highest priority was tearing them down. But they were not rebuilding. It just was not happening. In Ithaca, homeowners were moving out and converting their houses into rentals. Neighborhoods were declining. The city decided to start a program to assist the public in buying homes by offering loans and grants. The department of planning and development tried, unsuccessfully, to run a program of housing rehabilitation from their office in city hall. The staff explained to Common Council that there would be a loss on each unit, and federal block grant funds would have to be used to cover the loss.

The first project was an old house that was given to the city by the county. It had been foreclosed on because it was in arrears on property taxes. With four feet of water in the basement and numerous other structural problems, it had to be gutted to the studs and sheathing and fully rebuilt, including a new roof, siding, mechanical equipment, interior surfaces, and appliances. Planning and development staff hired an architect to draw up plans for the rehabilitation, and a builder was selected through the normal competitive bid process that the city was required by law to use. In the end the project cost a total of $28,000, and when the rehabilitation was completed the house sold for $24,000. Just as staff had predicted, they lost money on the deal, but the city had a fully rehabilitated building, up to code in every way, that would last for another twenty or thirty years without further major investment.

The only thing that the council heard was that they had lost $4,000. The elected officials wouldn't stand for that. They failed to see the potential long-term benefits, and they became reluctant to do any more of these transactions.

The Urban Reinvestment Task Force in Washington, DC, had begun looking around the country to find out how cities revitalized themselves. In Pittsburgh in 1968 they found Dorothy Mae Richardson, who had started a campaign for better housing in her neighborhood on the North Side of Pittsburgh. Dorothy Mae Richardson worked with city bankers and government officials to convince sixteen financial institutions to make conventional loans for the betterment of her North Side community. Her legacy was an organization named Neighborhood Housing Services of Pittsburgh, which eventually became the model for community-based housing initiatives throughout the country. Its partnership model, which included neighborhood residents, local government, and the business community, proved to be a highly successful formula for city revitalization.

In 1978, Congress chartered the Neighborhood Reinvestment Corporation, with a mission to re-create Neighborhood Housing Services of Pittsburgh's housing program on a national scale. It went to work under the name NeighborWorks America providing grants and technical service in support of community development in urban, suburban, and rural communities across the country. Their slogan: "Working together for strong communities." NeighborWorks America aimed to create opportunities for people to live in affordable homes, improve their lives, and strengthen their communities. This organization was to become the model for Ithaca Neighborhood Housing Services (INHS).

In Ithaca, when the city's initial efforts had foundered, Citizens Savings Bank president Ken Myers said his bank would participate in a program for the betterment of Ithaca's housing *provided the program was not run from city hall*. It had to be through a separate organization.

Under Thys's continued leadership, Ithaca joined the growing network of successful Neighborhood Housing Services operations, and Ithaca Neighborhood Housing Services was formed as a not-for-profit with an independent board of directors not directly responsible to any elected officials. As Thys has said, the goal of INHS was to try to find a way to reverse the decline of downtown Ithaca by *fixing homes up* rather than *tearing them down*.

Thys was instrumental in the formation of INHS. He believed, and had stated publicly, that a city cannot be a great city if it has either *a weak downtown* or *failing residential neighborhoods.* Thys found that INHS proved the efficacy of public-private partnership in the residential sector. Just as, years after the formation of INHS, the business improvement district successfully directed and focused development in the central core, using aspects of private-public partnerships such as tax abatements and IURA loans, INHS in partnership with city government, local lending institutions, and the affected neighborhoods themselves had earlier changed the face of Ithaca's residential neighborhoods. Neither could do the entire job themselves as effectively as they could do it together.

Starting with helping homeowners maintain or improve their homes with low-cost loans and other types of home-repair assistance, INHS soon began acquiring and redeveloping dilapidated rental properties, constructing new homes and rentals, and helping community members buy their first homes.

When Thys began working on the INHS concept, the planning department performed a housing survey of the downtown neighborhoods on the Northside and Southside of Ithaca, using five categories of exterior condition for buildings: 85 percent of the houses were in the lowest categories, with only 15 percent in the "good" or "excellent" category.

The INHS mission is to help people of modest income to locate and remain in high-quality housing in the Ithaca area. Their method is to provide low-interest loans to first-time home buyers and both low-interest loans and technical assistance to homeowners seeking home improvement projects. They own and manage rental units, rehab older homes, and provide home-repair assistance to seniors.

In 1984, Thys hired Paul Mazzarella as a planner on his staff in the planning and development department. Paul had developed an interest in governmental politics and public service during his studies as an undergraduate at Duke. He graduated with a master's degree in planning from Cornell in 1979, and after working five years in Lansing, Michigan, and Amherst, Massachusetts, Paul came to Ithaca and started working under Thys. He became interested in neighborhood civic groups and joined the INHS House Recycling Committee. Paul aspired to become director of planning for the city of Ithaca, but, as he somewhat humorously puts it, "When it became apparent that Thys was never going to leave," he applied for the job as the executive director of Ithaca Neighborhood Housing Services. As he tells the story, he took over at a time when "INHS was at its worst position in its entire history. It was a lender, and it had run out of funds to lend. Most of its programs had come to a standstill, and there was an insurrection by the staff."

Paul found he needed to rebuild the finances and restore confidence in the organization. He set to work and learned how to get the money to make loans. He learned how the capital markets work and how to gain access to capital. He learned the government process for grants and loans. He learned that, for the most part, private conventional sources considered low-income housing high risk. Most investors would look at what his organization does and wouldn't want anything to do with it.

Over the years, with the increasing success of INHS, the Ithaca nonprofit housing world has gained in stature. A stable organization with a strong balance sheet can leverage money from many sources. Paul can now go to local banks and find them extremely supportive. Now most of the loans are underwritten based on the project itself.

Paul attends national conferences for NeighborWorks America and finds there are many nonprofit housing organizations with varying degrees of capacity and success. Not everybody enjoys the close financial relationship with their city that INHS does in Ithaca. Much of the federal money, such as the CDBG funds given to the city, come to INHS. When we paid off the balance of the HUD loan from the refinancing of our Collegetown Eddygate project, for instance, the city gave the funds to INHS with the restriction (by HUD regulations) that they could only be reused to finance rental projects that benefited the low-income bracket, as they had been used originally at Eddygate.

The ensuing city administrations in Ithaca have seen fit to support INHS, and Paul has been there more than twenty-five years now. "It is not partisan in any way," he says. "Colleagues in some other cities tell stories of new mayors coming in and cutting them off."

In 2002, INHS became a community development financial institution (CDFI), a designation by the US Department of the Treasury. To qualify, they had to show that the primary lending target is low-income households. There are fifteen hundred CDFIs in the country focusing on housing, economic development, and credit. CDFI also provides training and capacity building for INHS. Every three years there is an audit of Paul's entire program policies and procedure. INHS always gets the highest rating.

Paul says that "INHS has been lucky. It escaped the severe problems of subprime lending and foreclosure, which could have wiped them out as it did in other communities in the 2008 financial crisis." Much of the growth of its assets has been due to the success of its lending and real estate development projects, both of which contribute to the financial stability of the organization.

Under Paul's direction, INHS has built assets of $24 million and has a solid track record with local banks. Recently he received a query from

Oppenheimer Funds. Although Ithaca is isolated from big money centers, he is learning to gain access to different opportunities, farther afield.

After decades on the job, Paul feels INHS has made a measurable and sustainable long-term impact on the community. It has made an important contribution in its efforts to assist homeownership and to create better-quality rental housing. It has turned the Northside and Southside neighborhoods around. In the beginning it was hard to sell a home in some of the poorer neighborhoods, but INHS activities have improved the housing market so that no place in Ithaca is now seen as a second-class community.

INHS staff can be proud of what it has accomplished. "Ithaca is small enough so our efforts actually can have an immediate visual impact," Paul says. "That might not be true in a larger city. There has been a lot of support from the city—the whole community has been supportive."

Why? "People are seeing you as successful and have confidence you will continue to be."

Personally, Paul has developed strong relationships in the community. Ithaca Neighborhood Housing Services is regarded as a partner, no scandal, no underhanded or criminal behavior. Bigger development can sometimes bring out antidevelopment sentiment—not for INHS. On the fourteen-member INHS board of directors, Paul has always had top bankers from local and regional banks such as Alternatives Federal Credit Union and M&T Bank. He also has an accountant, David Sprague, and from city government, Thys Van Cort.

Some Ithaca developers have criticized INHS, saying that because they get grants from the government, it "must make it easy." But as Paul points out, "Those grants have strings attached—real constraints. For instance, rents are restricted, our projects have rent or income restrictions that can last up to fifty years. Our Community Housing Trust program creates homes that are permanently affordable. A buyer is limited in what he can take out of the deal. (This avoids speculation: If the market goes up, it keeps the price tamped down.) [The price for a house can] only increase in relation to [area] median income, so future low-income buyers will be able to afford them. In addition, you have to deal with HUD or New York State laws and policies for low- to moderate-income housing, which makes it harder to run a business."

Some developers have said, "INHS is in competition, building units that sell at prices lower than the market; it's an unfair advantage." Paul's answer: "We are doing this to serve a low-income population who probably won't be able to rent from you at market rates anyway. The rental portfolio will be held forever; these buildings are not built as speculative ventures that will be sold at a significant profit if the market goes up. On the houses that we renovate and sell, INHS retains ownership of the land and leases it to the home buyer. It is a government subsidy, and in exchange for the lower acquisition price, the buyer is limited in what he can take out of the deal—no more than the rate of inflation."

The goal of INHS is community sustainability, environmental sustainability, and financial sustainability.

When Paul speaks to different civic groups, a typical reaction is "This is un-American. It's like socialism." His response: "You may be skeptical, but we have a whole lot of buyers."

Are they cutting into the market? "Yes," says Paul, "but INHS is serving a segment of the market that consists entirely of low-income renters and buyers. Private developers do not target this segment because the income that they would receive is too low to be financially viable. The nonprofit sector operates in an entirely different world, with different financing, a different market, and different goals."

Many developers see INHS as beneficial to the city, increasing the desirability of the Ithaca community overall. Today, nearly forty years after the planning department did the original survey on the Northside and Southside housing stock, the findings have been reversed: 85 percent of the houses were rated in the top two categories and only 15 percent in the lowest two categories. As Thys says, "It isn't an understatement to say that Ithaca Neighborhood Housing Services has transformed downtown's neighborhoods."

Today, with both the renovations of older buildings and construction of new projects, INHS has become one of the largest real estate developers in Ithaca. The house recycling program has become one of INHS's most visible and valuable programs. They find the worst house on each block, do a gut-rehab job on it, and sell it to a neighborhood (usually minority) family. INHS also owns and manages over three hundred units (and growing) of rental housing for low- and moderate-income families and individuals.

Paul operates with a staff of thirty-eight in property management and maintenance. Most of them are long tenured, so they build up their skills. Two of his people are designated strictly to originating loans. INHS also provides education and counseling to the public, thus creating knowledgeable and better-qualified consumers. With home improvement loans, INHS inspects houses and helps to manage work. A couple of his people focus on real estate development, looking for projects, doing the design, financing, and construction management.

In 2016, they had twenty-eight buildings and 351 rental units, with another 115 units under construction. The number of houses they have been involved in renovating and selling to low-income owners (who often put in sweat equity and use INHS-arranged financing) is now over fifteen hundred. Their mission: neighborhood revitalization and affordable housing. These activities, driven by Paul with the active engagement of the INHS board of directors, are changing not only the lives of low-income people, but by the ripple effect, lives throughout the community.

# CHAPTER 18

# THE WHOLE COUNTY (1974-2010)

## The South Hill Business Campus

Not all development in the Ithaca area takes place within the twenty-two-block boundaries of the BID. INHS works to improve housing all over the city. TCAD and the IDA have their impact helping create jobs by supporting business throughout the county. Cornell itself is the primary economic driver for the Ithaca economy—not only through their enrollment of twenty-one thousand students, but also by employing faculty and staff of over 8,700, being a major recipient of national research grants, and building and rebuilding the campus. In 2010, Cornell came out with a strategic plan, outlined in "Cornell University at Its Sesquicentennial," projecting growth and development for the university for the next *fifty* years—inspiring confidence and laying out plans for the long term.

The Downtown Ithaca Alliance maintains that the health of downtown directly affects the desirability of the university and its ability as a place to attract top-notch students and faculty—"*Picture downtown boarded up . . .*"—and conversely a healthy university has a direct impact on the health of downtown. As it had done in the zoning review for the Southwest, the DIA jealously guards against all development that could diminish the appeal and strength of the downtown retail and office market. It is a delicate balance.

Andy Sciarabba began serving as my accountant in the late 1970s and stayed with me as a trusted consultant until 2010 or so, when we both retired. He was still my consultant in March of 2004, and he was about to build the largest project competing with downtown office space that Ithaca had ever experienced. When he announced his plans to buy the vacant 275,000-square-foot, seventy-two-acre National Cash Register plant on South Hill across from Ithaca College, it sent a shudder through the BID membership. The BID so far had been successful in limiting the size of retail development in the Southwest to no stores under 5,000 square feet, thereby protecting the downtown retail market as much as possible. We could not limit overall development in the Southwest part of town and had chosen instead to support it for the benefit of the city rather than risk that its tax benefits move outside the city limits to nearby Lansing. At the same time, since big-box development was no longer a possibility downtown, we had promoted the specialty stores that tend to cluster in restored downtowns, as is the trend nationwide.

Andy's new "South Hill Business Campus," as he explained it, would draw professional offices (of whatever size) and light industry from throughout the community. In fact he was already in the process of making a deal with Challenge Industries across the street from Gateway to relocate there. Their exit from downtown could potentially take six hundred "clients" and a hundred or more staff out of the central business district. I was worried, because even our new Gateway offices and our Center Ithaca offices had some turnover. Change is a part of the business. Would our office tenants exit to the South Hill Business Campus with its virtually unlimited free parking and only a five-minute drive from downtown? We had 140 parking spaces at Gateway, but somehow it was never enough for our mixed-use site, with restaurants, the residents, clients, and office workers all vying for space.

In the early '70s, Andy had worked at Touche Ross in Rochester as a certified public accountant (CPA). He had clients who were developers, so he took a course in real estate to better understand the process. He moved to Ithaca in 1974 to cover Touche Ross's ongoing audit contracts with the National Housing Partnership for two projects being developed by the local developer Dave Abbott—350 units of tax-credit housing on West Hill, and another 394 units at Maplewood near Cornell.

Working with real estate developers had stimulated Andy to become more entrepreneurial, so he could afford, as he said, "to do things." He didn't want just to retire on a pension. He and another accountant at Touche Ross, Ken Walker, who had helped with the first BID attempt, joined forces and set up their own CPA firm in Ithaca, Sciarabba Walker & Co., where Andy managed the production and Ken handled the administration.

Shortly after Andy arrived in Ithaca, the YMCA on the corner of Buffalo and Tioga Streets burned down and was completely destroyed. The Y raised funds, and in a controversial move, left for the suburbs in Lansing. Many downtown residents felt the inner-city youth needed the Y more than the "rich kids" in the suburbs, but it moved.

The Y offered its corner site at 200 East Buffalo for sale. Andy had the thought, why not form a partnership with some of his clients? Doctors, lawyers, professionals—they all need office space. They could join together and buy the Y site. In 1978 he bid successfully on the land, and since sprin-klers were required for buildings over five stories, they built the new 200 East Buffalo Street building five stories high with a single elevator. HOLT Architects designed the new office building and Andy had it preleased even before it was built. He and Ken raised the equity with their partners through borrowings. At that time, there was no such thing as Excel: he did all the financial-analysis spreadsheets by hand.

It was during this time that Andy advised me on establishing a devel-opment team for my Ravenwood project. When I asked him who the best professionals in the city were, he recommended some of the colleagues who had helped him develop the 200 East Buffalo building—David Taube at HOLT Architects, George Gesslein at Citizens Savings Bank, and Jim Kerrigan, attorney.

Andy had made his mark as a real estate developer in Ithaca, long before the South Hill Business Campus. In 1967, as part of the urban renewal program, the Hotel Ithaca site on the corner of State and Aurora Streets had been demolished. Jim Rothschild built a new department store on the site in the late 1970s, complete with a modern escalator, the first in Ithaca. He operated it until the early 1980s, when, after years of losses, Citizens Savings Bank foreclosed on the real estate. In 1987, George Gesslein at Citizens Savings Bank called Stu Lewis, a second-generation retailer who owned five retail clothing stores—one at the mall in Lansing, one in Col-legetown, and three in downtown. Perhaps Stu would like to buy the Roth-schild's Building? Stu knew retail, and he and Andy were friends. In early 1988, Stu, Ken, and Andy formed Comex Plaza Associates. They began negotiations with Iszard's Department Store to lease the entire building, and submitted an offer to purchase the Rothschild's Building, contingent on funding from Citizens Savings Bank, and signing the lease with Iszard's.

Later in 1988, having signed a long-term lease with Iszard's, and with financing from Citizens Savings Bank, they purchased the building. A year later, S. F. Iszard's was acquired by McCurdy and Company, which oper-ated the department store until 1998, when they negotiated a lease buyout with Comex and closed their operation. After three failed attempts, it was apparent that a department store in downtown Ithaca was no longer fea-sible. The partners used the buyout funds to redevelop the building into a mixed-use retail and office building.

By then, Andy and Ken had developed a network of over twenty-five hundred clients for their accounting business. Andy began sifting through the client base to find potential tenants for a renovated, adaptive reuse in their vacant building on the Commons. Comex was able to lease the 20,000-square-foot second floor to Thomas Associates Architects with its

180 employees. Thomas designed, and Comex built out, a quarter-million-dollar renovation to create the architecture firm's new space. It was the first truly class A office space ever built in Ithaca. The design included a lobby fountain and a waterfall, dozens of plants. It had a fishpond. It had what seemed like an acre of open space divided by partitions all on one floor for the design team. It included huge picture windows on two sides looking out on the Commons. It had a large conference room, and a lineup of private offices for the principals. Gone was the escalator from the department store. The first floor became an extension campus for Tompkins Cortland Community College, a Taco Bell belonging to a friend of Andy's, and a pizza parlor, and in the rear, and partially under the parking garage, 10,000 square feet was converted into support offices for the Tompkins Trust Company Bank, which was less than a block away.

The project was an immediate success for both Comex and for downtown. Andy orchestrated this first venture in redevelopment with the help of his partners. It had taken less than a year. They had brought in investors for the equity, which together with a loan from the bank had paid for the renovations.

In 1985, prior to the Comex purchase of the Rothschild's Building and Andy's initial efforts in downtown revitalization, I received a call from a Realtor regarding purchase of the old tennis court building in Lansing that Joe Ciaschi had developed and later turned into a roller skating rink in front of the Pyramid Mall fronting on Triphammer Road. I was focused on my Collegetown projects and finishing Eddygate at the time and not at all interested in a project near the mall, so I gave Andy a call about it.

Andy had the unusual ability to look at a vacant Butler building with green metal roofing, nearly the length of a football field, and envision it rebuilt as a strip mall and rented to successful small tenants. In 1985, that is exactly what he did. He negotiated two six-month options for $5,000 each to give himself time to finance and purchase the building, and he began finding partners and tenants before he and Ken even owned it. They raised $400,000 in equity by selling a 40 percent ownership to thirteen limited partners, offering them a 10 percent preferred return, noncompounded. They kept 60 percent of the building for themselves and turned it into a successful strip mall, housing a computer store, florist, dance studio, yoga studio, a vet, dog day care, and a medical laboratory.

In 1989 Andy purchased a vacant car dealership building across Triphammer Road from the Pyramid Mall and their new strip mall and turned it into a one-story office building. A year later he negotiated to purchase an unbuildable vacant lot on the corner of North Triphammer and Graham Roads. He secured it and then approached the owner of the adjoining property,

**Figure 18.1** Andy's mall. This was once a Butler building, a tennis court, and later a roller-skating rink. Photo by Jon Reis.

a single-family residence, and negotiated the purchase of that house. He moved the house to a nearby site, joined the two vacant sites into one, and built a two-story professional office building, which was mostly preleased.

Andy surrounds himself with electrical and plumbing contractors, land-scapers, and plowing operators. He pays a retainer on all his properties to keep the HVAC units serviced and functioning. If there is something he can't do, he brings in subcontractors. All his commercial leases are triple net—utilities, taxes, and common-area maintenance paid for by the tenant.

He also undertook a number of community projects in Lansing. He put together an elaborate 501(c)3 charitable corporation to construct the Community Recreational Center, Inc. He received New York State grants through the efforts of Senator Nozzolio ($125,000) and Senator Seward ($250,000), funds that, with senate approval, they could direct to community projects. With the grants, private donations from the community, and IDA bonds, he had assembled over $4 million—enough to build a hockey rink and soccer fields. The Rink opened in 1995 after a ten-year effort. The Field opened in 2001.

Andy then bought a fifteen-acre corner property at the very north end of Lansing and sold the front corner to Xtra Mart—to construct a convenience store and gas station in an area that was served by neither. It was a four- to five-mile drive to significant services at the time. The Lansing Xtra Mart became the highest-volume store in the entire national chain. In 2010 he met with a former manager of the supermarket chain Price Chopper. Andy's question to him: "Would you have any interest in managing and owning a share of a new grocery store in Lansing?" He would, and with eight investors—four at 8.33 percent, including the manager, and the others at 10 percent—Andy opened the Lansing Market, retaining the balance of the ownership himself. He felt it was important that his manager have "skin in the game." Initially the project was a slight disappointment and early on required a capital call; however, today it is holding its own in the competitive grocery market, and the Town of Lansing is very excited about it.

Shortly after the Lansing Market project, Andy got a call from the local Montessori school. Would he buy the old lumberyard at the corner of Peruville and Triphammer Roads that was up for auction and help them establish a new home for the school? He was the only one to bid on it. He renovated the lumberyard building for the school, which moved in four months later. Along with four adjoining parcels, he and his partners now owned thirty acres of highly visible land on a major highway. He worked with the town to develop another 150-acre site for an industrial park, negotiating with the state to lift zoning restrictions on it and develop a comprehensive plan for area growth, all within the county guidelines, and with designated, protected open spaces. T. G. Miller, Engineers and Surveyors, designed seven or eight big lots for the industrial park.

There were no doctors in the town of Lansing, no incentives for development, and no basic services. HOLT Architects assisted in holding public hearings at which citizens could express their concerns and develop incentives to build traffic flow. Andy promoted a density policy, and an incentive zone to protect farmlands, separate from residential and industrial areas.

Reflecting on his work in Lansing, Andy said, "This community has been good to me. That's why I do the projects—the ice rink, the soccer field, the industrial park. A CPA deals with historic info—tax compliance—and the intangible. Real estate is tangible." Andy likes that—the "hard stuff." If he weren't a CPA, he said, he'd have been a contractor.

Andy sees what he does as a benefit to the community. His business tenants are hiring people at a good wage. They are generating a flow of food, goods, and jobs. They support scores of families and affect people's lives in a positive way. "You give back—the rink, the grocery store. You use your experience. You know it's right." And he loves making it happen, despite the occasional "dagger in his back." Andy breathes credibility and integrity. As he says, he has "honored his word" from day one.

It was in 2004 that Mike Stamm, president of Tompkins County Area Development, called Andy to tell him that the CEO of Axiom wanted to sell their seventy-two-acre parcel and the 275,000-square-foot former National Cash Register building, built in 1957, for $4.5 million. It had some environmental issues.

Andy didn't hesitate; he immediately called the CEO of Axiom, whom he knew to be a former CPA, and told him he would like to take a look at the building. They met in Ithaca. "Why don't you stay in the building?" Andy asked. The issue was the environmental cleanup. The CEO said the cost to clean up had been estimated at $2.5 million, and Axiom would prefer to sell to a developer who would assume the entire liability. Andy could buy it and take over the remediation.

He brought in an experienced engineering firm from Syracuse to look at the cost of environmental cleanup. The engineering firm developed a work plan for remediation of radon and air changing, plus cleanup of trichloroethylene (TCE), an industrial degreaser from earlier manufacturing processes that had contaminated the groundwater—estimated cost $3.5 million.

Andy offered $1 million for the building. Axiom's CEO mentioned that Ithaca Space Systems, a tenant, wanted to negotiate four one-year leases with a six-month out. "Let me think about it," Andy said. Axiom and Andy settled at $1.6 million—$5.82 per square foot for the building—including the seventy-two acres of land five blocks up South Hill from downtown.

He raised $600,000 from investors and found that a $1 million note with $250,000 down got the numbers to work. He also asked for and was awarded an IDA PILOT (payment in lieu of taxes), based on a $1.6 million assessment, for seven years, gradually adjusting to 100 percent assessment thereafter. After the acquisition, Chemung Canal Trust Company took the financing package, because Tompkins Trust Company (TTC) would not finance it without proportional personal guarantees. Chemung Canal Trust Company was new in town, just breaking into the market, and they eagerly took the loan without a personal guarantee from Andy.

Andy told Linda Luciano, the facilities manager of the building, that he wouldn't buy it unless Linda came with it as the industrial engineer and property manager. His management fee from tenants in the building was less than $100,000; from this he paid Linda's salary and benefits.

Andy quickly rented office space to Better Housing for Tompkins County, and to True Walsh and Miller, a law firm that relocated from downtown. Axiom stayed on, and several other professionals came up from downtown. Therm, a local company producing turbine blades, which had contracted for a new project with Pratt & Whitney, opened a new, small manufacturing center on the old factory floor.

Andy kept going back to Chemung for funds to finance tenant build-outs and energy improvements. "Chemung was fantastic," he said.

**Figure 18.2** Axiom, the seventy-two-acre former National Cash Register site, now Andy's South Hill Business Campus. Photo by Jon Reis.

He had taken over the old Axiom building in December of 2004, and the building received its permanent certificate of completion from the Department of Environmental Conservation (DEC) in 2009. At the time he had purchased it, the cost for heat and domestic hot water was $6,000 per month. He hired Taitem Engineering to do an energy survey. With a $1 million New York State Energy Research & Development Authority (NYSERDA) loan at 3.25 percent interest, he replaced all windows with energy-saving ones, replaced the boiler with a more efficient one, and thereby was able to lower the energy bill to $600 per month! The DEC cleanup process removed the environmental liability from the site, and Andy and his investors received a 10 percent tax credit on all the money they had spent for renovation and cleanup. The property grossed $650,000 its first two years at 40 percent occupancy, and increased by another $120,000 per year at 90 percent occupancy.

Once he received the certificate of completion from the state DEC, he met again with Chemung to request a refinance of the entire project with a permanent mortgage. He had a debt service coverage of 2.3 (banks usually require 1.25); they turned it down. They had taken all the risk and now they backed down. Andy sold fourteen acres of land to Ithaca College, kept his $650,000 in reserve and went elsewhere.

I followed Andy's progress during the time he was redeveloping South Hill Business Campus. He was successful in attracting Challenge Industries

away from their downtown site across from Gateway. It was this site that
local real estate broker and developer Bryan Warren and his partners Newman Development would later purchase for his Seneca Way development.

Although I lived with a continual concern that Gateway and Center
Ithaca might lose tenants to Andy, none of our tenants ended up relocating to the 275,000-square-foot business park on South Hill. My favorite
question for him during the five years it took to solve the environmental
issues and stabilize the property was—"Hey Andy, are you rented up there
yet on South Hill?!" "It's coming, it's coming," he'd reply.

Andy had been an invaluable member of my development team over four
decades. We had immense respect for each other. Obviously his devotion to
Ithaca extended far beyond the downtown business improvement district
that I had so carefully focused on. I asked him once why he had developed
so far afield. His spontaneous reply: "The city is not the be-all and end-
all to everybody. It's important to address the needs of the whole county."

As involved as I was in downtown, I couldn't help but agree. Andy
was right.

# CHAPTER 19

# LOOKING BACK AT THE STRATEGIC PLAN (2000–2010)

## The End of a Decade

The first decade of the strategic plan had passed. What had Ithaca achieved? We had a new office and apartment complex at Gateway, a new Hilton Garden Inn, and hundreds of Cornell employees working at Seneca Place. The county had just opened a new library downtown, and the city had opened a new parking garage on Cayuga Street. Stores on the Commons were filled. The Commons had had a minor renovation with a new fountain, brick pavers, and new lights. The BID had a full schedule of events—some new, like the Art in the Heart program bringing art onto the Commons, plus a full season of outdoor concerts during the summer. Thanks to Historic Ithaca, the State Theatre, albeit on shaky ground financially, had been spared the demolition ball and was drawing some thirty thousand people a year to its shows. Another historic building, the Clinton House, was still intact and was home to a charter school with over 150 students.

Our marketing director at the BID had been working in collaboration with the Tompkins County Chamber of Commerce to promote downtown Ithaca and the Finger Lakes region, which includes scores of wineries. We were approached by a travel writer for the *Philadelphia Inquirer*. For a fee, she would come to town for a few days and write a promotional piece on the area. The Tompkins County Chamber of Commerce and the Downtown Ithaca Alliance collaborated financially, and Ithaca was featured in a full-page article in the Philadelphia Sunday paper. In addition, many other publications had begun naming Ithaca, New York, as a great place to live and work. The following are some of the accolades Ithaca received between the founding of the BID in 1997 and the end of the first decade of the strategic plan in 2010:

- "America's Most Enlightened City," *Utne Reader*, May 1997
- "American Values: Where to Buy a Retirement Home," *SmartMoney*, February 2002
- "Best Places to Vacation," *Money* magazine, April 2002
- "100 Great Escapes: Top-10 Trips," *Travel & Leisure*, March–April 2002
- "America's Five Best Mountain Biking Towns," *Bike*, June 2002
- "Best Lesbian Places to Live: The Ten Lesbian-Friendliest Cities in the USA," *Girlfriends*, November 2002
- "Best Healthy City in the Northeast," *Organic Style*, September–October 2003
- "Number-One Emerging City," *Cities Ranked and Rated* by Bert Sperling and Peter Sander (Wiley, 2004)
- "12 Great Places to Retire," *Kiplinger's Personal Finance*, March 2005
- Fourth in *Relocate America*'s "Top 100 Places to Live in 2006," April 2006
- No. 1 city for knowledge workers in "College Towns Are at the Heart of the Knowledge Sector Economy," *Expansion Management*, March–April 2006
- Eighth in "50 Smart Places to Live," *Kiplinger's Personal Finance*, June 2006
- Seventeenth nationwide among the "Best Places for Business and Careers," *Forbes Magazine*, April 2006
- First in "12 Great Places You've Never Heard Of," *Mother Earth News*, July–August 2006
- One of the "12 Hippest Hometowns for Vegetarians," *VegNews*, July–August 2006
- Third in *Relocate America*'s "Top 100 Places to Live in 2007," April 2007
- Second in "Best Green Places to Live," *Country Home*, April 2007
- Ithaca schools ranked second nationwide among metro areas under five hundred thousand by *Expansion Management*, December 2007
- Third in Farmers Insurance study, "Most Secure Places to Live: Small Towns," December 2007

- Second in *SmartMoney* magazine's "7 Best Places to Retire in an Economic Downturn," February 2008
- Third among "America's Smartest Cities," by *Forbes Magazine*, February 2008
- A top-ten global travel destination chosen by Gore-Tex and the Adventure Travel Trade Association, April 2008
- Cornell University named best employer for people over fifty by *AARP: The Magazine*, September 2008
- Sixth in "The 20 Best Towns in America" by *Outside Magazine*, August 2008
- No. 1 "green commuter" city by *AARP: The Magazine*, September 2008
- First among "Best Middle Class Housing Markets" by Forbes.com, December 4, 2008
- One of the "10 Best Cities for Job-Seeking Retirees," by *US News & World Report*, January 22, 2009
- Fourth among the "Best Places to Retire for Wine Lovers," by *US News & World Report* online, May 2009
- One of the top one hundred American cities by Relocate-America. com, April 2009
- Seventh in "America's Brainiest Metros," by *The Daily Beast*, August 2010
- First among 350 US metro areas as the best place for recent college graduates, by *The Daily Beast*, June 2010
- Sixth in "America's Foodiest Towns" (population under 250,000), by *Bon Appétit*, September 2010
- No. 1 "Best College Town" (population under 250,000) by the American Institute for Economic Research, September 2010

No wonder Ithacans were proud. Thanks to the activities of the city planners, the BID and its membership, and the activity of the developers, Ithaca had kept the lights on. It was growing. It was being recognized nationally. *"Picture downtown boarded up . . ."* It wasn't going to happen. Thanks also to the early efforts of Historic Ithaca, Thys and the department of planning and development, the strategic plan and the efforts of Gary and the business improvement district board and membership, an active and supportive Common Council, the Tompkins County Industrial Development Agency tax abatement policy, there were many positives driving Ithaca to the top.

**Figure 19.1** Apple Harvest Festival takes place every fall on the Commons. Photo courtesy of the DIA.

**Figure 19.2** Hilby, the "Skinny German Juggling Boy," performs at an event downtown. Photo by Jon Reis.

**Figure 19.3** Street scene at the Apple Harvest Festival. Photo courtesy of the DIA.

**Figure19.4** Apple Harvest Festival downtown on the Ithaca Commons. Photo by Sarah Resman/ *Ithaca Voice*.

# CHAPTER 20

# LOOKING AHEAD (2010–20)

## The 2020 Strategic Plan

The 2010 strategic plan had successfully guided the activities of the BID for a decade. It was time to look ahead to 2020. The original strategic plan stemmed from the need to convince Thomas Associates Architects to keep their 180 jobs downtown. In order to be convinced that it would be worthwhile to expand their offices in downtown rather than move out of town, Thomas needed to know what the plan was for downtown Ithaca. As part of the process for developing the plan, Gary Ferguson, newly arrived in 1999 as the executive director of the business improvement district, and with input from his board of directors, held community meetings, did surveys, and performed a feasibility study to confirm that downtown Ithaca was indeed poised for growth—provided the community accepted it and had the courage to proceed. The 2010 plan laid out exactly what the goals, strategies, and action plans were for promoting significant growth within the twenty-two blocks of the BID, and Ithaca had been successful in achieving most of its goals over the past decade.

In the opening pages of the 2020 strategic plan Gary writes, "One should never start planning from the beginning. Rather, one should build upon the accumulated wisdom and thinking that has come before us." He continues, "So it is that this *Downtown Ithaca 2020 Strategic Plan* derives its inspiration from two of the great community place-making planners and thinkers of the past hundred years—William H. Whyte and Jane Jacobs. Whyte and Jacobs both preached the message that strong urban places that work best for people are ones that have developed from the grass roots upward, and not imposed upon a community from above. It is with that spirit that the Downtown Ithaca Alliance met with and collected input from hundreds of residents and users of downtown, to capture their passion, their imagination, their concerns and their dreams."

Beginning in 2008 and in preparation for the 2020 plan, Gary held meetings that systematically undertook a series of community conversations with downtown stakeholders, city officials, and the greater Ithaca community to collect input and thoughts about the future of downtown. As Gary states in the plan, "Downtown strategic plans draw their inspiration from the passion, opinions and dreams of the community."

The process included a variety of methods. Always working closely with his board of directors, and with their approval, in 2007 Gary commissioned a retail market report from the Toronto-based Urban Marketing Collaborative. They determined that downtown was able to support an additional 95,000 square feet of new retail space. In 2008 and 2009, the DIA commissioned a student in the master's degree program of public administration at Cornell University, Brianna Olson, to conduct a volumetric study in order to physically verify the capacity of downtown to accommodate additional residential and office development. Based on all of the vacant and infill sites built out to a revised zoning code, she calculated an ambitious 1.4 million square feet of potential development space—with 355,000 in office, and 1,075,000 square feet in residential.

Also in 2008 the DIA hired WB&A, a local market research firm, to survey two outlying areas that served as sources for the downtown Ithaca tourists and visitors, to spot trends and public perceptions of downtown needing work. In 2009 the DIA conducted an online survey that gave all Ithaca residents an opportunity to speak out about downtown, and to which 250 responded. Additionally during 2008 and 2009 they held outreach meetings with two dozen community groups and organizations to identify issues and challenges that needed to be addressed. BID stakeholders—property owners, retailers, and downtown tenants—were invited to comment. A final formal public meeting was held at the Tompkins County Public Library to solicit input from anyone who had not yet had or taken an opportunity to comment on the issues that should be addressed in the 2020 strategic plan.

Gary requested, and received, a grant for the DIA from the American Institute of Architects to bring their Sustainability Design Assistance Team (SDAT) for two visits to Ithaca. It was an eye-opener for the community, as eight trained architects and city planners who had never before been to Ithaca took detailed close-up pictures of deteriorating sidewalks, the broken benches on the Commons, the crumbling infrastructure that we all had "forgotten to see" during the day, and then showed them in their public presentations in the evening. They were the second set of eyes that every community, every developer, every politician needs in order to see their downtown as a visitor or a tourist sees it.

Inviting them to Ithaca was another stroke of genius on Gary's part. Those two visits of the SDAT probably more than any one thing gave the city, the DIA, and the public the impetus to clean up the trash, repair the sidewalks and benches, rehabilitate the facades of downtown buildings, continue with our agenda for housing, and eventually tear up and rebuild the forty-year-old and now severely deteriorated Commons.

As Gary states in the 2020 strategic plan, the entire process of outreach and surveys was undertaken with the idea of "gaining community input in order to 'help frame future policies and sustainability solutions' for downtown and the City." And building on the accumulated wisdom and thinking that had gone before us, the 2010 strategic plan and the city's zoning code were also used in compilation of the *Downtown Ithaca 2020 Strategic Plan.*

The findings of the surveys, reports, and community outreach initiatives resulted in a plan considerably more expanded than that of 2010. It set forth a "three-pronged package" to revitalize the urban core and reduce regional sprawl, and introduced the concept of reducing our community carbon footprint. It also included bolstering tourism and strengthening the linkages between our institutions of higher education and downtown.

As with the previous plan and based on the SDAT recommendations, it called for building five hundred more residential units in downtown, and it expanded the downtown vision outside of the BID boundaries to include an additional one thousand units of housing in the greater urban area—fifteen hundred residential units in total. It called for rebuilding the entire Commons to enhance its commercial and community appeal. It called for turning our pedestrian mall into a "transit hub" with a streetcar or other form of transit running down its center, connecting it to Cornell University and Ithaca College, and even farther out to the waterfront on the west end of town, all in an effort to stimulate corridor development and to bring more people quickly and easily to the center of the city. By making downtown more accessible, more green, more desirable as a place to live, work, and play, we would be reducing the carbon footprint, diminishing sprawl to the countryside, and making the university and college a stronger part of the downtown economy—thereby meeting the overall goals of the three-pronged plan.

The plan adopted comprehensive "key concepts," which included creating mixed-use development and a dense urban core; reducing automobile usage downtown; utilizing the principles of infill development; recognizing the transition zones at the perimeter of downtown—gradually reducing building height as one approaches the residential part of town surrounding the four sides of the core business district; preserving and enhancing the retail streetscape (for instance, no offices allowed in the ground-floor retail lineup); and recognizing downtown as the center of the community and a leader in green practices and sustainability.

The plan was ambitious. It called for building 78,000 square feet of new retail, another 200,000 square feet of offices, meeting parking needs by mobilizing public awareness toward walking, bicycling, and alternative modes of transportation, as well as a review and possible reassignment of downtown parking management and Commons maintenance. It called for updating (rebuilding) the Commons according to the extensive plan by the Sasaki firm from Boston, which had been presented to and approved by the city council. It called for extending the Six Mile Creek walkway (the Gateway walkway) as a trail into the gorge. This would connect the Commons with the nature preserve—picture a Sunday walk with your dog from the heart of downtown, through Gateway, into the gorge, with the possibility of continuing for six miles into this lovely natural preserve. It stated its commitment to diversity—in hiring, in store ownership, in the overall acceptance and appeal to all ethnicities, all sexual orientations.

The plan called for at least ten new pedestrian-generating projects in downtown, which had already incorporated dozens of successful ones, including city hall, the Cinemapolis movie theatre, the county courthouse and office complex, the Community School of Music and Arts, five downtown banks, more than ten churches, the new Hilton Hotel, the History Center, the Holiday Inn, the Kitchen Theatre, the internationally known Moosewood Restaurant, plus an additional fifty-five restaurants within two blocks of the Commons, the post office, the Tompkins County Public Library, the State Theatre, the TC3 extension campus, the Ithaca Town Hall, and the New Roots Charter School in the Clinton House. Gary has said that typically, individual retailers or restaurants would not be considered pedestrian traffic generators unless they had extraordinary drawing power or marketing appeal such as Moosewood, which caused them to serve as anchor businesses.

One of the important things our board of directors had organized were fact-finding trips to other communities with pedestrian malls. Eighteen of us traveled overnight on a hired bus to Charlottesville, Virginia, to see their historic pedestrian mall anchored at one end by the Sheraton Hotel and at the other by the Dave Matthews Bandstand. We had previously seen Charlottesville's 1,100-seat, restored Paramount Theater, built in 1931 as a movie theater, closed in 1974, renovated in the 1990s, and reopened in 2004 after a $16.2 million complete restoration funded by private donations. This was an inspiration for what could be done at our 1,600-seat State Theatre in downtown Ithaca. A group traveled to the Burlington, Vermont, Church Street Mall and saw their impressive signage, artwork, brickwork, and very successful urban setting. We had also been to the Boulder, Colorado, downtown with its Pearl Street Mall, which is as well designed as Burlington's.

Gary was particularly adept at looking at other successful areas and identifying just why they worked so well. He determined that one of the major factors for a successful downtown is the clustering of pedestrian traffic generators. He also pointed out that "the decision to locate a community traffic generator often turns on economic factors that might steer projects away from downtown. Helping leaders understand that these attractions provide more benefit to the community when they are clustered versus in disparate locations will be a key objective of the Downtown Ithaca Alliance."

He added, "A primary goal of the *Downtown Ithaca 2020 Strategic Plan* is to adopt a strategy of clustering pedestrian traffic generators in downtown, in an effort to provide a large-enough base of patrons and customers to support the type of downtown commerce that area residents desire."

The 2020 strategic plan's list of potential pedestrian traffic generators included another school, a Finger Lakes Wine Center, a nightclub, a teen activity center, a new History Center, a new city and county administration facility, a welcome/visitor center, expansion of Hotel Ithaca (a former Holiday Inn), construction of another new hotel, an artist incubator or clustered studio project, and a music club.

To explain the concept, Gary quotes from an article he had written earlier on the "Characteristics of Successful Small City Downtowns." He begins by asking: "Why are some downtowns more successful than others? What causes a downtown to be healthy and vibrant?" He then lists in the plan results from a 2005 study of eleven great US small-city downtowns, which he had undertaken with a grant from Cornell:

> One shared attribute of successful downtowns was the clustering of many pedestrian traffic generators within walking distance of each other. These attractions were each able to lure pedestrian traffic to their own particular activity, be it a museum, a civic building, or an entertainment establishment. When they were clustered, however, their impact appeared to multiply exponentially. By concentrating traffic generators within close proximity of each other, the downtown was able to reap overlapping synergistic benefits, because patrons of one attraction were more likely to frequent others close by. This results in an increased length of stay and the likelihood of increased expenditures within the district. In simple terms, the more traffic generators, the better. The closer together they are, the better, and the more diverse and varied the traffic generators, the better still.

In many respects, the clustering of traffic generators in a walkable down-town district replicates or simulates downtowns of old. Most of our down-towns were plotted and set up in times predating the automobile. Walking and biking were the predominant modes of transportation, and clustering uses within easy walking distance was both practical and efficient. Clus-tering resulted in strong, overlapping pedestrian traffic patterns.

The new plan also proposed a program to undertake opportunistic land banking of key downtown properties. The city, or an organization such as the DIA, could actually purchase and hold strategic downtown proper-ties until a preferred developer could be found and a well-planned project undertaken. It called for amendments to downtown zoning to improve the viability of key downtown parcels for future infill and redevelopment activity; it called for improving the tax abatement incentives and creating additional meeting and conference space, plus the addition of a third and even a fourth hotel during the period 2010–20.

It called for a new city and county administration building and a new teen activity center. It set out a plan to modify the 100 block of West State Street and the 300 block of East State Street for inclusion into the pedes-trian mall, or in the alternative for periodic, temporary closure to accom-modate special events and community activities.

The 2020 strategic plan was comprehensive (ninety-two pages), giving great detail on accessibility, how to serve seniors and youth, the provision of cultural arts programs, entertainment, and historic preservation, and how to market downtown—complete with goals, strategies, and action steps. It became a visionary, practical guidebook on development in downtown Ithaca for the next decade.

CHAPTER 21

# DENSITY
### Seneca Way (2010–12)—One Vote!

Density had always been at the heart of the BID strategy for developing downtown. Ithaca was a small town with few buildings more than four stories high. It was regarded by many as built on a "human" scale. Creating density in downtown obviously has many advantages: the infrastructure— roads, sidewalks, sewers, water supply, and utilities—already exists, and up to a point it does not have to be expanded to serve additional buildings. Building in the areas surrounding the city chews up farmland and the outdoor environment that is so important to the natural, green lifestyle most people in Ithaca cherish and enjoy. Our Finger Lakes Land Trust even solicits donations for purchasing unspoiled areas and establishing conservation easements on existing farmland and natural areas. They have established the "Emerald Necklace" of trails and green space surrounding the city that tie in with several of the nearby state parks and national forests. Concentrating new development in the already developed infrastructure of the central downtown area assists in minimizing the impact of adding more people into our growing community.

To create density required that we examine the zoning for downtown. Although a few buildings, such as the twelve-story Holiday Inn tower in the early 1980s, had received height variances for up to 130 feet, it was a cumbersome and very time-consuming process for developers to have to apply for a height variance for each project. It would be much more efficient if we could simply rezone our downtown to support vertical density. The DIA together with the city planning department led the charge at city hall to do just that. Part of the 2020 strategic plan for the second decade of the twenty-first century—approved in concept by the city—included both design and shadow studies, which showed the shadow the proposed building would create on the sidewalks, streets, and surrounding structures at various times of day. It provided an idea of what could be built in downtown provided the zoning was increased to as high as 140 feet in the central core and gradually stepped down closer to the surrounding residential streets and houses. Not everybody was happy, however, with the idea of growing our human-scale downtown into what some considered a more chasm-like environment.

We had been fortunate with the Gateway project to receive a height variance for the two phases we had envisioned—the original warehouse now converted to an office tower was already six stories high, and the plan was to add a second six-story luxury apartment tower. Thys and I had worked together on the Gateway project to come up with a plan that would be appealing to the public as well as the planning department. Thys asked how high we wanted to go—sixty-five feet or up to eighty-five feet? The city and county had already implemented the tax abatement to stimulate development within the twenty-two-block BID district. The idea of building up to eighty-five feet would mean we could add two more floors, and I was unsure whether it would be prudent to take the risk of adding more than thirty high-end apartments. Since the tax abatement was based on building to the maximum permitted height, I chose the more conservative sixty-five feet. We were redeveloping a derelict four-acre site in downtown, which in itself would have general appeal, but I didn't want to push public opinion by going up higher than the existing old warehouse building on the site. Thys and I had additionally come up with the idea of granting an easement to the city along Six Mile Creek for a public walkway. It was possibly in part due to this that the entire concept swept through the planning and zoning process without opposition. Gateway was granted a variance to build out the four acres with a height of sixty-five feet, a stone-dust path on the public easement along the creek, and 140 parking spaces.

Across State Street from Gateway, and also at the foot of State Street hill, was the one-story former lingerie factory that Dave Abbott had established in the 1950s, after his return from service as a marine in World War II, by transforming an old bowling alley. When the lingerie factory closed, Dave rented the building to Challenge Industries, which, for twenty-five years, employed disabled persons who could be trained to sort and stamp mailings for local businesses, package foodstuffs for industries, and perform custodial duties for businesses who would hire Challenge, and whose clients would be supervised for up to 125 hours in order to learn a skill or trade. We knew their policies, for we had hired one of their clients very successfully as a custodian at Eddygate. His supervisor had worked with him to learn the job until he had it down perfectly.

Challenge was an independent not-for-profit, and it was facing hard times. Their director determined that they could improve their financial

situation if they sold their downtown building and moved to Andy Sciarabba's proposed South Hill Business Campus. It took them a year to make
the decision and complete the move. Another friend, Bryan Warren, purchased the Challenge building with the idea of demolishing it and going up
six stories—a height on par with Gateway across the street. The problem:
the Challenge site was zoned for a maximum of two stories and about the
only practical thing that could be built in this high-traffic location was a
gas station. The city was considering, but had not yet passed, a new zoning ordinance. Bryan would require a height and use various to build his
six-story office/apartment building.

As Gateway had received a variance for sixty-five feet across the street
and along the creek, it seemed reasonable that Bryan should receive a variance to do his project. He commissioned HOLT Architects to design the
building and prepare a rendering to present to the planning department,
since he would need their recommendation to apply to the zoning department for both the height variance and a change-of-use variance from a
two-story structure or a gas station to a six-story office/apartment building
with underground parking. From the DIA point of view it was a perfect
project that furthered the DIA strategy of creating density in our downtown. It was not of a scale that seemed disproportionate to the surrounding neighborhood, particularly with both Gateway buildings at six stories
right across the street. It would add space for two major offices, thirty-eight
apartments, and sixty parking spaces. But it was not to be.

Ithaca is an Ivy League intellectual town, with Cornell University being
a major influence on how our population "thinks." Ithaca College and
Tompkins Cortland Community College are also factors in this collective
"thinking." It is a standing joke in Ithaca—but not far from the truth—to
say, "Everyone in Ithaca has an opinion, " and they are most willing to
express it. The Challenge site was at the base of the State Street hill, and
behind it and farther up the hill on Seneca Street were mostly single-family
homes—many belonging to professors and staff at the university. At the
first public hearing held by the board of planning and development, the
neighbors had organized and turned out as a group to oppose the project.
They did not want their view of the city to be obstructed by a new building.
They did not want the noise of construction. They feared the disruption to
their peace and quiet by additional traffic and a building full of new tenants.
Never mind that their houses were farther up the hill and would mostly
look out over the top of the new building proposed to be built below them.

The role that the business improvement district had taken on since its
inception was to support an agenda of growth and development, based on
*density* for our downtown core. The DIA sprang into action. First, several

of us met with Bryan to encourage him and his partners to stick with the process. When it comes to public hearings at city hall, it is not unusual to run into the proverbial buzz saw. I told Bryan that our Eddygate project had won by *one vote*. I told him of the many hoops I had had to jump through at Gateway across the street, even though the public process there had been relatively benign. Gary organized the members of the BID to write letters to the editor of our local newspaper in support of the project. Bryan and his group redesigned the building slightly, stepping it down to improve the neighbors' view. He returned to the board of planning and development (BPD), this time with vocal support from the downtown merchants and property owners in the DIA. The neighbors up the hill from the project returned as well, just as vocal, and even better organized than before.

The site-plan review process held by the BPD is an opportunity for the public to have input and help shape or in some cases overturn a project. Growth solely for growth's sake is not recognized as desirable in Ithaca. From my point of view over the three decades that I had been in front of the board with various designs and requests for buildings, I had grown philosophical both about the planning and development board process and the outcome. My sincere feeling was that a project would likely be better for having been through the public review and planning process. Adapting one's project to the needs and sometimes even the aesthetic suggestions of surrounding property owners and neighbors can often improve what is built. The developer and the architect were, in general, wise to listen. However, in this instance, our support group felt this was a firm case of NIMBY: "Not in my backyard!" Bryan's concept was an excellent one for providing housing, offices, and parking at the eastern entrance to downtown, and the design by HOLT Architects, the firm I had used on all my projects, was excellent. We were up against neighbors who would settle for nothing above the two stories currently permitted by zoning.

On questions of zoning variances, it is the role of the BPD to hear arguments for and against a project and then pass on their recommendation to the board of zoning appeals (BZA), where the final decision will be made after another public hearing held by them. In addition to BZA approval, proposed projects need site-plan review approval by the BPD. Since site-plan approval is a discretionary act by a governmental agency, under New York State law "environment review" is triggered. Environment review can take anywhere from one month to years, depending on the complexity of the project and the amount of controversy it has engendered. It can also involve one or more public hearings.

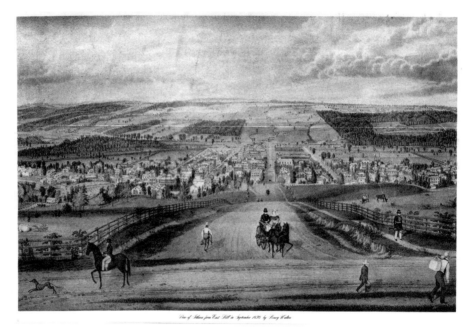

**Figure 21.1** *The East View of Ithaca*, lithograph by Henry Walton, 1836. Photo courtesy of the History Center of Tompkins County.

I made a final public appeal for Bryan's project with a letter to our local newspaper, the *Ithaca Journal*. (Permission to reprint this letter was granted by the *Ithaca Journal*.)

### A Challenge!

If you are a neighbor living uphill from the old Challenge Industries site at the foot of State Street hill, you may be familiar with the 1836 Walton lithograph of Ithaca from the vantage point of East Hill. Down below in the town, one views a few church steeples and a respectable cluster of two- and three-story buildings. In the foreground, where Cornell University now stands, one looks over the livestock and farm fences down Seneca Street to the town.

If you are a member of the Ithaca City Council, you know the growth on the West End that has moved the retail center from the Commons to bigger stores there. You know the number of buildings off the tax rolls. You may have even attended the recent Sustainability Design Assistance Team (SDAT) conference. Eight architects and city planners from across the country came to Ithaca to study and recommend what we could do to improve the sustainability of our City. [This is the group brought to town by Gary and the DIA.] Their recommendation: "We need to find reinforcement for retail as the major traffic generator in the central core of downtown."

That reinforcement, they reasoned, is housing. The trend today, not just in Ithaca but across the country, is for people to live downtown, close to work, shops, stores, entertainment, and services. SDAT recommended a total of 1,500 units be constructed downtown.

The Challenge Building is a derelict building past saving. Between Challenge Industries and Tetra Tech, more than 250 workers and clients have left downtown. If we are not willing to face reasonable development in our downtown, many more businesses will exit. It is density alone that will make downtown economically viable. We need more housing, more offices, and more specialty retail.

Bryan Warren is the third generation of the Warren Real Estate family. Bryan built the new "Class A" brick Colonial style building at Community Corners. He has a sterling reputation for quality projects. He has assembled the best possible local development team for his project, and he has listened to neighborhood concerns. Typical of everything Warren does, this will be a project of the highest design and construction standards, one of which all Ithacans will be proud.

As council members, as mayor, as volunteer members of the Planning Board and BZA, we expect you to have the courage to lead and to make decisions for the greater good of Ithaca—its residents and its businesses. You, better than any of us, see the big picture of economic development, and understand what is needed to keep downtown economically viable.

As neighbors, remember that your house was once farmland. Someone had the vision to develop East Hill as a residential neighborhood serving the community with housing. Your houses sit well aloft this proposed downtown building. The proposed Warren project on the Challenge site is a perfect blend of residential and commercial in a transition zone between East Hill residential and downtown commercial. We have an able developer, a beautiful design; we should do this project!

It's probably fair to say that the article had little effect on the neighbors. Given the public opposition of the neighbors, and the equally strong support of the members of the DIA, the board of planning and development sent the project on to the board of zoning appeals with no recommendation for approval or disapproval. It was a draw. The board of planning and development made no recommendation. The board of zoning appeals members would have to make up their own minds after again listening to vehement public comment both for and against.

There was one absentee from the five-member board at the first BZA meeting. It resulted in a tie vote of 2–2, which meant no approval. There was again one absentee at the next month's meeting—whether by design or not, we'll never know. Our support team feared being stuck again in a tie. While there would be no further opportunity for public comment at the second BZA meeting, all meetings were open to the public, so the neighbors could show up and turn their heads back and forth with nods of vehement disapproval, and the twenty-member support team from the DIA could bob their heads up and down with equally vehement nods of approval as the four members of the board of zoning appeals present discussed the pros and cons of the Seneca Way project among themselves.

At the last minute, the chair of the BZA, who at the initial meeting had voted against the project, resulting in a tie vote and no approval, unexpectedly changed his vote, and suddenly there were three for, and one against the project.

*It had passed!* The height and use variances had been approved by the BZA. Bryan's project later sailed through site plan and environmental reviews and was able to proceed. We were elated. Maybe the letter to the *Ithaca Journal* had played a part, but certainly the unwavering support of the downtown merchants and property owners of the DIA membership had resulted in official approval of the vision for density that our business improvement district had set forth in their strategic plan for downtown Ithaca. A single vote had kept the DIA and Bryan's plans on track.

**Figure 21.2** The old Challenge Industries building. It was demolished to make way for the building on the right in figure 21.3. Photo courtesy of Newman Development.

**Figure 21.3** "Seneca Way" on the right. The Gateway Commons luxury apartment building is on the left, with downtown and the Commons in the center background. Photo by Van Zandbergen Photography.

The following press release is an excellent summary of the project written by Jeff Smetana, the project manager for the Newman Development Group, Bryan's development partner from Binghamton:

### *Seneca Way Ground Breaking November 16, 2012*

#### Construction to Start at 140 Seneca Way

New luxury apartments and Class A offices are coming to downtown Ithaca, as the ground-breaking ceremony today signals the start of construction at 140 Seneca Way. Mayor Svante Myrick will join the developer, bankers and other public officials as redevelopment of this prominent City site gets underway.

"This project will continue the revitalization of the City by keeping residents and quality businesses downtown," said Bryan Warren, owner of Warren Real Estate and a partner in the project. The project will include 38 apartments plus offices on the first floor, which have been pre-leased to two prominent organizations in Ithaca, Warren Real Estate and the Park Foundation.

"We hope Seneca Way will be the place to live in downtown Ithaca," said Warren. "Living one block from the Commons, you're at the center of everything," he said, "and the apartments will be very large, beautifully designed and with lots of upscale amenities. So, you can really have it all." The 38 apartments will have spacious floor plans, designer kitchens and quality finishes, plus many premium amenities, including a private health club, roof terrace, under-building parking, bicycle storage and storage rooms. The building will also include many green features, which will help promote a sustainable and healthy lifestyle.

"I'm also proud to have Warren Real Estate as the anchor tenant," added Warren. "We're committed to promoting the success of the City and are very excited to be part of that with this project."

140 Seneca Way is being co-developed by Newman Development Group, which is based in Binghamton and has additional offices in Philadelphia and San Francisco. Newman Development has 30 years of successful experience with projects throughout the region and across the country.

"We wanted to do something significant that would have a positive impact on the City," said Marc Newman, Managing Member of Newman Development, "and I believe that we've done that with an exceptional new project within the downtown business district. Revitalizing our cities needs to be done building by building and block by block," he said, "and here we're transforming a blighted and obsolete property into a beautiful and dynamic building that will be a great place for people to live and work downtown."

Mr. Newman also explained that part of Newman Development's continuing and strengthening interest in Ithaca is due to several of the firm's partners being proud alumni of Cornell University and Ithaca College.

Plans for the project started more than three years ago. "We had a number of significant hurdles to overcome," said Jeff Smetana, Vice President of Newman Development, "but we had a great deal of support from the City. The Planning and Development Office and Building Department really worked with us to resolve problems and respond to issues, so that ultimately we have a project that will be a great addition to the City." Construction will be completed by fall 2013 and the apartments are expected to attract young professionals, empty nesters and others looking to enjoy the convenience and quality of life available in downtown Ithaca.

Development of the project is supported by a complex financing structure that includes a New Markets Tax Credit allocation provided by the National Development Council, as well as additional financing from M&T Bank, Tompkins Trust Company and PNC Bank. The design of the project was by HOLT Architects. Construction will be performed by Northeast United Corp., which is part of the Newman Development Group.

# CHAPTER 22

# COLLEGETOWN TERRACE (2007–17)

## Breaking out of the Mold

Ithaca is a city of many hills, numerous waterfalls, and three major "creeks," as they are termed in upstate parlance. One could call them "rivers" or "streams" or, if you live in the country, "cricks," but here they are creeks. Up State Street hill from downtown, a developer, John Novarr, was slowly buying up old houses along State Street. This was a little less than three blocks above the Gateway site and the central core of the business improvement district, and up the creek. (Six Mile Creek also runs below the cliff at the edge of the site.) Over a period of a year and a half, John, who was a native Ithacan, former house painter, former Cornell

**Figure 22.1** Aerial view of Collegetown Terrace. Photo by Jon Reis.

University architecture student (he completed two-thirds of his degree), and an experienced contractor, had purchased nineteen houses in varying states of disrepair and varying degrees of historical significance.

John had been a major Ithaca developer over the years. He had an appreciation of historic buildings and in 1971 had participated as a painter and contractor, with a group of dedicated young volunteers, in the renovation of one of Ithaca's most significant architectural icons, the historic Clinton House, after Historic Ithaca saved it from demolition. John started his own construction company and, over time, purchased and renovated the old Ithaca Sign Works and the old Thomas-Morse Aircraft buildings on the west side of town, which he renovated and turned into offices. He owned a few lovely historic buildings in the Collegetown area, which he rented— as did most landlords in the area—to Cornell University students, and he had also been one of the principals in the 312 College Avenue project built by Integrated Acquisition & Development.

In 1981 John had purchased the former nurses' dormitory, originally built in 1913, adjacent to the vacant Ithaca Hospital up the hill from downtown. He bought it from Ithaca College, which had used the nurses' quarters as student dorm rooms and was in the process of consolidating and expanding on South Hill. With the buildings came another several acres of woods and a separate structure that housed the heating plant for the complex. In 1998 he purchased the hospital and subsequently renovated the hospital and the nurses' quarters into a total of over six hundred single rooms for rent to students. He built out an Arts and Crafts restaurant there, in keeping with the architecture of the hospital building. Keeping the tall chimney, and maintaining the industrial look, he turned the heating plant into a series of sixteen unique apartments with steep stairs in steel plate, industrial stainless-steel counters and tables, all in compact one-bedroom units, perfect for students. There was nothing else like it in town, and on this site John had parking, acres of it.

One of his most successful projects had been the purchase and renovation of the 1923 Baldridge House, an English Tudor stone and half-timbered house that had been home to some of Ithaca's wealthiest families. Cornell purchased it in 1963 and sold it again in 1969. It sat unused for many years, until in 1987, as the market changed, John had the foresight and skill to buy it and renovate it using his own construction crews. He and his wife lived there for four years and then sold it back to Cornell for a substantial profit. He had done well on this transaction.

John formed a partnership with developers Stan Goldberg and Manley Thayler, and together they developed College Circle Apartments adjacent to the Ithaca College (IC) campus on South Hill, which they

**Figure 22.2** The Baldridge House, home to some of Ithaca's wealthiest families over the years. Photo by Jon Reis.

rented to over three hundred IC students. They had narrowly escaped financial disaster when enrollment dropped in the late 1980s, and the college retained its students on campus. The students stopped leasing at College Circle, which caused the partners to default on their financing. The loan was called; a balloon payment was due; the bank wanted to be paid; and the three partners couldn't do it. Their attorney negotiated a write-down on the mortgage, and they were able to retain ownership. The bank came out clean, and John and his group were able to refinance at a much lower interest rate. They ran College Circle Apartments for another three years until a local firm purchased the property. Eventually, Ithaca College bought that firm out.

John Novarr's comment about the whole situation: "I learned a lesson: You don't want to be a big fish in a small pond, particularly when the water control is in somebody else's hands!"

John had not developed anything in the central core of Ithaca, and in fact had intentionally steered clear of downtown. His new project, only blocks up the hill from downtown, was, since mainly targeting a Cornell student tenancy, unlikely to have significant impact on the central business district. He began purchasing houses along the 600–800 blocks of East State Street in 2007, just before the year-and-a-half moratorium on Collegetown construction went into effect. During that time he thought about long-term planning and came up with the concept of Collegetown Terrace Apartments.

It was not an easy project. John had carefully purchased each of the nineteen buildings through a local Realtor, paying asking prices with no contingencies to avoid owners suspecting that anyone was planning an assemblage. If word were to get out that a single developer was buying, prices would definitely rise. Miraculously, for such a small town, word never got out. Not until after John owned three blocks along East State Street, as well as his initial acquisition of the old Tompkins County Hospital and nursing home behind the State Street buildings, along the cliff edge above Six Mile Creek.

John is well-rounded, easygoing, a collector of art objects and antiques, and a wine connoisseur. He is shrewd and patient and has consistently been a visionary and positive force in Ithaca's development for well over forty years. John is also a force to be reckoned with.

Initial design for his Collegetown Terrace project called for demolition of all but three of the original buildings on the 16.4 acres he had assembled. He projected that, overall, seven new buildings would be constructed. He kept the three buildings in the historic district, plus he would be building several hundred apartments, with a total of 1,245 student bedrooms, and 650 parking spaces. All the new parking was to be constructed under the buildings, neatly concealed and taking advantage of the steep grade of the site so that drivers could enter on the downhill side of the buildings into what, from a cost standpoint, would simply be a somewhat deeper foundation than he would have to construct anyway to support the buildings. The three buildings remaining on the site would be Quarry Arms—the old City of Ithaca Hospital, now single-bedroom apartments; Casa Roma, a thirty-plus apartment unit he had built shortly after acquiring the original parcel from Ithaca College; and the Boiler Works Apartments, his highly original reconstruction of the old heating plant for the ingenious complex of sixteen units.

John's initial acquisition and renovation of the old hospital site comprised 635 bedrooms and 430 parking spaces. After the expanded vision for the State Street location, his plans were to double the capacity on the State Street site. It was not to be so simple.

Whenever a project is to be considered at a meeting of the Ithaca Planning Board, it is a legal requirement that all neighbors within two hundred feet of the site receive notification of the meeting. The agenda is also published at city hall and in legal notices in the local paper, the *Ithaca Journal*. The Collegetown Terrace project was scheduled for its environmental review in late May of 2009.

A number of neighbors attended the planning board meeting, and after John's architect laid out the plans, the neighbors to the east of the project and in the general East Hill/Belle Sherman area spoke out in opposition. At 1,245 rooms, the project was too big. It would worsen traffic on small roads. It would threaten historic buildings; while Novarr was keeping three historically designated buildings, some felt that all the rest of the buildings marked to be torn down should instead be renovated.

John responded by saying that many of the houses in the area were run-down or uninhabitable and that the new apartments would be safer for students. The biggest opposition, however, was to his original design with long, serpentine buildings for three blocks right along State Street. The neighbors felt these long buildings would destroy the residential feel and fabric of the neighborhood. Three blocks, with three long buildings three stories high, with more behind on a topography that slopes downhill toward Six Mile Creek, and a proposed increase to five, and later six stories, would require a zoning variance. Some neighbors felt this would devastate the small-town feel of Ithaca, particularly at this eastern entrance to the main part of town. John's project would definitely need a variance. To its credit, the planning board typically pays close attention to the neighborhood reaction, as well as to its expressions of support. At this point, the neighbors had him, and his project was stalled.

John and his partners already owned the entire site. He had been successful with his adaptive reuse of the old hospital into student housing. Boiler Works Apartments was a gem. Casa Roma had been successful. He was a developer, and quite experienced with both City Hall and neighborhood opposition.

Over the next two years John and his development team, ikon.5 Architects from Princeton, New Jersey, worked back and forth with the neighbors, members of Historic Ithaca, the ILPC, and city officials, particularly those representing the neighborhood. They changed the design to small three-story town houses lining State Street and located the five-and six-story serpentine buildings back behind the street facade and down the slope to a less prominent location. They reorganized traffic flow at the complicated intersection by giving the city a right-of-way to expand State Street east from Eddy Street, which allowed an extra lane of traffic, a bike lane, and a turn lane. In addition, they contributed a new traffic light and pedestrian crossing. They also agreed to restore, rather than demolish, the Williams House, originally built for businessman Roger B. Williams, and which became the home of the first president of Ithaca College. Although it is historically significant and stands at the very focal point of the project at the top of State Street hill where four major streets come together, the Williams House is not a protected building.

In all respects, this was an exciting project, breaking the mold of typical small-scale Ithaca development. At 1,245 beds, Collegetown Terrace would be the largest housing project ever attempted outside the Cornell campus. John's plan was to build it in at least four phases over six years, so the impact on other student landlords might be minimal. Of course it also might not be. We all waited somewhat apprehensively to see the outcome.

The project was approved and peaked out at close to 860,000 square feet in sixteen buildings, many more than the original seven anticipated, but not as massive and prominent along the street front as originally conceived. The central building along State Street contained a full gym with a two-story glass facade, which could be viewed in its entirety by the public, while driving up or down State Street hill. All units were fully furnished, with the usual amenities of Internet, security, and even multiple study rooms where residents could work together on group projects.

Collegetown Terrace would be developed three blocks from downtown and approximately ten blocks from the heart of the university—about a fifteen-minute walk for most students, who wanted to live as close as possible to the heart of campus. It is a steep hill to downtown and a gentle grade to the university. If the project were like other student developments on the hill, students would in general prefer not to traverse the steep hill, especially in winter, so Collegetown Terrace would likely have little perceivable impact on downtown retail. On the other hand, it might affect downtown vacancy rates, for graduate students could live there instead of downtown. Maybe some of the students would come down for events, but mostly they would be Cornell-oriented for meals, shopping, and classes and would tend to stay in Collegetown up on the hill for their evening entertainment.

John met with Tompkins Consolidated Area Transit (TCAT) and arranged for a complimentary bus service to campus by way of Collegetown, to run Monday through Friday every ten minutes from 7:30 a.m. to 11:30 a.m. and hourly from 12:15 p.m. to 4:15 p.m. In addition, the new number 10 bus that had been added to the TCAT network, and which ran every ten minutes from downtown through campus from 7:00 a.m. to 10:00 p.m. every day except Sunday, stopped practically at the front door of John's project. A student using a university-supplied bus pass could make it from the heart of campus to Collegetown Terrace in less than five minutes on the bus. They could also ride downtown on the number 10 bus, if they were so inclined, in less than three.

The clearing away of existing houses began in the fall of 2011, and construction started immediately thereafter. The first two phases were built by contractor Haynor Hoyt, with Welliver taking over on phases 3 and 4.

John Novarr was a lesson in patience, in buying strategically, in preserving the historic environment, and in working with the neighbors and the ILPC to create, through compromise, an acceptable design.

Would this project have happened without the activities and culture of growth created by the BID three blocks down the hill? Maybe it would have, but together, this interface of private development, the university's need for more housing, and the new dynamic of a revitalized downtown

**Figure 22.3** Collegetown Terrace, 2015. Nearly 1 million square feet of new student housing. Photo by Jon Reis.

**Figure 22.4** Collegetown Terrace, 2015. Nearly 1 million square feet of new student housing. Photo by Jon Reis.

very likely kept 1,245 beds worth of *density* from moving to the far side of campus, or outside the city limits—or very possibly not being built at all.

John, with his drive, his vision, and his patience, had built a truly remarkable addition to the Ithaca community.

# CHAPTER 23

# COMMUNITY FOCUS (1828–2008)

## Avoiding a Bankruptcy

There are over four hundred registered not-for-profits in Ithaca. It is not atypical that Carol and I selectively join boards and assist in their guidance and development. Carol spent nine years on the board of the Sciencenter, our local children's museum. She was on the board of the Tompkins Cortland Community College Foundation, and she was chair of the Women's Fund Advisory Committee of the Community Foundation of Tompkins County.

In addition to serving fifteen years as founding member and president of our business improvement district, I had also spent six- to nine-year terms on various boards, including Ithaca Alpha House, a local drug rehab facility; McGraw House, a senior housing facility; Cayuga Medical Center, our local hospital; and Kendal at Ithaca, a very upscale assisted-living facility developed near Cornell. Serving as volunteers in these various organizations was a natural outgrowth of our strong and ever-prevalent desire to help build a vibrant Ithaca community. Carol joined the board of Historic Ithaca in 2003.

Historic Ithaca was founded in 1966 by the Ithaca Downtown Business Women association, as a reaction to urban renewal and the subsequent demolition of cherished historic structures. Their mission included educating the public about the value of Ithaca's architectural heritage and preserving specific buildings downtown. If all the old buildings were torn down to make way for new, Ithaca would be a more modern city, but with the university and its Gothic stone edifices, with city churches dating back over a hundred years, and with an enviable natural environment, it became important to many to keep at least the core of the historic area intact. Historic Ithaca adopted the preservation of the historic environment as its primary mission.

As James Howard Kunstler had pointed out to the DIA years before, it is primarily in our downtowns that we have the opportunity to preserve the past and to keep the memory of our roots intact, not by preserving junk, but by selecting the key buildings—the Chryslers, the Empire States, the four-story stone facades lining our old streets—and keeping these buildings alive through renovations and updating, keeping them here for us, our children, and our children's children to enjoy. Picture the inner city of Paris, Stockholm, or London, or your own city, torn down and lost to posterity. That is what our historic preservation group, Historic Ithaca, holds as their mission—preservation of Ithaca's historic architecture.

In the early 1970s, motivated by the vision of urban renewal, the owner of the Clinton House, David Saperstone, was ready to tear the building down for use as a development site. Historic Ithaca had raised the funds and purchased it from him in 1972.

The Clinton House is a prime example of Ithaca's historic classic architecture. Built in 1828 as a hotel—the largest hotel west of the Hudson at the time—the Clinton House has been an icon in downtown Ithaca for nearly two centuries. The Historic Ithaca board of directors, along with local preservationists Victoria Romanoff and Connie Saltonstall, led a team of volunteers who worked for two years to successfully save and renovate the building, converting it into professional office spaces, including an office for the Historic Ithaca organization itself. It operated profitably as a rental property, actually bringing in enough income for Historic Ithaca to cover both their building and staff expenses for twenty-five years.

**Figure 23.1** The Clinton House was built in 1828. Photo courtesy of the History Center of Tompkins County.

Photograph by Constance Saltonstall

# SAVED FROM THE WRECKING BALL

## PRESERVING THE CLINTON HOUSE & OTHER STORIES FROM ITHACA'S EARLY HISTORIC PRESERVATION DAYS

FREE DISCUSSION at THE HISTORY CENTER
MARCH 5 at 2 PM
401 EAST STATE STREET
WITH VICTORIA ROMANOFF, CAROL SISLER, MICHAEL BACON, FRED SCHWARTZ, & OTHERS

ALSO ON DISPLAY AT THE HISTORY CENTER, MARCH 1-26:

### IT TAKES MORE THAN NOSTALGIA
CELEBRATING 50 YEARS OF HISTORIC ITHACA & COMMUNITY PRESERVATION

 NEW YORK STATE OF OPPORTUNITY | Council on the Arts   Historic Ithaca and The History Center events are made possible by the New York State Council on the Arts with the support of Governor Andrew M. Cuomo and the New York State Legislature.

THE HISTORY CENTER
in Tompkins County
www.thehistorycenter.net

www.historicithaca.org

**Figure 23.2** Advertisement for a 2016 public lecture on the preservation of the Clinton House. Poster courtesy of Historic Ithaca.

In 1980 another historic building in downtown was under threat of demolition by its owner, Tompkins County. The Boardman House was derelict. After significant public outcry over announced plans for its demolition, a sale was orchestrated by Historic Ithaca, from the county to Joe Ciaschi, a major developer famous for his restoration of the old Lehigh Valley train station, which he turned into a restaurant on the west side of town in 1966, and Clinton Hall, adjacent to the Clinton House. Joe would renovate the Boardman House and turn it into lovely offices.

In 1992 Joe also purchased the State Theatre to save it from demolition. It was built on West State Street in 1915, as a car dealership and garage. In 1926, The Berinstein family purchased the building, and hired architect Victor Rigaumont to design and oversee the transformation of the garage and showroom into a cinema and vaudeville palace. Rigaumont incorporated elements of the Moorish and Renaissance revival styles and the collegiate Gothic of Cornell University. Opening night as a vaudeville house was December 6, 1928.

**Figure 23.3** The Boardman House, 1867. Photo courtesy of the History Center of Tompkins County.

**Figure 23.4** The State Theatre, ca. 1957. Photo courtesy of the History Center of Tompkins County.

It operated as such until the early '50s, when it was converted, as so many vaudeville theaters were, into a movie house. It served Ithaca successfully, screening movies for nearly three decades, but eventually declined and became derelict even after another local development group, the Puryears, revitalized it by turning the balcony into a second movie screen.

As happened with so many downtown theaters across the country, the State Theatre succumbed to competition from national chain movie theaters built in suburban malls during this period. It failed again and was closed for a third time. Ciaschi purchased the building but could never figure out a use for it as a theater. Step in Historic Ithaca.

To everyone's relief, in 1998 the board of Historic Ithaca voted to purchase the building from Ciaschi to save it from demolition. It was the last of seventeen theaters that had been built in Ithaca during the past century; of these only the State Theatre remained. Under Historic Ithaca's guidance, funds were raised from the city of Ithaca and many generous donors. After its initial stabilization and renovation by volunteers, funded by events and donations, the city invested nearly $2 million in a new roof, boiler, and plaster renovation, generally saving the structure from the elements.

Historic Ithaca did not intend to go into the business of running a theater and producing shows, but it became apparent that rather than just sitting there as an empty museum, this building might serve the community and perhaps could cover its overhead if they were to produce live theater—and that is what they did. They hired a young producer, Matt Joslyn, to bring Broadway shows to the city. Matt developed a convincing business plan, and the board raised enough money from donors to support the first season, and the second. It was then that financial reality began to creep in.

Ithaca is a small town. It has the cultural amenities of Cornell and Ithaca College, both of which bring international events to town—mostly music. Both have legitimate theaters on campus. There is probably enough "highbrow" entertainment in town already to satisfy our small population, many of whom are willing to travel the four hours to New York to see the best theater in the country. Broadway in Ithaca was intriguing and enjoyed by many residents, although far too few to fill the State Theatre's sixteen-hundred-seat house, and far too few to cover the cost of bringing in Broadway touring companies. Historic Ithaca went into debt. The Clinton House was paid for—it had no debt. It operated successfully, but was not profitable enough to cover the $250,000 annual shortfall that was resulting from trying to produce expensive Broadway shows in Ithaca, so they took out a private mortgage on the Clinton House to survive.

A community theater in downtown was recognized as extremely important to the revitalization of downtown Ithaca. It was part of the Downtown Ithaca Alliance's "arts, dining, and entertainment" plan, which all knew to be key to the redevelopment of downtowns, and not exclusively in Ithaca; it is a nationwide phenomenon. Historic Ithaca attempted to change the programming at the State, bringing only a few Broadway shows a year, and making the majority of shows music acts—cheaper to produce and probably more of a draw to the general public. Ultimately Matt Joslyn had to be let go, and he went on to Minneapolis, a larger market, where his talents as a Broadway producer could be better utilized.

It was then that Historic Ithaca hired Dan Smalls, a former Cornell student who, while still in school in the early '80s, had produced shows at a local nightclub, the Haunt, and who had moved to Boston and become the promoter of the band Phish. He was now in his mid-thirties and quite experienced. He had a vision and he had contacts for producing popular music shows with nationally known groups that might prove to be successful—if it was not too late.

Carol was still on the board of Historic Ithaca, and at her request I had met with the executive director and attempted to assist the organization in financially restructuring themselves. It quickly became apparent that they could not make it. At home one night, Carol invited me into her study and asked me to take a final look at the figures. I did, and said there was simply no way this organization could survive. She grew quiet, and then in her seldom-used emphatic voice suggested that I "get out, and close the door!" I did. Carol proceeded to get on the phone and raise $60,000 from friends and donors, which was the amount the organization needed at that time to continue.

But too much debt had accumulated. In a last-ditch effort to keep Historic Ithaca solvent, I went to the bank and asked them for a personal note for $250,000. I rounded up five friends, and we each agreed to guarantee $50,000 of the note. At that time neither I, nor anyone else, knew the *true* financial picture. I found out later.

Step in Jeb Brooks. Jeb was a friend of Historic Ithaca. He had been very successful in real estate, primarily in Boston. He had lent enough money to the Historic Ithaca organization over several years to keep it afloat while it continued trying to produce Broadway shows. He was financially astute, and when he updated his analysis of the finances of the Clinton House and his investment with Historic Ithaca, he determined there was not enough equity left in the Clinton House to justify further advances. He had close to $1 million at risk, secured by a first mortgage on the building, and not only did he now decline to make further advances, but Jeb wanted to be repaid. He was patient. He was understanding. He totally supported the mission of Historic Ithaca, but as a businessman he saw that the organization could not continue, and he asked to be repaid.

So my friends and I had $250,000 at risk, and Jeb had $1 million at risk. The State Theatre was going to close, and Historic Ithaca faced bankruptcy.

One of the advantages of being on the board of the Downtown Ithaca Alliance is that you get an overview of downtown and the dynamics at work there. Retail is important. People living in downtown are important. Restaurants, art galleries, and yes, theaters, are all important. And let's not forget parking, cleanliness, and police protection. Not only did we have all of these areas of focus as concerns, but by now we also had a very workable vision for the future. Thanks to Gary's expertise and vision, we had developed our first ten-year strategic plan for downtown Ithaca and were working on our second. We had built more housing. We had added a new 750-space parking garage. Gateway and Seneca Place had supplied 140,000 square feet of new office space to downtown. We knew that density rather than urban sprawl was important to the preservation of our natural landscape, to our health, and to the continuation of our downtown's health and well-being. Just as with Gateway, I had heard this over and over again, and just as with Gateway, I had begun to "believe my own hype." Loss of the State Theatre would be a disaster for downtown.

Carol and I decided that we had to do what we could to save the State Theatre and the Clinton House. These two properties were vital to the overall vision for revitalization of our downtown. And now more than ever, with our portfolio of Center Ithaca, both Gateway properties, and our offices and two other apartment buildings downtown, we had to make this work. Even for our own self-interest, we had to make this work, and for the preservation of Ithaca as a small city, I was convinced that we had to make it work. Over and over the images of downtown boarded up, the State Theatre boarded up, the Clinton House demolished for a modern, cheaply built economy-class office building or "motor-hotel"—as had been the plan with urban renewal in the 1960s—kept returning. Something had to be done.

Dan Smalls and I met. Could we take his vision for a fully operational theater producing primarily popular music and include community events like the Ithaca Ballet, Running to Places (a hugely popular high-school community theater organization), and other college and miscellaneous rentals—all this together—and make it work financially? Dan began work on developing a plan for the production side, while I began work on the financing angle. Together, with the help of our shrewd and experienced consultant, the late Andrew Dixon, we wrote a forty-page business plan and went to the bank. Actually I invited three bankers to a meeting with our attorney, Elena Flash, in her office overlooking the Commons. We presented our business plan. There was discussion. Not one banker felt their bank could take the risk of investing in a run-down ninety-year-old theater and a two-hundred-year-old Greek Revival building, no matter how historic. Even as a group they declined. Three bank presidents, and not one would support our plan. This is the first time I had ever raised my voice in the presence of a banker.

"You absolutely have to do this!" I spoke too loudly. They listened again. "Carol and I will personally guarantee both the loan on the Clinton House and the State Theatre. Both are vital to downtown. If they are boarded up, downtown will be headed that way. We are on the verge of creating a hugely successful downtown. If we fail to keep the State Theatre going, we will be headed downhill." They listened and shook their heads. Greg Hartz, president of Tompkins Trust Company, our 180-year-old community bank, finally paused and said, "Given your passion"—and probably our guarantee—"TTC would consider it."

The entire package was one of the most fascinating real estate transactions Carol and I have ever attempted. Dan, Andrew Dixon, and I developed a business plan that would keep the theater operational, and it would happen by our purchasing the Clinton House for enough to cover its approximately $400,000 in payables to local vendors, the $1 million owed to Jeb Brooks, and the $250,000 owed to Tompkins Trust Company by the five of us who had guaranteed it. Earlier, out of desperation, Historic Ithaca had put the Clinton House up for sale by sealed bids in an effort to stave off bankruptcy. The bids they received ranged from $350,000 to $500,000. As we had calculated, they owed $1.65 million.

Historic Ithaca's attorney was also one of our attorneys, John Hinchcliff at Miller Mayer. He agreed to handle the transaction for both parties. Elena Flash, also at Miller Mayer, who had handled our real estate transactions for twenty-five years, would agree to represent us. It is *not* usual for a single firm to represent both parties in a real estate transaction. What happens if you disagree? What happens if you come to blows? Both parties had to agree to sign a conflict-of-interest agreement absolving the law firm of responsibility should either of their clients disagree or sue for damages. We did so willingly—we were all among friends here.

Dan and I prepared the business plan, which included a list of Historic Ithaca's payables. We knew the amount of the debt. From the bidding, we knew that at a fire sale the Clinton House would bring no more than $500,000 into the coffers of Historic Ithaca. Since there was a first mortgage of nearly $1 million on the building, anything Historic Ithaca took in would have to go first toward the mortgage. In addition, there was well over $400,000 owed to dozens of local businesses that had extended credit to keep the Clinton House and State Theatre afloat. These local businesses would all have to absorb the loss—not a pretty thought. My friends and I would have to make good on our $250,000 guarantee to the Tompkins Trust Company. It was a mess.

Our goal was to move quickly—help the Historic Ithaca organization avoid bankruptcy—pay all the local vendors and suppliers, pay Jeb Brooks, pay off our $250,000 note, and clear up its financial problems, thereby keeping the theater open and saving the Clinton House and the State Theatre from a fire sale and probable demolition. Our business plan proposed that Carol and I would take over ownership of the Clinton House for $1.2 million. In addition, provided the Ithaca Urban Renewal Agency would lend the funds, we would agree to purchase the State Theatre for $450,000, then spin it off into a not-for-profit—the State Theatre of Ithaca, Inc.—and we would also guarantee the theater's debt to the IURA.

I went to see Nels Bohn, director of the Ithaca Urban Renewal Agency. The IURA had helped on Gateway by relending the funds we had paid back from Eddygate. This organization existed to help local projects for the "public good." One criterion was job creation. According to the business plan Dan and I had prepared, we would be keeping two full-time jobs and adding three more to the State Theatre payroll, thus allowing one of the biggest draws for downtown to remain operational and intact. This would all benefit the community. Nels accepted our business plan and financial projections, and after weeks of meetings and negotiations, he called to let me know that the IURA board had approved a loan of $450,000 to our newly formed not-for-profit—at the favorable interest rate of 2 percent.

Based on our business plan, Tompkins Trust Company agreed to lend $975,000 on the Clinton House toward the project. This, together with the IURA funds, would give us $1,425,000. We needed an additional $225,000 to make our purchase price of $1.65 million. We raised another $75,000 from three friends who agreed to invest $25,000 each for a 6 percent ownership position, and our family business was prepared to make up the difference of $150,000. $1.65 million. We were there.

It was then that I revisited the numbers provided by Historic Ithaca. They had undercalculated the payables by $100,000. I rechecked our spreadsheet. We could still purchase the Clinton House and run the theater, but we would have to put in an additional $100,000 to make the deal work. It was the first time I had ever gone to the attorney of a seller, who of course happened to be our own attorney, and told him that we needed to pay more for the building than the price we had negotiated with his client. I called John and told him, "John, I just recalculated all the figures from Historic Ithaca, and we need to pay an additional $100,000 to avoid Historic Ithaca having to file for bankruptcy. We need to increase the purchase price for the entire package by $100,000 to $1,750,000!" John told me he had also just recalculated the numbers and reached the same conclusion. "I was about to call you," he said. Adding up all the payables and all the debt, we now needed $1.75 million to keep Historic Ithaca from going bankrupt, keep the State Theatre from closing, and pay off all creditors.

Our business increased its investment in the deal by $100,000, so were now committing to a total of $250,000. We could now close the deal and bail out this important community organization so that they could continue their mission of historic preservation. The buildings would not be sold at a fire sale, and best of all, if it worked out as projected, we had a fully functioning sixteen-hundred-seat State Theatre and a viable business plan that would keep it operational as a major draw for our downtown. It was years later, in 1973, that I found out Historic Ithaca had paid $83,000 for their original purchase of the Clinton House.

At the closing, we wrote Jeb a check for his first-mortgage payoff. He totally surprised us by redonating $100,000 toward keeping the theater open for the first year. He was obviously pleased at the outcome. Carol, Dan, and I were ecstatic that we had the operating funds to assist the theater in its first year of operation.

While pleased that their organization had avoided bankruptcy, the president of the board and the executive director both felt they had failed in their mission of historic preservation. They had lost the Clinton House, and they had lost the State Theatre. They now had only one asset left, Significant Elements, their restoration company charged with preserving historic architectural artifacts.

**Figure 23.5** Mack and Carol Travis (2008). It all worked out in the end! Photo by Carl Mazzocone.

We suggested that they look at things differently. They had not failed. They had preserved two magnificent historic structures. Historic Ithaca's mission had never been to act as a landlord. Certainly their mission was not to produce theatrical productions and run a theater; it was historic preservation—and by saving the Clinton House two and a half decades ago and the State Theatre a decade ago, they had fulfilled their mission. Both buildings would have been sold and torn down, resulting in a huge loss in Ithaca's historic architectural legacy. They had completely fulfilled their mission and could now focus on the job of historic preservation and public education without the worry of also trying to assume the roles of landlord and theatrical producers. Carol remained on their board, and that is what they have done.

This focus of the BID on recognizing the importance of our historic legacy, and the need for a successful theater downtown, had made a great impression on us. Having a sympathetic bank, and the power of the Ithaca Urban Renewal Agency—now focused on preservation rather than demolition—were major forces that enabled this community-oriented acquisition to succeed.

# CHAPTER 24

# OPPORTUNITIES (2008-15)
## A Successful Collaboration

Arts, dining, and entertainment lie at the heart of downtown revitalization. In studying other cities, and in listening to Gary, who was a wealth of experience, Ithaca had learned this dynamic well. People like to visit art galleries, and many were springing up downtown. They enjoy attending live theater. In addition to providing office space to both professional and arts organizations, the Clinton House also housed a truly avant-garde seventy-five-seat theater on the ground floor—the Kitchen Theatre—whose tagline was "Important conversations happen in the Kitchen!" Many people have a great fondness for concerts, and they love eating out. Downtown was alive with over fifty restaurants and bars within two blocks of the Commons—"more restaurants per capita than New York City," our convention and visitors bureau liked to brag. Arts, dining, and entertainment. Thanks to the involvement of the city leaders, store owners, and property owners, thanks to active developers and the Downtown Ithaca Alliance with its strategic plan, Ithaca was following the formula for developing a successful downtown.

Running a theater is not like managing an office building or apartments. Emotions run higher in a theater. Staff, volunteers, maintenance and custodial workers, the producer, the board of directors—all feel a dedication to perfection, and all of us are "onstage" for the public. No one is anonymous. Hundreds, even thousands, of people will come nightly to see what *"you"* have done—it better be good. And good it was!

Saving Jeb's donation for down the road, Carol and I covered payroll for two months, while Dan Smalls made the theater operational again. Our three-member board of directors grew quickly to five, then six, and finally to fifteen members. The shows were magnificent. Dan served as our exclusive talent buyer, and his strategy was to find shows traveling between New York or Boston on their way to Cleveland, Chicago, and beyond, and book them as "fill-ins," perhaps on a weeknight at a deep discount. Performers who had never come to upstate New York were now coming to town—Joan Baez, Arlo Guthrie, Gordon Lightfoot, even Eric Clapton and Bobby McFerrin. Comedians like Ron White and Lewis Black. Ithaca was a small town, but it now boasted a beautiful sixteen-hundred-seat theater, with perfect acoustics and a ready-made audience of twenty-five thousand students, plus a more mature population of nearly one hundred thousand, within five miles of our downtown. The shows at the State Theatre could *put people in seats.*

The State Theatre became a focal point for donors and volunteers who felt they could make a difference. Jeb's initial donation was critical to the theater being able to stay open the first year, but beyond that, it was imperative that we raise significant funds. Carol and I had developed a financial model for the Clinton House that made it self-sufficient. With the many office rentals, and with the Kitchen Theatre on the first floor, we could cover the cost of the mortgage, utilities, taxes, and management, and even have money left over to pay a small return to the investors.

In 2008, my son, Frost, who had now earned a degree in real estate development from Cornell and had been working with a firm in New York City, returned to Ithaca and took over the management of our entire real estate portfolio. His mother had recently joined the board of the newly formed New Roots Charter School (NRCS), which was looking for a home. Frost showed them the first floor of the Clinton House, which was currently occupied by several arts organizations and the theater; the space might fit the school's needs for a home, provided we could conveniently relocate the tenants.

It wasn't certain that this two-hundred-year-old building would actually suffice, or even meet building code for a school—it was a long shot. Frost worked with HOLT Architects and the city building inspectors. Surprisingly, they found it could work. The entire building would have to be sprinklered, firewalls would have to be built between adjoining tenancies. New bathrooms would have to be constructed. Somehow, we managed to continue to accommodate the Kitchen Theatre, but all the other current first-floor tenants would have to leave. Was it worth it? Would it be possible, given that the entire renovation would also have to meet the ILPC standards for historic preservation?

What followed was an exercise in patience and creativity and relied to a large degree on serendipity—all forces that over the years have had much to do with the dynamic of the development process of every project. Frost talked with the Tompkins County Visitors Center, which also served as a ticket center for local theaters and was located on the first floor. He showed them that he had an even more suitable space for them in Center Ithaca, our high-traffic building on the Commons. They agreed, and he worked out a deal to rebuild the space to their specs and relocate them. For the remaining arts organizations—the Community Arts Partnership, the Hangar Theatre business office, and the Cayuga Chamber Orchestra, he again found space in vacancies we happened to have at Center Ithaca. We definitely did not want to lose the Kitchen Theatre, as they paid a reasonable rent, and Frost felt sure that he could work things out in such a way that they could share space with the school.

He negotiated a thirty-page operating agreement between the New Roots Charter School and the theater. The school could use the entire first floor, including the theater, during the day. They designed their furniture to roll to the side, and the theater could use the lobby, the reception desk, and the theater after five o'clock in the evening. The theater found rehearsal space around the corner on State Street. Everything was set. Tenants were relocated and happy in their new spaces. The theater and school had cooperatively agreed to cohabit the first floor and most of the second floor. A half-million-dollar renovation was completed, and the school moved in and began with teaching over 150 students their first year.

About a year later, the Kitchen Theatre informed us that they wanted to leave. For many reasons, we wanted to keep them downtown. They were a good draw for the restaurants; downtown would certainly suffer by their departure. They paid a good rent; without them, how could we, as landlords, keep the building solvent? They told us they needed to stay through the first year of their lease in order to have time to raise the money and to build their new theater, five blocks away from the center of downtown, but after that, they wanted out.

NRCS was supported by state funds as part of the city of Ithaca school system, so they could cover the additional rent to have the space all to themselves. However, they were under severe criticism from two women who opposed every move the school made. The two critics, former teachers in the public school system, wrote article after article to the newspaper denigrating the New Roots Charter School; they attended every board meeting, as they had the right to do, since this was a public school. Fortunately, the school's enrollment was expanding, and by the time the Kitchen Theatre had built out their new space, New Roots could, despite the criticism from the two critics, afford to take over and pay rent on the entire first floor.

Not only that, the State Theatre had a large vacant office space on the second floor of the theater only a block away from the Clinton House, and the theater could certainly use the income. As president of the board of the State Theatre, I suggested that the board negotiate an arms-length deal with NRCS and renovate two large offices into classrooms for the school. In addition, the theater could sweeten the deal by giving the school the right to use the stage and sixteen-hundred-seat theater for assemblies, graduation, and other group meetings and activities, especially as these events were usually held during the day, when the theater was mostly idle. I was criticized by one of our very active and outspoken board members for taking theater space for one of my own tenants. However, in my mind and in the minds of the majority of the board, the need for funds to run the theater took precedence, and the State Theatre board of directors overrode the one critic, who subsequently resigned from the board. To me, the entire transaction, from the purchase of both historic buildings, to the relocation of tenants from the Clinton House, to the rental of the upstairs offices as classrooms, had been about making our downtown more active and vital. I was sorry to lose the board member, but I like to think that time has proven me right.

I continually returned to the vision of downtown boarded up and vacant, but now it was as if I awoke from the nightmare. We had 150 students taking classes in the Clinton House and walking the Commons after school. We had sold-out shows to sixteen hundred theater patrons, and we had two classic historic buildings vibrant and contributing to the activity and excitement of downtown, all of which went a long way toward countering my nightmarish vision of what could have happened if we, and many others, had just given up on downtown. When restaurant owner and chef Lex Chutintaranond told me that if the State Theatre had not been opened and running, he would not have redeveloped a derelict building on the Commons into Mia, his first-class restaurant, with nine apartments above, I knew for certain we had done the right thing. It was a pleasure to pass by his restaurant on evenings when the theater had a show playing and to see it bursting at the seams with patrons.

To assist the school in expanding their enrollment, during their first two years of operation our company donated the services of our long-time public relations specialist, David Plaine. David assisted the school in designing and placing banners advertising the New Roots Charter School on the sides of the city buses. David helped them design an entire PR campaign that contributed significantly to the school's stability and success.

Development does not unfold in a prescribed and predictable way. It takes on a life of its own. Opportunities often appear out of nowhere. By being ready for the unexpected, by taking advantage of opportunities as they appear, one can become a successful player. The acquisition and renovation, the establishment of viable and active community assets such as the New Roots Charter School and the State Theatre, brought great new vitality to our downtown, and great personal satisfaction to all of us who made it happen—all of these activities have been driven by focusing on the fulfillment of the strategic plan for downtown. All of us were "shaping a city."

CHAPTER 25

# NONPROFIT SURVIVAL

### How to Improve the Bottom Line through Real Estate Ownership

In a city with over four hundred not-for-profit organizations, requests for donations arrive almost daily either in one's mailbox or email in-box or over the phone. In addition to requests from the fund-raisers for each non-profit, Ithaca also has the Legacy Foundation of Tompkins County, the Community Foundation of Tompkins County, and United Way, all asking for donations to disperse among their supplicants. In running the State Theatre, we became one more not-for-profit with our hand out for dona-tions. Our budget quickly grew to $800,000 annually, then $900,000, and then to nearly $1 million. We hired an executive director, a market-ing assistant, and box office staff—all positions necessary for the efficient operation of the theater. Our paid sponsorships in the community grew, as small businesses saw the State Theatre was a viable organization that could reach fifty to sixty thousand patrons a year with its program and mailings, but still there was never enough money. It was a theater, and the-aters, as with most cultural organizations, require community financial support, well beyond the sale of tickets, to survive.

Carl Haynes had been successful establishing his extension campus for Tompkins Cortland Community College in downtown Ithaca by purchasing the M&T Bank building from Ciminelli. TC3 was now a permanent player and had joined the educational powerhouse composed of Cornell Univer-sity, Ithaca College, and now TC3. Together these educational institutions bring close to thirty thousand students into the Ithaca area, in which our major industry has evolved from industrial and auto parts at BorgWarner, and cash registers at National Cash Register, to education.

Prior to joining the faculty at TC3, Carl had been a real estate developer. Over lunch one day, I asked him to review a preliminary draft of a book I was writing, *Creating an Independent Income in Real Estate.* I thought the book might appeal to students at the community college level interested in entering the field, and asked Carl if he would write a statement to include in the introduction in support of the text. Carl agreed and proceeded to tell me of his own real estate career. In the '80s he had purchased four hundred acres of land at the north end of Cayuga Lake. He developed the land into building lots and made enough money to pay cash for a farm in the area. He then decided to take a position teaching and eventually became president of TC3. Carl understood the power of real estate to create an income stream. He extrapolated that if it worked for an individual, as it had for him, it could work for a nonprofit organization like TC3.

Carol had joined Carl's TC3 Foundation. She, too, understood real estate. Carl had created the foundation to hold and manage real estate for the benefit of the college, and under his guidance, it purchased two derelict dormitory buildings next to the college. They had been built as dorms for the students but were a financial failure, and he was able to pick them up at a low cost. He raised money through the NYS Dormitory Authority to renovate them, and now successfully ran them as a profit center for the college. During our lunch, Carl complimented me on my book, and he also made the following statement: "Nonprofits simply do not realize the power that real estate ownership can have for improving their bottom line."

He elaborated on his plans to expand the campus in downtown Ithaca and went on to share his experiences in real estate, starting from his rental quarters in the basement of the former Rothschild Building, to purchasing the six-story M&T Bank building. As the deal developed, Carl's vision had grown to include relocating the TC3 campus to the upper two floors of the M&T Bank building, keeping the bank in their rental space on the ground floor, and renting the remaining three floors as a source of income. He again explained how it had worked—as a nonprofit organization, TC3 could receive the building as a tax-deductible gift from Ciminelli, who wrote off the purchase as a contribution to the Ithaca community, and Carl could use it as a source of rental income for the college.

As our State Theatre developed over the years, I thought many times of Carl's statement. How could the theater, as a not-for-profit, use real estate to improve its bottom line? How could it become the owner of additional income property? Gary Ferguson agreed with this possibility of the State Theatre getting into real estate. Prior to taking the job as director of Ithaca's business improvement district, Gary had worked in Dayton, Ohio, as assistant director of their BID, and he knew his counterpart in Cleveland. Gary and I planned a road trip.

Cleveland, Ohio, is a classic city whose downtown has imploded. As shops and residents left for the suburbs, many old buildings, from warehouses to department stores, were demolished to make room for parking lots. Like missing teeth in the facades of block after block, they stood out in this bedraggled downtown. However, many other buildings were gentrified as developers purchased them for a fraction of their original value—some had even been given to developers by the city for a dollar. We met one developer-architect, Jonathan Sandvick, who had worked magic with what is called adaptive reuse on over sixty projects. Cleveland's downtown was beginning to come alive again, as young people and professionals moved into old industrial lofts, old department stores, and old office buildings that had been transformed into modern, attractive retail spaces, with grocery stores on the first floor and offices and apartments on the upper floors. We saw the Ithaca dynamic, as laid out in our strategic plan, repeated on a much larger scale here.

Our host took us to the west end of Euclid Avenue, a magnificent, wide boulevard that housed Cleveland's theater district—in the 1920s, five theaters had been constructed within two blocks of each other. As the city declined in the '70s, and under the influence of urban renewal, developers were anxious to purchase and demolish the theaters to make more parking lots for downtown. Instead, Cleveland's Playhouse Square historic preservation group stepped in and over time purchased all five theaters and saved them from demolition. Today they have all been fully restored. Many of the shows Dan books for Ithaca are on their way to play in Cleveland, whose largest theater, at thirty-five hundred seats, with its sweeping stairs and marble balustrades, dwarfs our little plaster-of-Paris sixteen-hundred-seat State Theatre, which would fit on the stage of these larger theaters.

We were struck by the beauty and foresight exhibited in the theater restorations. Our host walked us across the street into a local bar and restaurant, where we happened upon and were introduced to the executive director of Playhouse Square, the organization that owned and operated the five theaters in downtown Cleveland. Yes, they were operating successfully. Yes, they still had to raise money from the community to survive. Yes, they had many sell-out shows, but it was always a struggle. However, they had something else. Playhouse Square, their director told us, owned a million square feet of prime real estate in the several blocks surrounding the five theaters. They owned a Westin Hotel; they owned apartment buildings; they owned office buildings; they had restaurants and retail, plus they managed another million square feet of commercial real estate in the suburbs. They owned major real estate holdings, and their manager confided that these holdings contributed over $400,000 to the bottom line of their nonprofit theaters. Carl was right, here was tangible proof that real estate can be a major contributor to the success of a nonprofit organization.

Gary and I left Cleveland without actually finding out how Playhouse Square had come by their real estate portfolio, but we were impressed. We returned home determined to make this concept a reality in Ithaca. We could form the State Theatre Foundation, just as Carl had set up the TC3 Foundation, and we could somehow acquire real estate, just as Cleveland had done with their Playhouse Square. In addition to producing shows, selling tickets and sponsorships, in addition to our traditional fund-raising efforts, we could add this real estate engine, which would contribute to the bottom line of the State Theatre.

For those not already invested in real property, buying and managing a building and making a profit can seem like a foreign country. What did it have to do with running a theater? What if something goes wrong? Hold a mortgage? What if we can't pay the mortgage? Our board of directors was understandably reluctant and cautious. By now we had a couple of developers, an architect, and a real estate attorney on the board. We proposed the formation of a foundation to own and manage property. The State Theatre itself would not be put at risk. If the State Theatre Foundation failed, other than a public nosebleed, it would not really affect the theatre. All losses would be the foundation's; all profits would be donated from the foundation to the theater. The full board listened and finally agreed. Following Carl Haynes's concept of real estate ownership as a way to improve the bottom line, and having seen it at work in Cleveland, our goal was to expand the real estate holdings of the State Theatre Foundation to the point where the theater could gain financial stability and independence. I had begun with a two-family house forty years earlier and built a substantial portfolio and corresponding income. Why couldn't we take the same concept and apply it to the theater?

Our first property was purchased with the assistance of a new, young board member, John Guttridge, who had recently purchased the local newspaper office and printing building on West State Street, one door down from the State Theatre, for his ever-expanding computer business. He found out that the former Family & Children's Services building two blocks away was up for sale, and it was a fire sale. Their organization desperately needed money. It had been on the market for two years at over $850,000, but no bites. John didn't have the cash to buy it himself, so he came to Travis Hyde. Frost and I discussed it with him. We agreed we would put up the cash and suggested that he should make a cash offer of $300,000. He made the offer, and Family and Children's Services accepted.

Since John had brought the building to us, we made it a three-way partnership. John would own one-third; my son, Frost, and my son-in-law, Chris Hyde, would own one-third; and the State Theatre, while not owning the property, would be entitled to an equitable one-third distribution of profits from the property. It worked like this: for every dollar distributed, John took twenty-five cents, Frost and Chris took twenty-five cents, the State Theatre Foundation took twenty-five cents, and twenty-five cents was retained in the building's capital improvement escrow to fund improvements whenever they would be needed. It was not a large building, and it was not going to add $400,000 to the bottom line of the State Theatre, but it was a start. It made more sense for private individuals—John, Frost, and Chris—to own the property, since the tax advantages would be lost on a nonprofit owning them, and we set up the distribution to the theater as a legal obligation to the owners. It would be a donation on their behalf.

The three owners undertook a major renovation of the building and turned it into a home for two major nonprofits on the first and second floors and two apartments on the third floor. Just as he had done so successfully at the Clinton House, Frost was able to move one nonprofit out of a building he and Chris were gutting and renovating on East State Street to a new office they would build for them at 204 Cayuga Street, and they would build a business incubator in their vacated space housing thirty-five start-up businesses in their new Carey Building.

We were following Carl Haynes's directive, and we were mimicking Cleveland's success at Playhouse Square. We felt we were taking our first step toward using real estate ownership as an additional income source for this community gem    the State Theatre.

# CHAPTER 26

# THE WOMEN'S COMMUNITY BUILDING (1960–2014)

## Breckenridge Place—Affordable Housing in the Heart of Downtown

The four corners of Seneca and Cayuga Streets form one of the busiest intersections within the BID boundary. Three of the four corners hold historic structures whose future has been closely guarded by Historic Ithaca and the ILPC. The Clinton House from 1828 sits at its strategic, stately location on the southwest corner facing east and up the hill toward Cornell. On the site across the street, on the southeast corner, sits the Masonic Temple with its two-story limestone-clad structure, built in 1926 in Egyptian revival style. It has been vacant for two decades. On the northeast corner is the Dewitt Mall, site of the former Dewitt High School from 1915–60 and the Dewitt Junior High from 1960–70. It was saved from demolition by architect Bill Downing, who, much to the dismay of several other developers, bought it in 1971 at a sealed-bid auction. The other developers later filed a lawsuit against the board of education for selling this 80,000-plus-square-foot, four-story structure to him for $20,000, or $4 per square foot. They lost their suit, and Bill spent over a million dollars improving the building in 1971, executing an extremely creative adaptive reuse of the structure by turning it into forty-eight apartments, offices, and an interior shopping mall. On the northwest corner was the one-story, very unhistorical Women's Community Building with offices, a cafeteria, and transient rooms for single women. This single-story, cinderblock building was built in 1960, designed with little character or historic reference.

Ithacans have always had a philanthropic spirit, and the City Federation of Women's Organizations (CFWO) was founded in 1910 with the mission to "support women and girls and to act as a catalyst for the improvement of the lives of women and girls in Tompkins County." It was a philanthropic organization concerned with "education, recreation, philanthropy, health, safety and civic betterment." In 1920 the federation purchased the first Women's Community Building (WCB) on the corner of Seneca and Cayuga Streets and established a recreational center, public restrooms, meeting rooms, and living quarters for single women and girls. In 1927 CFWO purchased the house next door that became a home for older women, and in the 1940s they opened a community nursery school.

In 1960, the two older houses were demolished and a one-story Women's Community Building was opened on the site, which included a community auditorium for up to 250 people and a commercial kitchen. This became the home for the famed Rotary Club pancake breakfast held annually around election time. It hosted public meetings too large for city hall and the occasional wedding, and it was also rented five days a week by the New Roots Charter School as their lunchroom. Even though the WCB rented office and auditorium space to various community organizations, the building was still losing money and the federation faced financial difficulties.

In 2010, as part of exploring options for the future of the organization, they asked if I would come in to assist them with planning an addition to the building, perhaps creating rental apartments to enhance their income. I met with them several times and laid out a conceptual plan for thirty or so units. Their board discussed it, but they ended up choosing another route.

During this same period, the federation met with Paul Mazzarella of INHS and Joe Bowes of PathStone to explore possible alternatives for the building. They discussed renovation of the existing structure; demolition and new construction; partnerships with other developers; and developing a new project on their own. After many months of consideration, the CFWO decided that their best option was to sell.

**Figure 26.1** The one-story Women's Community Building at Seneca and Cayuga Streets, demolished in 2012 and replaced with fifty units of affordable housing. Photo by Rachel Philipson.

This was a shock for New Roots and their 150 students, who needed lunch served daily. It was an inconvenience for organizations like the Rotary Club, the city, and the county, which counted on the large public meeting space at a nominal rent. I began formulating a plan to meet with Jason Fane. The vacant two-story building across the street from the Clinton House had a commercial kitchen, a gym, and a large meeting hall, all of which could very nicely fill the gap after the Women's Community Building was sold, and it had a huge for sale sign on the side along Seneca Street.

Meanwhile, INHS and a Rochester developer, PathStone, became very interested in developing an affordable housing project on the WCB site. INHS, from its founding by Thys Van Cort and its guidance for twenty years by Paul, had renovated over fifteen hundred houses in Ithaca. It had also built several "affordable" housing complexes on the outskirts of town. Partnering with PathStone permitted INHS to work with a developer that was experienced in funding affordable housing through tax credits and other highly competitive governmental aid programs. PathStone would navigate the tax-credit and regulatory programs, thereby bringing the funding along with their construction expertise to the project. Paul would bring the not-for-profit status of INHS that was needed for the building of affordable housing, and in addition he would navigate city hall and the intricate permitting process. The developer would make money up-front from developers' fees and construction profit. INHS would receive its income from the management of the units contracted for a fifty-year period. The community would benefit by having permanent affordable workforce housing at rents to be set by HUD for the income bracket of 50 percent of the area's median income.

Paul looked at the Women's Community Building on the northwest corner of Seneca and Cayuga Streets. It was one block from the Commons—easy walking distance to all that the center of the city had to offer in the way of restaurants, shopping, art galleries, and cultural events. The State Theatre was a block away. INHS began the conceptual design for the WCB site with some simple sketches by HOLT Architects.

The current B3 zoning on the site allowed only 50 percent lot coverage and required forty parking spaces. Could INHS get a variance or a zoning change for the site? HOLT calculated that the ideal for maximizing use of the site would be a six-story building, sixty feet in height, with no parking and 100 percent lot coverage. This was consistent with the zoning requirements of the CBD 60 zone, which existed on the other three corners of this intersection and throughout much of the area around the Commons. Sixty feet would not overshadow the Clinton House or the Dewitt Mall, and at six stories it would be three stories lower than the Seneca Place and Hilton

Garden Inn projects less than half a block away. It would show sensitivity to the stepping down at the edge of the central business district, as specified in the *Downtown Ithaca 2020 Strategic Plan*. HOLT calculated the new building could accommodate fifty units—one- and two-bedroom units on the upper floor, and a large public-meeting area on the first floor. As their plans developed, and word got out that INHS was considering purchase of the WCB, they were strongly encouraged by the BID and city hall to replace the commercial kitchen and the 250-seat meeting room for public use on the ground floor as part of the project.

Paul and the INHS board, in partnership with PathStone, worked with HOLT to design a building that would be sixty feet high and with 100 percent lot coverage, considering that the city was promoting density. Would they agree?

INHS made a formal purchase offer on the Women's Community Building, but before accepting, the federation had to be convinced that their project could work. The idea of affordable housing a block from the Commons had considerable appeal to their board. It was in keeping with the civic-betterment and equal-treatment aspect of their mission. They were also looking forward to converting their real estate asset into an endowment that would enable CFWO to make grants to deserving women in need. Retaining the public area on the first floor had appeal as well, but how long would they have to wait for INHS to pull it together?

Overall the INHS project was receiving good public support; however, it definitely was not receiving support from an important neighbor who would need to be notified beforehand and listened to at the public hearing for the site-plan review and the required variance to build. Bill Downing was the owner of Dewitt Mall directly across the street from the WCB.

When Bill renovated the old Dewitt School in 1971, he placed his architectural offices on the top floor, where over a dozen architects and staff now worked under his guidance. Next door on the top floor, he and his wife, Alison, had developed a penthouse extending out onto the roof, tastefully set back from the building edge, complete with decks and planters. It was a haven that few knew of except those who attended the parties they held for the artistic and professorial friends they invited. His management office for the building was a doorstep away from the entrance to their penthouse.

I had met Bill in his office a few times to discuss the possible purchase of his Dewitt building. He was in his eighties now, and as I had done many times before, I offered to purchase, and have Bill and Alison hold the mortgage—providing them both a lifetime of regular income without the hassle of management. Bill was friendly but not interested. He was, however, interested in talking about the new "low-income housing" being

**Figure 26.2** The former Dewitt High School and Junior High. An adaptive reuse project (1971) by architect Bill Downing with forty-eight apartments and sixteen shops and restaurants. Photo provided by the History Center of Tompkins County.

proposed by INHS across the street. Bill had previously served on the board of INHS, and years ago had been the one to invite me for a fund-raising bus tour of the many restored INHS properties in the city. That had been my first introduction to the landmark work they were doing in restoring the housing stock and in giving low-income buyers an opportunity to own their home, but now Bill was concerned. Fifty units? Low-income housing? Maybe drug dealers? Trash and filth in the streets? No parking? Bill did not have a good feeling about the proposed INHS project.

I listened. In my role as president of the BID and chair of the DIA's business retention and development committee, my priority quickly shifted from trying to buy Bill's building to instilling confidence in him that this project would upgrade downtown, not drag it down. Affordable housing was a stated and definite goal of the Downtown Ithaca Alliance's 2020 strategic plan. I went to see Paul and told him of Bill's concerns—he'd heard it before on other INHS rental projects on Quarry Street and Floral Avenue. NIMBY—not in my backyard!

He had answers. INHS now owned and *managed* 175 units of housing, which they rented in several complexes throughout the community. They seldom, if ever, had a problem on their properties. These were working-class people for the most part, not drug dealers, and many were elderly. Many were workers, with jobs in the community. The last thing INHS tenants wanted was police on the site and trash and disarray where they lived. Paul ran a tight ship with the INHS properties. They were good neighbors. I returned to Bill and reassured him that this was not a project that would negatively impact his prized Dewitt Mall. I also explained that it was a project the BID fully supported and was part of the downtown Ithaca strategic plan. It should sail through city hall. Bill had been a founding member of the INHS board. He listened and, though remaining skeptical, agreed that he would not speak out publicly against it.

Meanwhile, the CFWO accepted the INHS purchase offer. INHS consulted with CFWO, and it was decided to name the new project Breckenridge Place in honor of Juanita Breckenridge Bates, a founding member of the City Federation of Women's Organizations in 1910 and an early leader of the women's rights movement in Tompkins County.

The Ithaca Urban Renewal Agency allocated $1 million toward the proposed development. INHS received commitments from the Tompkins County Community Housing Affordability Program, the New York State Housing Trust Fund Corporation, NeighborWorks America, and the Federal Home Loan Bank of New York, administered by the Tompkins Trust Company; INHS and PathStone also put in equity. With the collective total of $14.5 million in funds from public resources, it was assured that Breckinridge Place would be a permanent and affordable, long-term community project.

There was one hitch though. Close to $800,000 of the IURA funds that were to be allotted for Breckenridge Place came from the repayment of the short-term loan that IURA had lent to Carol and me to cover shortfalls at the end of the Gateway project. According to HUD regulations those funds had to be used for low-income housing. No matter how many times they were recycled through the CDBG, the funds had to remain permanently available for low-income housing projects. The idea of a commercial restaurant and public community room that could be used by members of the public with all ranges of income was not permissible. Paul said, "We asked our funders if we could make it open to the public, and they responded that in accord with the rules, only people with a median income equal to the people who live there are allowed to use it."

The ground floor could be used for a smaller meeting room related to activities for residents and staff of the building, but not as a public meeting space. INHS and PathStone worked with HOLT to redesign the ground floor into a small community room, offices, a laundry, and ten parking spaces, and a drive-through on the west side underneath the structure on the ground floor. The public kitchen and meeting room were not to be. The need for Jason's Masonic Temple became all the more apparent.

There is statewide competition for the allotment of NYS affordable housing funds, and Breckenridge Place did not receive approval in the following
annual round of funding; it would now have to wait a year and reapply.
CFWO agreed to extend their deal to purchase with INHS for another
twelve months. Finally, on September 23, 2011, the *Ithaca Journal* quoted
Paul Mazzarella:

> In New York State, only 27 multifamily rental projects received funding this
> year, and Breckenridge Place was the only project in this region. The success
> of Breckenridge Place is clearly tied to the strong support provided by our
> community. Elected officials, business leaders and residents all recognized
> the benefits of affordable housing and rallied behind this project.

They were funded! Janis Graham, president of the board of directors of
the CFWO, commented:

> I'm delighted that this project is moving forward. This is the culmination of
> years of effort by the CFWO to transition from being a landlord to becom-
> ing a grant-making organization. The resources that we gain from the sale
> of the Women's Community Building will enable us to fund worthy proj-
> ects that support our mission. The sale to INHS is a fitting reflection of the
> CFWO's community-minded history and spirit.

Joseph Bowes, a senior real estate developer for PathStone Corporation,
said:

> Our concept for this project was to deliberately link affordable housing with
> the economic success of Ithaca's downtown. Residents living at Breckenridge
> will shop downtown, use the library, walk to work and go to neighborhood
> schools—they'll be helping to create a more vibrant downtown. We're very
> pleased that New York State recognized and supported this effort.

In a publicity piece, HOLT Architects described the architecture of the
building as follows:

> The project is designed with fifty 1- and 2-bedroom apartments on the upper
> five floors, with offices and common space on the ground floor. The design
> reflects the architectural fabric of downtown Ithaca with a glazed storefront
> system enclosing some of the more public spaces on the street side of the lowest
> floor and brick with more residential-scale windows on the five floors above.
> The massing of the building also takes its cues from its surrounding context.

The building hugs the street on the sides that are closest to the downtown, reflecting the larger scale of buildings on that side, but is then set back from the property line to allow relief to the residential structures to the north. The facade articulation will echo the styles and details of the surrounding buildings without mimicking, rather interpreting historic details and integrating them into a contemporary yet timeless composition.

The building was designed to meet the Enterprise Green Communities Criteria, the NYS Division of Housing and Community Renewal green criteria, and was awarded platinum certification by LEED (Leadership in Energy and Environmental Design), LEED's highest designation for sustainability.

In the spring of 2014, the dedication ceremony for Breckenridge Place was held in the small community room on the ground floor. It was attended by both local and state officials including a representative from the Department of Housing and Community Renewal. Many local developers attended as well, curious to see what fifty units of affordable housing in the heart of downtown would look like. Although the building was already 100 percent leased, residents opened their apartments to the invited guests, and tours were given after the ceremony.

**Figure 26.3** Breckenridge Place. Fifty units of affordable housing and one of the most attractive new buildings in downtown Ithaca. Photo by Jason Henderson.

Our young mayor, Svante Myrick, spoke at the dedication in May of 2014. He had been elected to Common Council even while still a student at Cornell. At that time, when he was twenty years old, he was the youngest African American in the history of our country to hold public office. At twenty-four he had been elected mayor of Ithaca—one of the youngest mayors in the country. I had attended a New York State mayor's conference in Syracuse with Gary not too long ago at which Svante had been introduced to speak about his vision for Ithaca. As might be expected, all the other mayors at the conference were well into their fifties and sixties. When Svante was introduced, he held up his right hand as though making an important point, and said, "What I lack in *experience*"—he paused, his hand still in the air—"I make up for in *ignorance.*" The audience roared, and he concluded, "I don't know it can't be done!" And that pretty well describes Svante's outlook and enthusiasm for his position as the leader of our dynamic and growing city of Ithaca.

At the dedication of Breckenridge Place, Svante stood at the podium to tell his story, a story nearly everyone in the room knew. Svante had been accepted on a scholarship to Cornell University. However, as a child in Florida, after his father left them, he and his brothers and sister had lived with their mother for a while in the back of their car and in homeless shelters. They had been unable to find affordable housing anywhere. Eventually they were admitted into an affordable housing complex two miles out of town. Every excursion into town meant a two-mile walk for the children—church, school, shopping, anything . . . two miles to town. Breckenridge Place would have been a dream come true for his family, he said—in the heart of downtown, it's only a few blocks to everything they needed.

What a gift to Ithaca to be able to have this INHS affordable housing project located in the very center of downtown.

Within a year of the completion of Breckenridge Place, INHS purchased the old P&C grocery store site in Northside for their 210 Hancock Street project. They constructed five rental town houses and seven for-sale town houses, plus an additional fifty-nine rental units that would be available to tenants with low to moderate annual incomes of $25,000–$50,000. They opened fully rented on August 1, 2017. The for-sale town houses were available for a clientele with annual income of $40,000–$55,000, who now, thanks to INHS, have an opportunity to purchase their own home.

**Figure 26.4** Affordable housing by INHS. Apartments at 210 Hancock Street on the site of the former P&C grocery store. Photo by author.

**Figure 26.5** Affordable housing by INHS. Town houses for sale at 210 Hancock Street. Photo by author.

# CHAPTER 27

# YOU DON'T ALWAYS WIN (2012–13)

## Public Service Meets an Immovable Object

Once the Women's Community Building was demolished, there was no home for the several nonprofit offices they rented to; neither was there any longer a public meeting space for several hundred people, nor a commercial kitchen for special events, such as the annual Rotary Club pancake breakfast. In addition, New Roots Charter School lost their use of the commercial kitchen and the lunchroom. Since it opened in 1960, the Women's Community Building had been devoted to serving the community, even to the point of providing housing for single women. Now it was gone. New Roots Charter School set up temporary lunch quarters at St. Catherine's, the Greek Orthodox church a block to the west.

The Masonic Temple was elegant in its quirky way. It had served as the Freemasons' meeting and event hall since it was built, but was closed in the early nineties, several years before Jason Fane purchased it. For a couple of years Jason leased it to an unsuccessful restaurant and an equally unsuccessful nightclub, but aside from these ill-fated endeavors, the building had been vacant for over fifteen years. What better use for the building than to turn it into a replacement venue for the nonprofit offices, public event space, and commercial kitchen that were being displaced from the Women's Community Building? The vacant two-story building across the street from the Clinton House had it all—it even had a gym—so it could very nicely fill the gap created by the loss of the Women's Community Building, and it did have a very noticeable for sale sign on the side along Seneca Street.

With the purchase of the old Masonic Temple, New Roots Charter School would be able to expand their operation to include a kitchen, lunchroom, auditorium, and gymnasium on the first floor. The final piece of the equation, in my mind, was to have the State Theatre, through its foundation, purchase the building from Jason; and own, manage, and rent it to the school at a reasonable rent, thereby enhancing the theater's bottom

**Figure 27.1** Masonic Temple at Seneca and Cayuga Streets. Photo by author.

line—just as Playhouse Square had done in Cleveland. Everybody would win—the nonprofits, the public, the school, the theater.

I made an appointment to meet Jason and lay out the plan for purchasing the building. Would he sell it—not to me, a competing developer, but to the State Theatre Foundation? Not only that, would he hold paper on the deal? It had been vacant for fifteen years, and some income would definitely be better than none. There was absolutely no downside for him. Or so I thought.

Jason did not get to where he was by being altruistic. He always thinks strategically. His Masonic Temple was on one of the most highly trafficked street corners in our town. With the proper zoning, it could be demolished and built as high as six stories—with a variance, maybe eight or nine stories. Jason figured he was sitting on a potential gold mine, provided he could redevelop the property. Never mind that it was vacant and not producing any income for him—he could afford to hold on to it and wait.

Instead of selling it to the State Theatre and holding a mortgage, he offered to rent it to the school for five years. I told him that would not work. The school needed to know they could be there for the long haul. I didn't tell Jason this, but renting directly to the school also destroyed my plans to imitate Cleveland, to establish ownership of commercial rental property that would provide income for the theater. Besides, his asking rent for the whole building was so high as to render the plan unworkable. He was renowned for charging rents that always pushed the market—hence the long-term vacancies and high turnovers in many of his downtown stores.

Jason faced a problem in his plans for the Masonic Temple. The building was on the historic register and therefore came under the aegis of the ILPC—the Ithaca Landmarks Preservation Commission. He could not demolish it, as it was protected by what local developers had affectionately come to call "the History Police." However, if he could show that he had been unable to rent it (his asking rents were high), or if he could claim hardship in not being able to sell it (his asking price was well beyond what was justifiable based on potential income), then the law allowed him to apply to the ILPC for a variance based on "hardship" and to be able to demolish it so he could put the land to use. Over the next few weeks I continued to negotiate with Jason to sell the building to the State Theatre for use by the New Roots Charter School.

Finally he said to me, "Bring me a signed purchase offer with no contingencies and a certified check for $1 million, and then I will have a decision to make." Given the square footage of the building, and the income it could produce renting to nonprofits and the school, I had calculated the value to be around $650,000, which was close to the county's assessed value of the property. But I felt that if we could somehow raise the money, he might sell it—he had said he would "have a decision to make." In my enthusiasm for the entire scheme, I took that as a positive sign.

The advantage of representing a nonprofit, such as the State Theatre, is that one has the potential of raising very inexpensive funds. Our State Theatre Foundation board of directors backed the idea. I had already spent two months attempting to negotiate with Jason. It took six more months of negotiations with lenders to put the package together. The Tompkins Trust Company said they would come in for $450,000 at 4 percent interest payable over twenty years, IURA would come in for $400,000 at 2 percent. We needed an additional half million to carry out the renovations we had designed for the school lunchroom, kitchen, and the nonprofit offices; we also needed to install an elevator and to take care of long-neglected maintenance. The local Park Foundation agreed to lend the State Theatre Foundation $500,000 at 0.5 percent interest—half a percent interest only—for ten years. It was almost a gift. Based on my financial projections, in ten years the foundation would be able to refinance and pay them off out of the proceeds. The numbers worked. Fully rented to the New Roots Charter School at reasonable rent, the State Theatre as owner could clear $50,000 a year. Our attorney drew up the purchase offer, and I personally signed the notes and borrowed all the money, convincing the lenders to put it in escrow at the Trust Company subject to closing the deal. All the lenders agreed to allow us to write Jason a check for $1 million to accompany the purchase offer.

Several times over the six months it took to assemble the funds, he had said publicly that the Masonic Temple was not for sale. However, I was taking him at his initial word—that if we gave him a no-contingency purchase offer and a certified check for $1 million, he would *have a decision to make*." How could he turn down $1 million when the building was worth far less than that? We continued with our plan to present him with the purchase offer and the check, then he would indeed have a decision to make.

Rather than trying to meet with him myself, for I sensed he was avoiding me, we sent John Guttridge. John was young, unassuming, and probably the last person Jason would expect to be presenting a purchase offer to him. John was also president of the State Theatre Foundation board, in whose name we anticipated purchasing the building.

John picked up the purchase offer from our attorney. He had a *copy* of the certified check, as the board didn't quite trust Jason to return a certified check for $1 million once he had it in hand, whether he sold to us or not. On leaving the attorney's office, John unexpectedly ran right into Jason on the Commons. Quick on his feet, and placing the offer in Jason's hands, he said, "Here is the State Theatre's purchase offer and a copy of the certified check for $1 million. Please review it, and let us know if you accept, and then we will provide the actual check." John said that a black look crossed Jason's brow as he realized that he had been presented with the purchase offer. It had been hand delivered, and he had taken it, so he could not say he didn't get it. Later we found out why he was disturbed. He must have looked at the offer, for later that day he sent me an email stating: *"The Masonic Temple is not now, nor will it ever be, for sale."* I had just wasted the better part of a year negotiating with Jason, raising the money to fulfill my public service vision for the community, but Jason was immovable.

I had led the banks, the IURA, the Park Foundation, the State Theatre board of directors, and the city officials on a wild-goose chase. I had sold the entire idea based on what he had told me—he "would have a decision to make." That had not exactly been a no. And in my mind, in my optimism, that was adequate reason for putting everybody through the process as though we had a firm deal. I was mistaken, badly mistaken. On a lonely day in February, I hosted a luncheon downtown with all the city officials, lenders, attorneys, and members of our board of directors who had helped put the deal together. I apologized for my misconception and our lack of success. No one blamed me, no one said they wished they hadn't been a part of it. All lamented that we had not been able to secure this building for community use and that it would continue to sit vacant.

At our luncheon, the head of the Ithaca Landmarks Preservation Commission informed us all of the good that came out of this—if there was anything that could be called good—was that Jason could no longer cite financial hardship and his inability to sell the project as a reason for allowing him to demolish the building, and "hardship" was about the only reason for which preservation law could permit demolition! We had made him a firm, no-contingency offer at an above-market sale price. The head of the ILPC said, "That should protect the building for at least the next three years"—which explained Jason's dark look when John had handed him the purchase offer and the copy of the certified check for $1 million. Now, from the ILPC point of view, it was checkmate. For the next three years, Jason would not be able to tear the building down. The historic Masonic Temple was preserved, at least temporarily. You don't always win, no matter how good an idea you have, but despite this setback I remained convinced that Carl Haynes was right and that the Cleveland example was a good one. Our State Theatre Foundation should continue to try to purchase real estate to improve the bottom line of the State Theatre.

# CHAPTER 28

# SHIFTING EMPHASIS (2013)

## A Family Business

My son, Frost, had graduated from Cornell's Baker Program in Real Estate in 2000. After graduating from American University in 1995 with a degree in English and medieval German literature, he had worked as a commercial fisherman off the coast of Alaska for five years. In my eyes, as distinctly different as commercial fishing and real estate development are from each other, his fishing experience had given him the temperament to live on the edge, which is a necessary part of the business. He was a survivor. He could cope with adversity.

After fishing, he worked for me for two years, running aspects of our real estate development and management business. However, Frost was anxious to grow his own real estate portfolio, and the graduate program in real estate at Cornell was a perfect fit. The idea in both our minds was that he would get his master's degree from Cornell and then come back to work for me to expand the business, but it didn't work out that way.

Six months into the program, Frost came into the office and said, "Gee, Dad, I'm awful sorry, but I want to go to work for a big real estate developer."

The Baker Program in Real Estate had obviously expanded his vision. My response was, "God bless you, Son. That's great." And I meant it, but I had also been conceptualizing a buyout of my partners with the idea that Frost could step in and run the business. I realized now I had to do what was in my own best interests, in the knowledge that Frost had his own career ahead of him, very possibly independent of me. I refinanced the four major properties in which I had general partners and, after twenty-two years, I bought my partners out.

At the end of his first year Frost's internship was with Tishman Speyer at the Chrysler Building in New York—he ran tenant improvements in the spire at the top of the building. The second year he interned for a real estate developer in New Jersey with thousands of units in the five boroughs of

New York City. He was hired to do acquisitions. Six years later he had a staff of eighty-four people working under him and was handling all of the company's apartment renovations.

Nine years after graduating from American University he had reconnected with a college sweetheart. He and Kate were married, bought a house in Edgewater, New Jersey, and within two years had started a family—they had a son. At some point, Frost decided that rather than work for someone else, he and Kate would prefer to return to Ithaca and become part of the family business. We worked out a succession with a professional management consultant, and within a year they were living in Ithaca and on a track to take over management of the business. Shortly after their arrival, my daughter and her husband, Chris, moved to Ithaca, and he became vice president of operations.

Late in July of 2013, David Skorton, the president of Cornell, called me: "Mack, would you consider renting the university your space in the Carey Building rent-free for a year?" I listened, obviously curious. David continued, "Cornell, Ithaca College, and TC3 are planning to apply for a New York State economic development grant of $1 million to set up a business incubator space, and it would improve our chances greatly if we could show that there is community support for the project." I was definitely listening. "The way it would work is this: if the grant is awarded, and if you build the space and also give us a year's free rent, we would apply the million dollars toward the project, the incubator would be launched and could then pay market rent going forward."

The two-story Carey Building was located a few doors from the east end of the Commons. It was built in 1924 and had a lovely brick facade. There was one problem. I didn't own it.

Frost and Kate, my daughter Elsa and her husband, Chris, however, had bought the building as one of their first acquisitions. I said to David, "I don't own the building directly—I assisted in the purchase of it, but Frost and his brother-in-law, Chris Hyde, are the principals. Let me talk to them and see what we can do."

When I had negotiated the purchase of the Gateway site across the intersection of State and Green Streets with Don and Sue Dickinson in 2001, they gave me an option on the Carey Building. I had long since released the option when they told me they had another buyer interested in it, and at the time I did not anticipate wanting to develop it. Don and Sue had done well in their real estate holdings over the past fifty years. Don had a soft spot in his heart for nonprofits, and had leased the upper floor of the two-story Carey Building to the Advocacy Center, a nonprofit organization that arranges safe havens for battered women. He had leased it for $6

**Figure 28.1** The two-story Carey Building, built in 1924. Photo by author.

per square foot, in a market that typically rented for at least double, and in some cases triple, that amount.

Frost, Kate, Chris, and Elsa had purchased the Carey Building with its first floor of retail and offices above. They had negotiated a no-cash deal with the Dickinsons, who held a first mortgage, and they continued to rent it to the existing tenants, including 4,500 square feet on the second floor for which the rent was $6 per square foot (about one-third of the market rate at that time). David had said that Cornell needed nearly 10,000 square feet for their business incubator. Another floor would have to be added to accommodate them. After I told Frost about President Skorton's call, he suddenly began seeing the two-story Carey Building through new eyes. Here was an offer of equity that could be used toward financing a new project. He quickly sketched out some possibilities. "Dad, if this were done right, it could be a seven-story overbuild with twenty apartments and offices and retail on the lower floors. It could be done in such a way as to preserve the historic facade, with the upper floors in a totally modern blend with what is there."

The building was not on the National Register of Historic Places, but it certainly had historic appeal and was one of the many buildings on and around the Commons that contributed to the charm of our downtown, much in the way the 1828 Clinton House and the 1928 State Theatre help keep the character and charm, and differentiate our downtown from the drab and repetitive suburban development denounced by Kunstler in *Home from Nowhere*. Frost gets it.

Frost had worked his way into our business. Sitting in my office one day, I told him as his father that we had different aims. He was in the "shoot for the moon" phase of his career, while I was in the "circle the wagons" phase of mine. With the help of a professional business consultant, we developed a succession plan that worked extremely well for us as Frost gradually took over the helm. I had spoken with him one day about the necessity of paying strict attention to detail and taking responsibility as the key person in a business with so many assets and so many details, and with so many people's livelihoods dependent on it. He said to me, "Dad, let me tell you a story," and he proceeded to tell me about commercial fishing in Alaska and being out in the Bering Sea at 2:00 a.m. one night in a storm with forty-foot waves, alone at the wheel holding the fishing boat on a radar marker, with six other guys trying to get some sleep down below. The sodium lights on the cabin roof shone on the marker. Suddenly a forty-foot wave crashed over and submerged the boat. All went dark. Frost said he glanced to the corner of the wheelhouse, where his survival suit lay on the floor. If he went for it, he knew the boat would broach to. It would turn sideways in the waves and be rolled over. He kept his hands steady on the wheel and waited. In a few moments, the boat resurfaced and the lights reappeared on the marker. I listened, and said to him, "You get it." From that story, I knew my son had the stamina and the guts to be a real estate developer.

Just as I would have done, Frost and Chris ran the numbers on the new concept. The million dollars from the NYS grant would help serve as equity on the new project. Since the Dickinsons already held paper in the form of a first mortgage on the Carey Building, provided that they would agree to subordinate to bank money for construction, provided the rental market for downtown apartments held, and if Frost and Chris could build the building at a reasonable cost—if everything came together, they calculated they could afford to give the second floor rent-free for the first year to Cornell, TC3, and Ithaca College, as requested, for their business incubator. In consultation with our contractor, Dick Schneider, they worked out a plan in which they would approach the construction in such a way that the incubator could occupy the second floor, even as construction continued for five stories above them. If the incubator would pay market rent of $18 per square foot beginning in the second year and going forward, they could catch up on the year's free rent, and the numbers would work.

I put Frost directly in touch with President Skorton, who turned the matter over to his staff for the final negotiations, and they worked out the free-rent-for-a-year deal in concept. They could live with the 9,000 square feet that the final build-out would be, and at the end of the day, Don and Sue Dickinson agreed to subordinate their mortgage to a first mortgage to be provided by Tompkins Trust Company for the construction. With this strong expression of "community support," the university, in collaboration with TC3 and Ithaca College, was successful in receiving the million-dollar grant from the state of New York to build "REV: Ithaca Startup Works," the new business incubator space in our downtown. Frost, Kate, Elsa, and Chris had a new project created essentially out of thin air—100 percent financing from the Dickinsons for the original purchase, $1 million "equity" from Cornell, and construction financing at market rates from the Trust Company—or so it seemed in concept. The project proved to be considerably more expensive than originally anticipated, and they needed to raise more equity.

As the lead developers, Frost and Chris would have to move quickly. The grant was awarded, and the space had to be designed, built, and ready for occupancy within a matter of months—at least the second floor had to be ready. It was an involved and complicated lease. REV would get the first year rent-free, and they could wait and take occupancy of the full 9,000 square feet once the third floor was built. They could expand into it as their own operations grew, and then market-rate rent would begin. Although Cornell, TC3, and Ithaca College had received approval for their grant, no funds would actually be awarded until completion of the project. The $1 million "equity" suddenly became pretty thin; not only would they have to find funds for construction prior to release of the grant, the Advocacy Center still had another two years on their lease. How could Frost and Chris possibly turn the concept for this project into reality?

Creating something out of nothing is the job of the developer. Taking an idea, a concept for a project, somehow assembling the funds—for it always takes money, even when you buy a building for "no-cash" as Frost and Chris and their wives had been successful in doing here. To move forward, you somehow have to find the money. Frost and I had many conversations about this; I wanted to support him. I had not amassed huge cash reserves, because for whatever reason every one of my projects had been built with seller financing, bank financing, and in some cases partner funds. I didn't have the cash to cover the required equity, but I did have substantial net worth tied up in the properties Carol and I owned.

We had built or acquired nearly two dozen properties during the thirty years of our marriage. We had sold some and refinanced others along the way to use the value of one to create equity for the next acquisition, and we retained ownership in some dozen and a half properties. We hadn't

discussed it at length, but it had been our unstated intent to relax at this
stage of our lives and live comfortably on what we had accumulated. Frost
and I had the discussion when he first came to work for us, that he could
do as I had done and start his own portfolio, buying a single-family house,
turning it over for a two-family, four-family, ten-family, and so on, or he
could "stand on our shoulders," using our resources, provided we agreed
that his projects made financial sense. In that way he could start his own
real estate portfolio on a larger scale. This is what we had decided to do.

The thrill of real estate development, of creating something from nothing,
of adding "0s" to your net worth, is addictive. It is something that serves
your own and the public's good. We all need shelter, a place to work, a
place to eat, a place to manufacture, a place to live out and enjoy our lives.
My son understood this, and he was ready. Frost and Chris had proven
themselves as managers, growing our business for the past five years. They
had increased the value of our portfolio by 30 percent since they took over
management of our apartments, retail, medical, and professional office
portfolio. Both of them were working closely with the Downtown Ithaca
Alliance on the Business Retention and Development Committee—Chris
had been elected chair of this important committee—and they were both
now becoming recognized as concerned and experienced real estate professionals who took their property ownership and stewardship seriously.
They worked for the good of the community in parallel with working for
their own good, and they had the support of their wives. The baton was
being passed.

Carol and I agreed to make a shift in emphasis from accumulating net
worth in our own properties to gifting and strengthening the portfolio of
the children, who of course were no longer children. We discussed it, and
Frost began a refinancing of our portfolio that would provide additional
equity for the Carey Building construction as well as for major improvements to Center Ithaca, our 144,000-square-foot building in the heart of
the Commons.

In addition, he and Chris would install solar panels and rebuild the
stone steps and underpinnings of the magnificent front porch of the Clinton
House. They would install roofs, new sidewalks, and new energy-efficient
boilers in all the properties, and upgrade kitchens and bathrooms where
needed. Their lists of major improvements were all undertaken with an eye
to improving the properties for the long term; they were committed. They
looked beyond current cash flow to the decades ahead for them and their
children. I was proud of them both. We were delighted to support them as
they took on the role of developers with a vision. They, too, were becoming part of the energy and dynamic of shaping a city.

We were able to raise the additional equity needed, and Frost and Chris were able to develop the Carey Building into the envisioned seven-story overbuild on a historically lovely building that would also fill Cornell, TC3, and Ithaca College's need for REV—the business incubator space that would bring new businesses and jobs to the downtown. The baton had definitely been passed on!

# CHAPTER 29

# DEVIL IN THE DETAILS (2014)
## Synergy and the Big Picture

With the equity problem having been solved at the Carey Building through major refinancing of our properties, the next concern was how to relocate the Advocacy Center, which would be out in the street if we didn't renew their lease. Their rent was so much lower than market that it would be difficult for them to find another location.

Frost and his new partner, John Guttridge, agreed that they would be a good fit in the property they had purchased at 204 North Tioga Street, in which the State Theatre Foundation was also a partner. They presented it to the board of the Advocacy Center, which, after considerable discussion, agreed to relocate and to pay a rent that, while not fully at market, was double what they had been paying at the Carey Building. Not only would they lease the new space, which Frost and John agreed to totally remodel, but they also requested an option to purchase the building within a twelve-month period. This would dovetail nicely with my desire to assist the State Theatre in improving their bottom line, since our written agreement stated that one-third of the final distribution of ongoing income and sale proceeds would be donated to the theater.

Renovating an old building is tricky business. At the Carey Building, Frost and his architect had to figure out how to keep the retail businesses on the first floor operational while renovating the second floor for the REV space, and on top of that, they would have to build five more stories of apartments. At the beginning of the process, the most critical aspect was getting city planning board approval for the design. In our city, *everyone* has an opinion. Seven stories was too tall. As designed, the overbuild needed more articulation in the facade. The new didn't match the old. Why not leave it as it is? Where will tenants park? (Never mind that the zoning did not require parking in the central business district.) And who will live there?

When David had first asked us to provide a year's free rent in exchange for a million-dollar investment in the building, Frost's mind began working overtime. He took a trip to New York City to look at Mayor Bloomberg's "Housing Museum," and came back with the idea of building "micro-units." From his initial description, it sounded as if this was simply a matter of constructing small studio or efficiency apartments, and in a way it was. The goal, however, was to fit a tenant's entire needs—kitchen, bathroom, living room, closets, and sleeping quarters—all into a single unit under three hundred square feet. Bloomberg felt this approach could help provide housing for many more people at an affordable rent in NYC. This was done in part through the use of built-ins: beds that folded up against the wall, armoires that served as dresser-and-closet combinations. Not spacious, but utilitarian. Not luxurious, but targeted at the younger working professionals—the millennials who were moving back to downtowns where the action was, and at this point in their lives just needed a clean, comfortable, well-located, and affordable place to live. This market had not yet been met in our downtown. Frost explained his concept to the department of planning and development, and they finally bought in. They approved a final design that met most of their concerns, and construction could be started.

He negotiated a contract for the construction with our good friend and contractor Dick Schneider, now of LeChase Construction, who had built 407 College Avenue, Gateway Center, and Gateway Plaza for me. Dick was skilled, patient, and willing to work with Frost and the architect to refine the design and construction details as they moved forward through the project. Solving the details of the interface between the old building and the new one became expensive, time-consuming, and almost overwhelming. Money flowed like water. They worked and reworked; they got Elwyn & Palmer, a local engineering company, involved and finally came up with a plan for a steel frame to be built above the second-floor office space, essentially a platform on which the upper five floors would rest. They tested the concrete columns in the basement and the foundation in key locations. What had seemed like a simple project in concept was turning out to be very complicated.

In the original construction, the columns in the basement were large enough and sturdy enough to support the building—they had been there, solid and substantial, for over ninety years—but during the testing, when the engineers drilled into the concrete of the columns, they found that the steel rebar ended a foot above the base of the columns. While their calculations showed that the size and load-bearing capacity of the original columns could support an overbuild of five stories, this new finding at the very base of the columns made going up five more stories too risky. This particular building's role in shaping a city would crumble in a heap if the project were attempted as designed. Finally, the engineers came up with a solution: they would dig down two feet around each column in the basement, pour a new

**Figure 29.1** Four-foot-high "collars" around each basement column support the seven-story overbuild at the Carey Building. Photo by author.

footer, and come up with a reinforced concrete collar several feet thick and four feet high around each column to provide the required additional support. This was expensive, but according to the engineer, it would work. One day, after the strengthening work was done, Dick's building superintendent said to me, "There's a million dollars sitting down there in the basement that no one will ever see!" None of that had been planned for.

Not only that, but as they dug around the exterior of the building to reinforce the footings to accept the added load, they found that a twenty-foot section of the foundation narrowed down from the typical twenty-four inches to little more than six inches. The contractor in 1924 must have run short of concrete!

Quite unlike developing a project on raw land in the suburbs or in the country, any building in the downtown is surrounded by neighbors, other property owners who have an interest in seeing what you are planning to build, what it will look like, what its use will be. Some may even have deed restrictions or rights-of-way over your parcel. The Carey Building was no different. The city owned a fifty-foot right-of-way and parking lot to the east, and a local developer and former council member, Joe Daley, owned property to the north and west. The city owned the street in front; Joe's property line on the west side came right up to the Carey Building footers. In fact, Frost found that underground, the Carey Building footers extended a foot or so onto Joe's property. Nothing to worry about, except they had no right to be there. Additionally, to correct the structural deficiency in the narrowed six-inch section of the existing Carey Building footer, it was necessary to come up with a solution. More money, more time. Dick and the engineers figured out that they could pour an interior footer and place an additional wall sintered and pinned to the six-inch poor excuse for a foundation. It would never be seen from the outside, and it would solve the problem of encroachment on Joe's property.

The Carey Building was Frost's first major development project. It was small in comparison to some of the developments going on in our downtown, but it was significant, and it was his. Surrounded as he was with a zero-lot-line on three sides, access to the rear over a three-foot, city-granted right-of-way and a ten-foot sliver of an access area behind the buildings, Frost needed staging room for the project. Toward this, the city granted access and air rights on the east side of the building. With a new, aggressive city attorney, what could easily have been granted in a neighborly fashion for free wound up costing an additional $50,000. He needed the access and air rights. The city attorney knew he needed them, but assumed he was doing his duty by ensuring the city gave away nothing they could extract money for, and he was immovable. He had the public trust to consider. I suppose he was right, but I have granted a number of easements to neighbors for zero dollars just in the spirit of neighborliness, to help them build a new project.

If he was going to be able to build up an additional five stories, Frost needed access through Joe Daley's property to the north. The crane, dumpsters, and scaffolding would all need space to operate if this building was to be built. Frost had a conversation with Joe, and he seemed amenable to granting access. Frost would pay him for the parking spaces he would temporarily lose the use of. Joe, now retired, thanks to the success of his real estate investments in downtown, left for one of his many trips abroad with his new wife. In his enthusiasm for moving forward, and based on his initial conversation with Joe, Frost told a local newspaper reporter that "all was going well for the project. The City had agreed to grant a right-of-way and use of their property to the east"—he didn't mention they were holding him up for $50,000. He said that "his neighbor to the north and west, Joe Daley, had agreed to grant use of his property for access and staging." The project appeared to be a go.

Publicity is important to a developer. A new project needs exposure, and the public wants to know what is going on as well. The *Ithaca Times* gave front-page coverage to the Carey Building project, with a picture of the new building—a rendering—and a headline to the effect that "All Approvals Are in Place," specifically mentioning that Joe Daley and the city had both granted access.

Timing is everything. Joe and his wife returned from Europe just in time to read the front-page headline. From Joe's point of view, he and Frost had had a casual conversation. Joe had never formally agreed to access and staging. Joe and Frost had never signed a written agreement nor had cost or timing been discussed. Joe was less than impressed.

As part of turning my business over to my son and son-in-law, I had gone through a several-year process of familiarizing and training both of them in the specifics of the business. We owned a dozen and a half properties of varying sizes and complexity. I had spent forty years buying, developing, selling older properties, developing new ones, and establishing management procedures that worked. Frost and Chris picked it up quickly and had proven themselves capable, trustworthy, and skilled at running our portfolio. I still met once a week with both of them, for an update and to discuss strategy and solutions for any problems that came up.

Frost and I were sitting in my old office, now his office, discussing the Carey Building project and the next steps, when our receptionist knocked and said Joe Daley was here for his appointment with Frost. I asked Frost if I should leave. He indicated I should stay, so I remained seated in my old leather armchair. Joe was a colleague; someone I had known peripherally for many years. He walked into the office, glanced at me in surprise, and said, "Oh, I didn't know you were going to be here. I guess I won't be able to be as blunt with Frost as I had planned!" We all laughed, but Joe proceeded to tell Frost that he was quite upset about reading the headline in the paper. He said Frost had no right to assume use of his property based on a casual conversation and without their having reached an agreement on price and terms.

I was slightly embarrassed for my son, but I had to agree with Joe. "Frost, you shouldn't have assumed; you have to work out every detail. You blew it, Joe's right." Joe softened a bit. He was right, they had not worked out the details, and based on Frost's presumptive behavior, he wasn't sure they were ever going to. He held the cards as to whether the project was going to proceed or not. This could prove to be another very expensive proposition for Frost, who had already been held up by the city for $50,000; in this business one can't always assume everything is sweetness and light. You can't blame a neighbor—be it a city or a fellow property owner—for following their own self-interest and extracting value from their property or their position. This is normal behavior in business. Fundamentally, we all operate from self-interest. The trick in my opinion is to expand one's vision and know that self-interest includes the interest of the greater community. If my project succeeds, so will your project. This is the attitude that I had taken years ago with Bloomfield/Schon as with every other interaction since Eddygate in 1982.

Over my forty-year career as a developer, I had often shared market and budget numbers; given tours of my properties to competitors; granted easements gratis; relocated my structures to avoid blocking access and even light to neighbors' properties, despite my prerogative to build right up against their building. Competition is healthy; however, over the years, I have found that cooperation can be even healthier. Working with the BID for fifteen years and my study of different communities and the dynamics of downtown development had proven this to me. Could we salvage this situation with Joe?

Joe had done well in Ithaca. He was a hands-on plumber and electrician. He did most of the maintenance work on the units he acquired, and several years ago he had purchased nearly a full city block owned by Roy Park, when it went up for sale at bargain-basement prices after he died. Roy was a very wealthy man, at one time number fourteen on the Forbes 400 list of the country's wealthiest. He had built a communications empire and happened to be based in Ithaca. When he died, New York State Governor Andrew Cuomo was quoted in our local paper as saying, "The taxes on Roy Park's estate will balance the State budget this year!" The governor later apologized for his tasteless remark.

His widow was a friend of ours. At dinner at her home one evening, she told us that Roy had taken over the Leonardo Hotel, a run-down flophouse, and the surrounding properties on Aurora Street and State Streets. In the early '90s, he had gone on to develop a four-story retail and apartment building on this site as his "gift to the city." He was rich enough that he didn't need to worry about wringing every penny out of his property investments. As part of settling his estate, his agent sold the properties as a package for a very reasonable price, and Joe, who had the experience of doing light construction, plumbing, and electrical work on his own apartments, had the foresight to pick them up, and he had done well. Joe loved going to New York City. He had remarried, bought a condo in the Village, and he and his wife now split their time between their condo in New York, their lake home in Ithaca, and their world travels.

With things somewhat settled down between Frost and Joe, they agreed to continue talking. Joe stood up to leave, and I told him that Carol and I had plans to be in New York the following week to see a show or two, and if it would fit for him and his wife, Rebecca, we would love to see their condo in the Village and take them out to dinner. Joe warmed to the idea. I told him we'd call to confirm, and we made a tentative date to meet.

Frost was improving in his mastery of dealing with the details, but I felt he still needed some support and assistance in making sure the Carey Building project didn't run off the rails and into the weeds. As with the six-inch-wide foundation, the devil was in the details.

Carol and I occasionally drive down to New York City to go to a Broadway show or the Metropolitan Opera and visit various art museums. While Ithaca is an enclave of nature and beauty that nourishes and supports us in so many ways, New York is still the heart of our culture and the most vibrant, fun city we have ever been in. I knew it well from my cab-driving days there

in the late '60s, and now I had money enough to enjoy it. My dinner invitation to Joe and Rebecca had not been the idle "Y'all come see us" that
had been the typical parting words in my youth in the South—I meant it.

Joe and Rebecca were pleased to see us when we arrived at their condominium in Greenwich Village. I was impressed when Joe told me he had
paid $2.5 million for a three-bedroom condo, estimating to myself that the
same space back in Ithaca might rent for as much as $2,500 a month, and
just the debt service on $2.5 million would be over $14,000 per month.
I found out later, from the local gossip, that Joe had refinanced his entire
Ithaca holdings to purchase the condo. I saw it as a choice he had made for
a lifestyle. And he and Rebecca were having fun. The building was four
stories, and its one elevator opened into the kitchen of their fourth-floor
condo. It was spacious and well located in the Village.

At dinner we got to know them. Joe and Rebecca had met one sunny day
walking the same direction on opposite sides of Houston Street in the Village.
Joe saw a very attractive red-haired woman across the street, in the shade,
and casually yelled over to her, "Why aren't you walking on the sunny side of
the street?" She looked over at a trim, fit, fifty-some-year-old guy brilliantly
lit in the sun, and she took the bait. A year later they were married with the
understanding that they would split their time between NYC and Ithaca,
plus all the world traveling they wanted to do. Joe was more than a plumber,
electrician, handyman, and local Common Council alderman in Ithaca. Joe
was an adventurer. At dinner, he told us he had gone to Oxford University to
study philosophy, and that one summer, hitchhiking through Greece, he was
sitting at a café at which, a table away, a group of young students and their
leaders were commiserating that their bus driver had contracted appendicitis
and they would not be able to go forward into Afghanistan and points further
east. Joe casually walked over to them—he was twenty-four at the time—and
said, "I heard your problem, and I can drive your bus." They thought it over
for a few minutes, and they agreed. He spent a few days learning to drive the
bus in the hills around Athens, and he was ready to go.

I was totally impressed with this fellow landlord and his gorgeous ballet-
dancer wife. Joe and I had followed similar paths in developing our real
estate portfolio, and we both had been very successful, but we had never
gotten to know each other. Joe had used his resources for freedom and
travel. I had chosen to remain in place in Ithaca and continue to initiate
projects that would benefit both us and our city. Carol and I traveled, but
only for weeks at a time, not months, as Joe and Rebecca had chosen to
do. They were off to Costa Rica for two months now.

We discussed Frost's faux pas in not fully negotiating all the details with
Joe for use of his property. Joe listened as I painted the downtown picture. He
knew it—how, with mutual cooperation, Lambrou and Ciminelli had been

able to develop the Hilton Garden Inn hotel and office building downtown; how Cornell, with a lot of negotiating, had agreed to move 380 employees downtown; how Carol and I had bought the State Theatre and the Clinton House to keep these important historical buildings viable. He had served on Common Council. He had worked on the committee for the redesign of the Commons. He saw the development by Bloomfield/Schon, and I told him of my role in assisting them, and how their new project actually improved our rental situation at Center Ithaca. Joe knew the big picture. He knew his livelihood depended on the overall economic health of downtown. He accepted that Frost's project would be one more building block in meeting the BID's goal of creating a more attractive and economically vibrant downtown. And he accepted my several repeated apologies for Frost's overlooking the importance of working a viable deal through with him before assuming he would grant the access and staging areas Frost needed.

Joe took this all in. He then shifted to thinking of the synergy that could happen between his property and the Carey Building—they could share underground utility easements, they could share trash areas. Joe would not miss the temporary use of the staging area on his property surrounding the Carey Building, provided Frost would reimburse him for the parking income he currently received. Frost's new tenants would strengthen Joe's many restaurant tenants around the corner on Aurora Street. He was in the process of negotiating a deal with the Patel family to build a new Canopy by Hilton hotel on the interior of his site and cross easements and right-of-ways for both Frost's current project and the hotel, as well as the Community School of Music and the Arts, could all be arranged to everyone's advantage.

**Figure 29.2** The Carey Building under construction. Photo by author.

**Figure 29.3** The new building. Its seven-story overbuild was completed in December 2016. Photo by Jon Reis.

We parted friends, and while our dinner had been strongly slanted toward resolving the issues on his Ithaca site between him and my son, a transformation had taken place—we had gotten to know Joe and Rebecca. He agreed to work out all the details with Frost once he returned, so now, not only had we made new friends, but Frost's project could proceed—cooperation, even in the midst of competition, like the rising tide, was floating all boats.

# CHAPTER 30

# COLTIVARE (2011–14)

## Farm to Bistro

Shaping our city has taken many forms. An extraordinary variety of forces have been at work to bring about the growth that has evolved over the nearly twenty-five years since the Downtown Vision Task Force submitted its report to Common Council, and the twenty years since the business improvement district was first conceptualized.

The DIA's vision from the two ten-year strategic plans; the housing study; the pioneering development of Gateway Center and Gateway Commons; the Seneca Place Hilton Hotel coupled with the implementation of Cornell University's agreement to move 380 employees downtown; growing and more sophisticated events like Art in the Heart through the summer, Apple Harvest Festival in the fall, and the Ithaca Chili Cook-Off in February; our business retention and recruitment efforts—all were paying off.

The strategic plan had included the goal of getting the three educational institutions—Cornell University, Ithaca College, and Tompkins Cortland Community College—more involved in downtown. Students and faculty are shoppers. The Seneca Place agreement with Cornell had increased the number of professionals working downtown by over four hundred, and had also justified the construction of the Cayuga Street parking garage with its 750 spaces.

Years ago, Carl Haynes, president of TC3, had spoken with me about the potential strength of real estate acquisition and ownership for nonprofit organizations. That conversation had been the impetus for my convincing the State Theatre board of directors to establish a foundation to own property for the benefit of the theater. It had been reinforced by the trip to Cleveland, where I'd seen Playhouse Square and their tremendous success owning real estate for the benefit of the five theaters there.

Carl earned an MBA degree from Syracuse University and a PhD (1980) in higher education from Cornell. With his business background and his entrepreneurial vision he had worked with his TC3 Foundation board to purchase the two student-residence buildings contiguous to the campus. Subsequently, over an eight-year time frame, the foundation had built an additional five residential buildings. In total the college could now house a total of 814 students. The rental revenue from the resident buildings met the operational costs and debt service and over time was projected to grow to provide a net cash flow to the foundation, which in turn would be used to support college needs.

In addition to his real estate successes both at the Dryden campus and in downtown Ithaca, Carl tells the story of attending the last session of a summer practicum in sustainable farming and local food systems, taught by one of his biology faculty members at West Haven Farm at EcoVillage at Ithaca in 2011. It was a hands-on course that covered a range of topics on approaches to sustainable farming. The last class included a wonderful dinner, after which he was scheduled to speak. In the Q&A following his talk he was asked why this course couldn't become a program at TC3, perhaps in cooperation with Cornell. A seed was planted.

He goes on to tell of attending a conference that same summer as a board member of CCID (Community Colleges for International Development) at Kirkwood Community College in Cedar Rapids, Iowa. Kirkwood Community College has its own recently opened hotel with a culinary lab, full restaurant, amphitheater, and conference center. The chair of the hotel and restaurant management program at TC3 had been advocating for a culinary arts program at the college, but they simply did not have the space to accommodate it. Carl, however, was inspired, and again serendipity intervened.

My wife sits on the board of directors of the TC3 Foundation. She said that when Carl presented his seed idea for the Farm to Bistro program, the foundation board picked it up immediately. The foundation had overseen the purchase and renovation of the nearly vacant student-residence buildings adjacent to the TC3 campus, and it was by now experienced in holding title to and managing real estate. Carl's new idea, prompted in part by Gary's input, involved opening another college facility in downtown Ithaca. Gary had shown Carl ten spaces for sale, not all of them within the BID district, but they were either too small or not sufficiently well located to take proper advantage of the downtown market. Gary then showed him the ground floor space of 17,300 square feet under the Cayuga Street parking garage, which was undeveloped but ready for retail. The building was located on a major downtown street across from the Holiday Inn.

It was not for sale, but it was definitely for rent. The space was net-leased by Bloomfield/ Schon as part of their deal with the city and would be developed by them on the ground floor of the new 750-space parking garage. Carl was ready to sign a lease with them, and Ken would even offer TC3 an option to buy out the leasehold at a later date. But there were many hoops he would have to jump through to do this in a prudent manner.

His idea was to create a sustainable organic farm on the eighty-eight acres the college owned adjacent to their Dryden campus. He would hire faculty and develop an associate's degree program to prepare students in a wide range of occupations either in agribusiness or food systems and distribution. Additionally, students interested in food preparation and service would work in a culinary center and restaurant in the downtown Ithaca facility. Carl labeled it a true "farm to bistro" concept.

The advantages were widespread. In response to significant growth in the hospitality and tourism industries in the region, the college would be establishing a unique culinary arts associate's degree, satisfying a growing need at the school. Not only would the program offer training in food preparation and service, it would also support the college's wine marketing associate's degree program. This concept called for opening a culinary center—a restaurant, bar, and banquet hall, with meeting rooms and classrooms for the students on site.

The TC3 farm would grow much of the food and deliver it to the culinary center. Students would prepare the food, serve it, and publicize their services. It would be called Coltivare, which in Italian means "to plant, grow, cultivate"—a clever all-encompassing name for an idea that would give students thorough understanding of and training in the process of growing food and bringing it to the table in the ever-expanding business of organic food service. It would open up job possibilities for dozens of students a year. At the same time, it would bring a new restaurant, banquet facility, and bar to downtown Ithaca. The farm would focus on organic practices, and Coltivare would emphasize regionally grown produce, wines, and brews. It was win-win on all fronts.

Philanthropy can be an important force in development. The local Park Foundation had provided $2 million for the purchase of the closed Woolworth building from Dave Abbott. With these funds as seed money, Tompkins County had been able to orchestrate the relocation of the county library into the newly renovated library just down the street from what would become the new Coltivare restaurant in the city-built Cayuga Street garage. Before he could sign a lease with the Bloomfield/Schon group, Carl needed money.

The community college had an extraordinarily generous benefactor who helped them in the development of the concept for the new Farm to Bistro program. Carl told me the amazing story of coming into his Dryden office at the college one day, and as he opened the door he looked down and saw an envelope directly at his feet. He reached down and opened it to find a check for $2 million from a member of his board of directors toward the development of his new Farm to Bistro brainchild. Over the years, Arthur Kuckes has been a great benefactor of TC3, giving millions of dollars to the college. Arthur's wife once told me about Arthur's philosophy of giving: "The big universities (Cornell, etc.) have plenty of wealthy alumni with larger pockets than mine. Here at TC3, I can make a difference in the lives of these students who want to become prepared to go out into the local workforce." This was grassroots philanthropy. Carl didn't even have to ask.

Carl needed still more money, however, before he could make the deal. In 2011, New York's Governor Cuomo had established ten Regional Economic Development Councils (REDCs), to develop long-term strategic plans for economic growth in their respective regions. Tompkins County was located in the Southern Tier Regional Economic Development Council. These are public-private partnerships made up of local experts and stakeholders from business, academia, local government, and nongovernmental organizations. These councils have had a tremendous impact on job growth and development in New York State. They operate through a community-based, bottom-up approach.

What could be more grassroots than TC3's farm to bistro concept? The Southern Tier REDC awarded a $2.3 million grant to the TC3 Foundation to help with the capital investment needed to build out the Farm to Bistro facilities (both farm and culinary). Ever the entrepreneur, Carl also had three regional banks represented on his board: Tompkins Trust Company (TTC), Manufacturers and Traders Trust (M&T), and National Bank & Trust (NB&T). All three agreed to provide interim construction financing to the project, as it can often take several years for the REDC grant funds to be released, and they committed to permanent long-term financing as well.

The support from the Southern Tier REDC, the major gift from Arthur Kuckes, a significant gift from the Wegmans grocery chain, and several smaller donations, along with the bank financing, provided the $7 million capital investment needed for the project. At last the TC3 Foundation could sign the lease with Bloomfield/Schon, and in his entrepreneurial fashion, in order to strengthen the possibilities of continued success for the project,

Carl negotiated an option to buy the leasehold for the space after a five-year period.

To design Coltivare, the TC3 Foundation board hired Andy Ramsgard, a renowned architect with a creative flair, who had designed the Mirbeau resort in nearby Skaneateles, as well as scores of upscale restaurants and homes in the upstate region and beyond.

With the help of the DIA, Carl orchestrated an event to break ground in the bare space that was to become the college's new teaching facility and the newest downtown restaurant. As was typical for our downtown ground-breaking events, all the local officials, the city planner, the mayor, DIA executive director Gary Ferguson, the developer Ken Schon—who had worked on the Cayuga Street project for seven years—and many downtown business owners and well-wishers attended. Carl himself spoke about the synergy between this professional teaching facility and the revitalization of our downtown. "This program," he said, "will provide up to sixty jobs equating to forty-five FTEs [full-time-equivalent jobs]. It will prepare graduates for a wide range of employment in restaurants, hospitality, tourism, food distribution, and agribusiness jobs, including those serving the wine industry through our wine marketing program."

He credited Gary Ferguson for his initial help in showing him the ten sites where he might locate his farm to bistro concept. He credited Ken and Steve, the developers, who had kept the property vacant and available on a handshake, for the year it took Carl to pull all the moving parts together. He credited his board of trustees, his foundation board, and the finance, property management, and executive committees of the foundation. He also gave great credit to the Culinary Arts Advisory Council, which included many local restaurateurs and managers from such establishments as the Statler Hotel at Cornell; the chair of SUNY's (the State University of New York) culinary programs; the executive chefs at the Cayuga Medical Center; and Wegmans. "The TC3 Bistro," he said, "is its own limited liability corporation [LLC], and we have already hired fifty employees. The college board of trustees, following our internal review processes, approved the curricula, as did SUNY [of which TC3 is a part] and the State Education Department."

When completed, the culinary teaching kitchen would boast workstations with commercial six-burner stoves, ovens, hoods, and a large flat-screen TV at each station that could beam in live sessions with chefs from Italy, France, or any other country whose cuisine the student chefs were studying. An additional kitchen served the 110-seat restaurant, routinely preparing lunch and dinner and occasionally serving banquets in the 200-seat banquet hall. A tiered classroom, with sinks, refrigeration, and a wine trough for tastings, provided the setting for classes in wine appreciation for both the students and the public. The bar and restaurant would be serviced by a combination of students and professional staff.

Coltivare was completed and opened in December 2014. Forty-five students enrolled in the culinary program for the first year, sixty in the second year, and in the third year, there were one hundred and eighty-five applications. Graduates are fully qualified to enter into the food service industry as chefs, servers, bartenders, and managers. Graduates from the sustainable farming and food systems program are prepared for agribusiness careers, as well as jobs in a wide range of food distribution–related fields. Experience growing the food served in Coltivare on the eighty-eight-acre farm trains young farmers. The TC3 program is designed to give students a hands-on experience in every aspect of the food production system and supports four degree programs: culinary arts, sustainable farming and food systems, wine marketing, and hotel and restaurant management.

Coltivare was a dream come true for Tompkins Cortland Community College, and for downtown Ithaca it has provided a new upscale restaurant with exceptional food and a banquet hall that will seat up to two hundred patrons. It became instantly popular and only added to the attraction of our central downtown business district. Their motto became *"Coltivare: Come taste what we teach."*

Like the other development projects taking place in downtown Ithaca, none of this would have happened without the vision, support, and coordination provided by Gary and the Downtown Ithaca Alliance, its board of directors, and its membership of over four hundred property owners, merchants, business owners, tenants, and city officials.

**Figure 30.1** Rendering of Coltivare, which now occupies 17,300 square feet on the ground floor of the Cayuga Street parking ramp. Photo courtesy of Tompkins Cortland Community College.

**Figure 30.2** Coltivare's state-of-the-art teaching kitchen. Photo courtesy of Tompkins Cortland Community College.

**Figure 30.3** The bar and dining room. "Come taste what we teach!" Photo courtesy of Tompkins Cortland Community College.

**Figure 30.4** The banquet hall seats two hundred. Photo courtesy of Jason Henderson.

# CHAPTER 31

# REZONING (2013–14)

## Overzealous?

The DIA was successful in its efforts to have the city council approve the rezoning package it had proposed for our central business district, and it hadn't taken the huge fight with the public or city hall that we had anticipated. The DIA's *density* concept of concentrating growth in higher buildings within the central core of downtown was continuing to work. The 2020 strategic plan and the shadow studies done by HOLT made higher buildings in the downtown seem more reasonable and acceptable to a majority of people—not to everyone, but a majority. Forty- and sixty-foot maximum zoning heights were increased to eighty-five (seven to eight stories), and in some cases, in the very central blocks around the Commons, to 120 or even 140 feet. Property owners and developers were pleased. This would be the beginning of development opportunities without having to take every proposed project in downtown through the variance process. The city was also pleased that tax revenues would increase, leading to further prosperity and the ability to fund sidewalk repair, road repair, and general improvement of the city infrastructure.

Frost's plan to construct an overbuild in Ithaca had been among the first projects to take advantage of the zoning change. Many overbuilds can be seen in New York City—preserving a historic building at the street level and up to its original height and then building a new modern structure—an overbuild—above it, sometimes dozens of stories high. There had been many infill projects on vacant or demolished sites in Ithaca, and there had also been many renovations, but no one had yet done an overbuild. By right, Frost could now build out the Carey Building, the two-story 1924 historic structure, to eighty-five feet—seven stories total. He still needed site plan and planning board approval of the project, but the height issue would not hold him back. He also applied for and received a tax abatement for the project—another incentive offered to attract development and create density in the central core of downtown.

Across the street, the new Marriott hotel, which had been in the development stage for seven years—refining design, clearing title for purchase of a two-foot-wide strip along Aurora Street still needed for road clearance from the city, and finding the right financing package—was finally ready to move forward. It, too, had applied for a tax abatement after much discussion at the IDA about paying a "living wage" to the hotel employees in exchange for the granting of the tax abatement. I wrote a statement for the IDA, which Frost was to read, as I was out of town and would miss a crucial meeting about the tax abatement:

> *Dear Members of the IDA:*
>
> At the end of the day, the businesses that survive are the ones in which the income exceeds the outflow. It is these businesses that are able to provide services and products to their customers, wages to their employees, and taxes to the governing authorities on an ongoing and sustainable basis.
>
> Every business on earth has risks associated with its start-up. Every business owner on earth must weigh the risks for success or failure, as he or she begins the long and complicated journey toward the decision to proceed, or not to proceed. Mr. Rimland is in the process of weighing his risks as he creates the new Hotel Ithaca—a four-star hotel that will attract visitors and tourists to our area; a project that, combined with a restaurant, will provide 120 jobs and a million dollars of combined sales tax and property tax revenues annually in the Ithaca community.
>
> As part of his negotiations with the city, he has agreed to provide living wages to the housekeeping staff equal to 156 percent of minimum wage. The cost of this will be another $50,000 per year to the project. Forcing additional wage concessions onto this project will upset the balance of risk beyond the level of tolerance acceptable to both himself and his lenders.
>
> We all want the most we can get for ourselves, for our community, for each other in life. If we push too hard to get it, if we become too involved in our personal agendas, if we lose sight of the big picture and how interrelated we are with each other, we run the risk, each of us, of ending up on the rocks with nothing.
>
> The IDA board can choose to support this project with the tools at its disposal—a forgiveness of sales tax and mortgage tax. As members of the Ithaca community, we ask that you do so.

Gary and members of the BID attended the IDA meeting to speak in favor of the project. The IDA voted to award the tax abatement without imposing further conditions on the developer.

Figure 31.1  The Ithaca Marriott Downtown hotel under construction, fall 2015. Photo by author.

Figure 31.2  Rendering of the completed Ithaca Marriott Downtown on the Commons. Photo courtesy of Urgo.

The public discussion of any project in downtown that was in some way receiving public support would invariably result in meeting after meeting of parties interested in seeing some item of their social agenda included. Years ago, at Eddygate, I had agreed to include a child-care center in order to receive the deciding vote from council member Carolyn Peterson, who twenty-five years later would become Ithaca's mayor. With the Gateway project, the Creek Walk had been the public concession that Thys and I had discussed, and which I willingly gave. At the Marriott, it became the living-wage issue. As developers, we were slowed down by these things , but looking at them from the viewpoint of the overall well-being of the community, one had to become philosophical and admit that some conditions required of the developer could be effective in extending more than just financial growth for the developers and their companies but also providing benefits for the community. It was a good balance—economic growth and community support—socially responsible business, but it also had to work economically.

Building Eddygate, during scores of hours in public meetings, I had learned to appreciate this public process. As one Common Council member, an attorney, had commented, "We are a nation of laws." I liked that. It gave me patience, for as frustrating as it was at times to attend and to experience the public process, it meant that one high-powered individual could not ride roughshod over others. The public process assured that every project would be aired, and everyone who wanted to speak for or against it would have the opportunity. This was indeed the democratic process. We had lobbied successfully to change our laws—the zoning laws—downtown, but there was still the control required by site-plan and planning review. One couldn't build without enduring public scrutiny of the design, and sometimes even the use of the building.

With support gained from the planning department, the DIA had been successful in the passage of Ithaca's revised zoning law. There was now a major tool for promoting density. The new ten-story Marriott, the seven-story Carey Building, David Lubin's proposed fourteen-story mixed-use retail, office, and apartment building on the Commons, all within a year of each other—even the three-year-long Commons redesign—were having a huge effect on increasing density in downtown. During the first ten-year plan, 2000–2010, even with having to obtain variances for height and usage, downtown had seen a new Hilton hotel, two new parking garages, all of the Bloomfield/Schon projects, the new library, numerous upper-story renovations on the Commons, the Gateway projects—over $100 million of development had taken place during this ten-year period. During the second period, 2010–20, in part due to the rezoning, we had planned another $150 million of development. It was a construction bonanza for our small town.

Ithaca had been successful, almost beyond belief. Our vacancy rate for housing however, was less than 0.5 percent. This statistic did not go unnoticed by the Campus Advantage Company, a national real estate developer based in Austin, Texas. Campus Advantage had developed over twenty-five thousand student-housing beds in thirty markets. They correctly interpreted this as indicating a very strong need for additional housing units in Ithaca.

Michael Orsak, the front man for Campus Advantage, had come to town to meet with the new city planner, JoAnn Cornish; our economic development director, Phyllisa "Philly" DeSarno; and our young and energetic (twenty-four-year-old) mayor, Svante Myrick. Michael called me as well, and asked to meet to discuss the status of student housing in Ithaca. I thought back to my support of Ken Schon and Steve Bloomfield, of Bryan Warren and his group, of Gus Lambrou and the one-story building that became the Hilton Garden Inn—of course I would meet with him.

When he revealed the scale of their proposed project for downtown—a 240-unit, 620-bedroom apartment community marketed to students—I was skeptical. When he further described the company's desire to attract both Cornell and Ithaca College students to live downtown, I was even more skeptical. In my experience, the two campuses seldom mixed. Ithaca College was on South Hill, and while excellent in some fields, IC had a reputation as a party school. Cornell was on East Hill, four times larger than Ithaca College and known to be a very serious academic institution. It had been my experience that it was difficult to get a significant number of students from either hill to move downtown to live. How much more difficult would it be to get them to share a building? Nonetheless, I agreed to assist Michael and his company by giving them our rental numbers in the Ithaca market, and I also suggested he contact Gary, executive director of our DIA.

After meeting with key people in Ithaca, Campus Advantage put in a purchase offer at an undisclosed price on the one-story Trebloc Building on the corner of Aurora and State Streets, owned by Rob Colbert. Rob is a shrewd businessman. Here was an opportunity to capitalize on the increased value brought to his site by the zoning change. A developer could take his one-story building, demolish it, and go up as high as twelve stories or 120 feet, right across the street from the 140-foot Marriott and the 85-foot Carey Building. Campus Advantage now controlled the site with their purchase option—it had to be exercised within a one-year period.

They hired a local architect-consultant, Scott Whitham, to handle their project at the local level, while bringing in their Austin, Texas, architect to design the entire project. From the beginning the project received mixed messages. It was appealing, because if they were successful, and if they could bring that many college students downtown, it would help the overall economy. It would help fill the bars and restaurants. It would help the shops. Many people, however, when they saw the renderings, the shadow studies, and the traffic count projections, grew quite concerned. Campus Advantage was an experienced developer. They understood the public process and were careful to design their proposed building exactly to the requirements of the new zoning law Ithaca had worked to pass. From their point of view, their project should have been a shoo-in for the Ithaca community with its vacancy rate for housing at less than half a percent.

At the first public hearing, many people said the building was too massive, too high, and should be redesigned—lowered in height, not be as

**Figure 31.3** An early rendering of the Trebloc site project before Campus Advantage articulated and stepped down the facade in response to public outcry. Photo of rendering courtesy of Campus Advantage.

massive. "But we designed it to the zoning law you yourselves passed as a city," was their response. "Then step it back from the curb, articulate the facade, do something to make it blend in and be more attractive," was the demand from the public. Needless to say, the Austin group left the meeting frustrated and confused. I spoke with Michael afterward and reassured him. This was Ithaca. It had taken me five years from start to finish to design and receive city approval for one of my projects. Ithaca was not your typical market—everyone has their opinion. Be patient, take the suggestions that were offered in the site-plan review—and they did.

At their next meeting, and their next, and on through the following year, they kept improving the design, making the facade more interesting with stepbacks, bay windows, and, at even more expense, a public plaza on the ground floor at the corner of Aurora and State Streets. I liked the design and expressed my opinion in a public meeting the next fall. I thought they had succeeded in designing a building that would be attractive, improve the housing stock downtown, and be successful. I was still leery about whether they would succeed in the student market, but with their massive experience, perhaps they knew things I didn't.

Many people, however, continued to speak out against the project. It was still too big. Too massive. My observation was that this was a matter of construction fatigue. Too much was being built downtown in a short span of time. "Our town is turning into a city," was often heard as a complaint. "We don't want any more students downtown. We don't want canyons between the buildings."

Later in 2015, in October, as Carol and I were driving down through the mountains of Pennsylvania on a trip to Washington, DC, a call came in on my cell phone. It was an extremely frustrated Michael. He said that during their visit to Ithaca for the Planning Board meetings in September, both Svante and Nate Shinagawa, a county legislator up for election in a new district, had pledged their support for the project, but when the campaign season started in October, they changed their stances in order to obtain votes. Michael said they asked Campus Advantage to withdraw their presentation to the Planning Board until after the November election. The project was dead prior even to arrival at the IDA for consideration of the project!

Did I have any advice on what they could do? Carol was driving. I put him on speakerphone. Carol suggested right away that they wait until after the election. Both the mayor and the county legislator were up for reelection. "Wait a couple of months and then bring it back for reconsideration," was her suggestion. I suggested that if they could make it work with two fewer stories, it might have a better chance of surviving the public process. And if there was any way they could perhaps team up with Ithaca Neighborhood Housing Services and offer a floor or two of affordable housing, and not such an emphasis on the student market, then it might serve to temper public opinion.

Michael told me they had over a million dollars already invested in design, options, and the preliminary market studies they had performed. I sympathized with him and repeated my experience of trying to develop in Ithaca. "It takes patience. It's a good project. Stick with it."

We didn't hear from Michael again, and in January we read in the *Ithaca Journal* that Campus Advantage had dropped their contract with Rob Colbert. They were packing their bags and leaving town.

Years later Michael had told me they had presented Svante with a much-reduced project, down to 179 units and 445 beds with several floors specially designed for market rate units and a reduced height from 116' to 85'. Svante had liked the revised project and promised to pledge his support for it publicly and with the IDA if they were to resubmit this revised plan. On December 8, he and Mike Peter, CEO for Campus Advantage, met in the mayor's office with both Rob Colbert and Svante. They discussed the new scale, and Svante reconfirmed his support. He let Rob know he could get the smaller deal done at 85'.

Rob was not happy. The city had just recently upzoned his property from 65' to 120' and he felt that the Design Board's and Svante's insistence on a smaller project was a "taking" of property rights. His land was zoned for 120' and not approving an "as of right" density was not legal. Rob threatened suit. Svante let him know they could likely get a design approved for 120' after years in court, but they would never get the IDA approval, as the tax abatement was not a property right but a subjective incentive. Without the tax abatement, the deal did not pencil. Unfortunately, a smaller-scale project would mean Rob's land was not worth as much as he thought it was at 120'.

Campus Advantage requested a proportional price reduction from Rob, as well as additional time, since they had lost three months, October to December, by dropping their request to the Planning Board. Understandably, Rob refused to negotiate. He had zoning for 120'.

None of this of course was known publicly, and Campus Advantage subsequently canceled their contract with Rob Colbert in mid-January.

Just because a city has passed zoning laws that permit a height limit of 140 feet, and use of the project for student housing is permitted by right, doesn't necessarily mean it will be approved. I privately wondered whether Campus Advantage had the right to sue the city, since they had properly followed every step of the process and had designed a building that should have been allowed by the zoning law, but that approach was never brought up. Meanwhile, an undisclosed developer had already stepped in and put a purchase offer on the site, again for an undisclosed amount, which was accepted by Rob.

Had Ithaca been overzealous in passing the revised zoning law? We had used it to attract new developers to Ithaca. We had the new Marriott hotel under construction at ten stories. A nearby Hilton Canopy hotel was in the planning stages. Why hadn't the city given the go-ahead to the Campus Advantage project as originally proposed?

My personal feeling was that not only was it just too much construction in too short a time for downtown residents, merchants, and property owners to assimilate, it was also a serious question as to whether we wanted to turn downtown into an undergraduate student "ghetto," as some people termed it. To that, I think the answer coming from the public was a resounding "*No!* Keep the students—particularly the undergraduates—up on the hills."

Grad students, professionals, the elderly, and affordable housing were all uses suggested to Campus Advantage, but that was simply not their area of focus. This was Ithaca, and the public in Ithaca has a significant voice in what happens in the way of real estate development. Because a zoning law had been passed bolstering density didn't necessarily mean that every project that complied would be built.

# CHAPTER 32

# CORNELL PROGRAM IN REAL ESTATE (2014–15)

## The Class

It is a truism to say that all real estate is local. If you understand the principles of developing in Ithaca, you can, in large part, take these principles home with you to Seoul, Beijing, Kansas City, Brooklyn, LA, or anywhere else in the world. Over the years, I had been invited by various Cornell professors to lecture about my development projects to their graduate students in the architecture, business, and hotel schools—a small-town, local developer lecturing to a body of international students, students who come from wealthy real estate families in China, Singapore, Australia, and South America, as well as major cities in the United States.

In 1995, Bob Abrams, a very successful real estate professional from New York City, was invited back to Cornell University to establish a graduate program in real estate. It was to be tucked neatly into a virtual space centered between the College of Architecture, Art, and Planning; the College of Human Ecology; the School of Hotel Administration; and the Johnson Graduate School of Business. It would be its own fully accredited program, and in addition to drawing from faculty in each of these academic disciplines it would be taught in part by hands-on professionals in the real estate investment and development business from around the world, many of whom had graduated from one of these professional graduate programs at Cornell and gone on to make successful careers for themselves.

In 1999, Bob Abrams was joined by Brad Olson, past president of various community development divisions of the Irvine Company in Orange County, California, and immediate past president of the Carson Companies—industrial and commercial developers and property managers based in Los Angeles County. Together, Bob and Brad developed an exceptional professional program in real estate (PRE), one that quickly rivaled the professional real estate studies programs at NYU, MIT, USC, and Columbia.

Among the internationally known and interesting speakers who visit the campus regularly to talk to and meet with the real estate students are Bob Toll, executive chairman of Toll Brothers, the largest luxury-home builder in the country; Larry Silverstein, who acquired and rebuilt on the World Trade Center site; and Richard Baker, the governor and executive chairman of Hudson's Bay Company, also owner of Saks Fifth Avenue and Lord & Taylor, whose name is now borne by the Cornell Baker Program in Real Estate. They all come as visiting lecturers or as participants in the Cornell Real Estate Distinguished Speaker Series and focus entirely on sharing their experiences with the PRE students.

In September of 2014, I received a call from Brad Olson. After ten years of chairing and teaching in the real estate program, Brad had retired in 2009. Several instructors had been hired in the interim, and Brad returned in 2014 for one last time to teach the Residential Development course he had pioneered in 2000. He asked me if I would be interested in teaching the 2015 spring semester course in residential development in the Baker Program, while the school sought a full-time replacement for his position. He said it would mean filling in as a visiting lecturer for a semester. I had written a book titled *Creating an Independent Income in Real Estate!*, which I handed out to incoming PRE students when Gary Ferguson and I were occasionally invited to give tours to orient the students to development in downtown Ithaca.

Prior to coming back to his alma mater to assist Bob Abrams in structuring the real estate program, Brad had been at the Irvine Company, one of the largest and most successful master-planned community developers in the United States. His community development divisions had responsibility for master planning, entitlement, and infrastructure, and for preparing land for sale/delivery to merchant builders and commercial developers for the development of thousands of attached and detached homes and related commercial developments. Brad said the Irvine Company had been in the development business since the 1920s, when the Irvine family had begun developing thousands of acres of vacant California land between the coast and the mountains. Brad understood green-site residential development. And this is what he had based his course on.

How would my experience developing and buying commercial and multi-family properties—mostly urban infill in Ithaca—fit into a course labeled "Residential Development"?

I had attended seminars at Wharton, NYU, Cornell, and Battelle Memorial Institute over the years, but my real estate development skills were essentially learned "on the streets." I have BA and MA degrees in acting and directing, plus five seasons of acting in summer stock theater, where I had played many lead and character roles. I had earned my Actors' Equity card as a professional actor.

In hindsight, I was aware that being an actor and director had been great preparation for a career in real estate development. It had enabled me to speak to bankers and politicians. I could assume the character that could deal with the plumbers and electricians, the contractors and the building inspectors—the one who could rent to doctors, students, lawyers, and merchants. But would the students understand the connection? Would they be interested in hearing about the purchase of a first single-family house in Ithaca for no money down and only because the buyer was dead broke? Brad's course had been focused on green-site suburban development—creating entire communities with a well-capitalized national developer. My course would likely switch the focus to financial survival and working one's way up in the world, handling the messy reconstruction of problem properties and urban infill.

Brad felt confident that the students would benefit from hearing these street-learned experiences. Maybe it's not that different building thousands of homes and building a sixty-unit apartment building. There is an intuitive process one follows—finding the property, or infill site, settling on the best use for the site, refining the concept, analyzing the financials, hiring an architect, finding the money, bidding the contractors, obtaining the permits, and finally building the project. Every developer goes through that process.

Brad agreed that the course focus could be changed from tract development and projects in major cities to urban infill. And rather than taking twenty-five students to another city, as they had done every year, the course could be taught using a local project. In fact, rather than study one site and have five or six teams develop the same project, as they had done the year before on a forty-five-acre monastery site being proposed by Toll Brothers in Philadelphia, he agreed when I suggested the class could develop three significantly different sites in Ithaca.

The principles would be the same. But here the students would be able to touch and see the sites. They could meet with the local officials and the neighbors who would influence the shape of their "virtual" development. Our company, Travis Hyde, owned one of the three sites—a one-story medical office building downtown that had recently been rezoned and could be redeveloped into six stories. Frost and Chris had also submitted an RFP and were under serious consideration for another of the sites—the long-vacant old Tompkins County Library building in downtown, which could be turned into thirty or forty apartments or condos. The third site would be an abandoned grocery store on four acres at the north edge of the city, which was being bid on by Ithaca Neighborhood Housing and would expose the students to the process of conceptualizing, financing, and selling the neighborhood on affordable housing in an urban setting.

Would the school be critical and regard it as self-interest on our part if we used sites that our company owned or that were under consideration for acquiring as the basis for the student projects? Brad thought there would be no problem with it. It would be an opportunity for the students to see firsthand how local development works; they would be guided by the people actually doing the development. It would provide them with a window into the entire process, from conceptualization through market study, design, bidding, financing, and construction. They would actually be exposed to projects that would very likely be built, and the students' ideas could possibly influence what would happen on these sites. Although Brad had agreed on a shift of emphasis from suburban development to urban infill, he suggested that for administrative reasons, we should keep it simple within the university bureaucracy and continue to call the course "Residential Development."

The course went well. I had planned to have all twenty-six lectures prepared in time for the first class at the end of January. Exactly two were prepared by the time I taught the first class. It was not impossible to keep ahead with class preparation throughout the semester—it was, however, an incredible amount of work.

Students saw photos from my first real estate project—a brownstone on West Eighty-Second Street in Manhattan. This building could have been bought—in fact an entire city block of brownstones could have been bought—for $40,000 each at that time. We checked online, and today, such a brownstone is selling for over $2.5 million. If a purchaser had made an investment of $40,000 to purchase the building in 1968 and forty-seven years later could sell it for $2.5 million, what was the return on that investment? A volunteer among the students did the math. He calculated it was about a 10 percent annual return—a good example of the power of appreciation, the power of compound interest, and the value of money. They had learned these concepts in other classes, and now they could see them at work.

Over time, the students saw photos from trips I had taken worldwide—a wealth of material showing urban development, urban infill from many cultures and centuries of human development, buildings and streets, architectural details and public amenities that worked—and those that did not—in cities from Amsterdam to Beijing, Stockholm to Moscow, Panama City to Nuuk, Greenland, to Machu Picchu, Peru, and closer to home from Cleveland, Ohio, to Poughkeepsie, New York. They saw detailed pictures of our local construction projects—from Ravenwood to Eddygate, Gateway, and

Center Ithaca, buildings they would know around town. They could see them from footers and foundations to rooftop and finishes—from ground-breaking to ribbon cutting and the management beyond. They heard and discussed the principles and process of residential development, the philosophy of urban infill, how Ithaca had been shaped with our strategic plans and our BID.

They heard about cultivating the "developer's mind-set": "Figure out what you want and have the courage to go for it. Accept your own greatest challenge." They read from a tiny book by Princeton professor Harry G. Frankfurt titled *On Bullshit*—twenty-seven weeks on the *New York Times* Best Seller list in 2005. The author quotes the philosopher Wittgenstein quoting Longfellow:

> In the elder days of art
> Builders wrought with greatest care
> Each minute and unseen part,
> For the Gods are everywhere.

"Don't compromise yourself; don't cut corners on quality. Speak the truth. Don't deceive. Build the best you can within your budget." They heard about my "obvious parallel" between sailing and real estate development—every single fitting on the sailboat has to be in place, every O-ring and cotter pin, or you don't sail that day. Details! And once sailing, the boat must be in perfect balance with the wind or you risk capsizing. But find the balance, set the sails perfectly for the conditions, and you can ride out even the heaviest storm. "Sailing," they heard, "is a perfect metaphor for real estate development—indeed for life."

As with Brad's previous classes, all of this was in preparation for the students to develop their own projects. Their class project was to be the focus of the course. They would learn how to find a site, develop a concept based on market research, perform a market study, review contracts, and hire an architect and engineers to design their project; prepare a financial analysis to determine if the project was feasible based on the design, construction costs, and the operating pro forma once completed; prepare both a construction and operational budget; find and bid the contractors to get the best price; and prepare a Gantt chart for planning out the construction schedule.

The students reviewed genuine AIA (American Institute of Architects) contracts. They looked at detailed spreadsheets from many years of development projects. For the Gantt chart, they saw the actual schedule used by our contractor, Dick Schneider, who had recently renovated the 153 guest rooms in Cornell's Statler Hotel—our classroom adjoined the hotel, so they could relate to that. The students had seminars on financial analysis, net present value, and internal rate of return. Many of them would go on to be analysts in large real estate firms worldwide.

Two teams tackled the medical office site. They were charged with keeping the one-story medical office operational while building it out into a six-story building on the site. After all, as part of the overall plan for downtown, no one wanted a viable business, particularly a downtown medical office, to close. They would have to negotiate with the city to acquire a neighboring parking lot on which to build their fully expanded building, which would include an overbuild above the medical office. They met with JoAnn Cornish, the new city planning director who had taken over Thys's position, to discuss the process and likelihood of being able to acquire the neighboring site from the city in order to design the maximum building possible while keeping the medical practice intact. They met with the building commissioner to talk about the construction process and inspections, and they researched the zoning codes online to learn exactly what they could build according to zoning requirements and whether they would need a variance.

The two library teams came up with different housing concepts for this site situated across the street from a city park. Both teams had private meetings with Frost, who, if he and Chris won the competition, would be the developer. He showed his idea for a forty- to sixty-unit building on the site, which depended on coordinating with Lifelong, the senior citizen center that was the neighbor at the back of the site. If Lifelong donated their property, they could end up with offices and a community room in the new building, and the project could have additional above-ground parking after demolition of the neighboring buildings—hence more units could be added. What market would the students choose to build for—seniors, students, professionals, working class residents, or individuals who qualified for affordable housing? Frost had been through the PRE. What were the obstacles they would have to overcome?

The single team assigned to the INHS grocery-store site researched and interviewed Paul Mazzarella, the head of INHS, to learn how to finance a project and navigate the complexities of tax credits to build subsidized affordable housing. The entire class visited each site.

To expose the students to many different types of residential real estate, we visited other types of infill developments, including a downtown neighborhood development where the developer, Sue Cosentini, utilized a single lot to build two houses—four total on two sites—and the students followed the zoning process she had to go through to create this unorthodox assemblage in downtown. PRE hired a bus to take the students on a field trip into the countryside to see another type of residential development—a housing alternative where a local contractor, Bruno Schickel, developed seventy acres of farmland into 140 tiny houses for under $100 per square foot—meeting a need for affordable single-family houses ten miles out of town. The bus took the class to the famed Eco-Village on West Hill, where single-family cooperative housing was built as row houses, keeping the farmland open, and with community dining rooms and meeting rooms for the residents, who could have their offices on-site and never need to leave.

The visiting lecturers were one of the highlights of the course. It was my turn to invite professionals to Cornell to share their experience as developers. These visiting professionals gave the students a hands-on perspective of what other projects could be built—how other cities could be shaped. A former mayor of Ithaca, Alan Cohen, had taken the position as city manager in Sunrise, Florida. He had attracted over *$1 billion* in development to this new and emerging city. Alan flew up from Florida to teach an entire class, showing how he coordinated the megadevelopment in Sunrise.

Steve Bloomfield came from Cincinnati and showed pictures of his many developments both in Cincinnati and in Ithaca. He went into detail about his negotiations with the city of Ithaca and the protracted battle with one particular local legislator over the rents they could charge in exchange for a tax abatement.

John Novarr spoke of his Collegetown Terrace project. He told the students of his development trajectory: studying architecture at Cornell, painting houses, becoming a building contractor, and then taking on renovations of historic buildings. He said, "People ask me why at sixty-five years old I am taking on a project like Collegetown Terrace." (It was reported to be over a $70 million development.) John's response: "Because I can. This isn't something I do for a hobby. It is my entire focus in life. It seems a shame to give it up just when you really know how to do it."

My son, Frost, spoke about his plans, in particular the acquisition of the Ithaca Gun Company site and the environmental cleanup. Paul Mazzarella spoke of Ithaca Neighborhood Housing Services and their philosophy of renovating rather than tearing down old housing, and the effect it has had on over fifteen hundred houses, significantly changing lives in the Ithaca community.

Gary Ferguson, executive director of our BID, the Downtown Ithaca Alliance, lectured on the necessity of creating a vision for a city with a strategic plan. He described the need for planning, the need for buy-in from developers, merchants, and city hall, and the process we had gone through to re-create Ithaca since he first came to town in 1999.

Jason Fane, Ithaca's largest landlord, came and spoke about his history of development in both Harlem and Ithaca—buying old properties, redeveloping them, and holding them until development was ripe and he could tear them down and build new buildings. He had done that very successfully in Collegetown and downtown Ithaca. In Harlem over a dozen years ago he had purchased a four-story building, which he rented out as offices and a community center. He said he calculated that Manhattan was "gentrifying" to the north at about a block and a half a year. In another ten years, he'd have an extremely valuable property in NYC.

He showed slides of his Toronto project, Chaz Yorkville, now under way with a forty-seven-story condominium building on the site of a building he had bought twenty years earlier and rented out until he felt the market demand called for condominiums.

Ninety percent of his 526 condo units had already been sold. He got the students' undivided attention when he urged them to go into run-down cities like Detroit and start buying on a "lot-a-month" program. "Buy a lot every month for $500, hold it, and someday someone will want that vacant lot, that city block, for many times what you paid for it," he urged them. He showed a photo of the ranch he had purchased in the path of development in Arizona.

Meanwhile, the students were grouped into teams and working hard as they prepared what would become close to one hundred pages for each of their team projects—a fully developed feasibility study on the medical

**Figure 32.1** Jason Fane (right), Ithaca's largest landlord, at his Chaz Yorkville property in Toronto. Photo courtesy of Jason Fane.

**Figure 32.2** Chaz Yorkville in Toronto, during construction, at eiqht stories hiqh. Photo courtesy of Jason Fane.

**Figure 32.3** The forty-seven-story Chaz Yorkville tower is visible in the distance, left of center. Photo courtesy of Jason Fane.

office, the old library, and the grocery-store site. They were learning how to be real estate developers. Several times during the semester they would present as teams to the entire class, and at the end of the semester they stood at the front of the room and gave polished presentations to fellow students, invited city officials, other PRE professors, and friends. They were presenting their findings as if to a bank or at a public hearing, complete with conceptual design drawings, market data, feasibility studies, and spreadsheet financial analysis on how best to develop their sites with regard to the city zoning plan, the financial reality of the market, and the overall strategic plan for the city of Ithaca.

The professional experiences I had shared, plus the expanded vision from the many visiting lecturers, became grist for their own development projects. They had learned principles of both residential and urban-infill development that they could take out into the real world.

It had been a rigorous class. In hindsight, the course had become a summary of *Shaping a City*, condensing my experience of forty years—the ethics, the principles of cooperation versus competition, the floating of all boats, the importance of a business improvement district, the importance of giving back with civic projects as well as continually growing one's own portfolio of real estate.

Several of the students said that this one class had taken 80 percent of their time during the semester to prepare all aspects of their feasibility study, but they had done it, and they could be proud. One student told the class of going for a job interview at a development firm in Boston during spring break. She took the draft of her class project and, based on the knowledge she exhibited in her feasibility study, was hired on the spot to begin after graduation.

As big a challenge as it had been, I was extremely pleased to have condensed my own forty years of real estate development experience into a series of lectures and projects that would help prepare these very intelligent Cornell graduate students for their own careers. Many of them will very possibly go on to help *shape their own cities.*

# CHAPTER 33

# A CORPORATE COMMITMENT (2016–18)
## Since 1836

Tompkins Trust Company has been operating in Ithaca for 180 years. It has serviced small businesses and shopkeepers, and has lent mortgages to construct a large portion of the Ithaca housing market. It has been the depository for the life savings of thousands of customers, and it has grown to be the employer of over three hundred workers locally and another eleven hundred in their subsidiaries around the state from Newburgh to Castile.

Ithaca is a small city, and the local bank, Tompkins Trust Company, understands the Ithaca psyche. It is sympathetic and takes the approach of nourishing local business. It has branches on all sides of town and has expanded by purchasing banks in surrounding communities. The bank and its parent company, Tompkins Financial Corporation, had determined it was time to review their strategy and performance and to see how best they could accommodate further expansion. Essentially, the shareholders own the bank, and they, as well as the community, must be taken care of. Is the bank running as profitably and efficiently as it can?

In an interview, Greg Hartz, the president, described the process the bank was going through. He said that the senior staff agreed it was time to take a serious look at consolidating several downtown locations. A new building in the suburbs with an abundance of free parking might be the most cost-effective way to bring about their expansion. All office functions could move from the several locations around town to a single building— somewhere else. The senior staff had considered the options. Should they join the flight to the suburbs?

Other businesses had done just that. When the YMCA went up in smoke in 1981, a new Y was constructed five miles out of town in the growing suburb of Lansing. Many people felt that the inner-city Ithaca children who needed it the most were seriously shortchanged by the relocation. However, the leaders of the Y found it was cheaper to build in Lansing rather than attempt an urban-infill project in downtown Ithaca.

The BID had played a major role in making the downtown as aesthetically and economically attractive as possible. New stores and businesses had been recruited. New buildings were being built. The tax abatement was in place to assist with new construction downtown. The History Center and Historic Ithaca were a major force in keeping the character of downtown intact by influencing local developers to preserve many of the old buildings, such as the Dewitt building and Clinton Hall. They had even taken the lead in the renovation of some, as they had with the 1828 Clinton House.

Officers of the bank had served on the board of directors of the Downtown Ithaca Alliance. It was obvious that the bank officers totally understood the interdependence of business activity and the well-being of the Ithaca community. They understood the impact their bank has on the local economy, being very active in Ithaca and a steady contributor to many of the not-for-profits that make Ithaca unique, and bank staff are encouraged to serve on the boards of the larger ones. The bank portfolio is heavily residential, including multifamily and single-family buildings. It has been involved in many of the main development projects that have taken place in Ithaca over the past two decades and is a very active small-business lender in the downtown community.

They understood what might happen if yet another major business were to leave downtown, particularly at a time when the trajectory for downtown growth was hanging in the balance. Is Ithaca, their major market, going to succeed as a downtown or is it not? Tompkins Trust Company had recently made a significant financial contribution to the redevelopment of the Commons. They understood that the robust health of the downtown is of benefit to the entire community, and they knew that the bank was an important economic engine for the continued and improved health of downtown.

The city and the Downtown Ithaca Alliance had carefully crafted plans for high-density zoning in the central core. The Commons was a vibrant place, and the main office of the bank was located at the heart of it. However, it is more expensive to build downtown, and parking is a major issue. Where do three hundred people, and even 350—which they were projecting at peak growth—park? It is cheaper to build on vacant land, even farmland, or in the suburbs. Was a consolidated bank campus located downtown in the best long-term interests of the bank?

Greg had served as president of Tompkins County Area Development, and with these questions in mind, he said that the Trust Company board hired a consulting firm to do an inventory and a thirty-year present-value calculation of all the spaces and leases the bank held in numerous locations downtown. They considered various options, with full or partial consolidation, and determined that full consolidating into one building would be best.

One huge driving force in making their decision, Greg said, was that as the bank was currently configured, it got none of the efficiency that comes from having people close by and together. If they chose to relocate into one building, it would be easier for customers to take care of a variety of financial needs without traveling all over town, and it was more efficient for the people who work together to be located together. As an example, the building could have one large break room that would make it easy to get to know your coworker.

But where should the building be located? Rural versus downtown? And if downtown, where? Greg said there is an argument for the rural setting—drive in, park for free, and go to work. Downtown could be a hassle, particularly with parking. Senior staff weighed the parking problem against the benefits of an urban setting—many places for lunch, many places for shopping, accessibility to many of their business customers. The senior management leaned heavily toward remaining downtown.

The bank hired the local firm of HOLT Architects to assess possible downtown locations. As it turned out, HOLT calculated that by tearing down the bank drive-through and relocating it to an existing parking area at street level under its building across the street, a large-enough footprint would be created to build the 110,000-square-foot seven-story building that would become the bank's new campus. The bank worked with the city to secure parking in existing garages and was able to assemble sufficient alternative parking to meet their needs, both through small nearby sites they owned and by leasing from several neighbors. They developed a transportation management plan, designed to help minimize single-occupancy vehicles in the city. Provisions were being made to encourage walking, biking, taking the bus, and ride sharing. As had happened to encourage other major developments downtown, based on the density of their proposed seven-story building, the bank was granted a twenty-year declining tax abatement by the local Industrial Development Agency.

Was this project controversial? As Greg Hartz says,

> I don't think any project ever receives 100 percent support, but for this one, we have actually had tremendous support from the city, the downtown business community, customers, employees, and shareholders. That said, any development project of this size will draw the interest of people who care about the long-term impacts on the community, and that is where I believe we are aligned—this project will enable Tompkins Trust Company and Tompkins Financial Corporation to keep and grow quality jobs not only in Tompkins County but also in the city's core. We are creating an environment in our town in which we create opportunities for employment. Cornell and Ithaca College are tremendous growth engines. Ithaca's steady growth over the past ten years translates into more housing and related services. The bank has developed an emphasis on entrepreneurship with the new business incubator space, REV [REV—as in "rev up"]. REV was the newly formed alliance between Cornell, Ithaca College, and TC3, located in the Carey Building, and the Cayuga Venture Fund, which funds start-up businesses.
>
> The support systems are in place in Ithaca. It is a highly recommended destination for retirement. For the baby-boomer generation, 80 percent of those in Ithaca who retire in the next ten years plan to stay here. Plus it is a destination for senior-type housing.

While the Trust Company is making close to a $32 million investment in a new building downtown, Greg Hartz emphasizes the point that "our company is not about a building. It is about the services we deliver to the community. We are spending shareholders' money. This is a significant investment for our company, and it is one our senior staff and board of directors believe is important to make. It is an investment in our company and the community."

"And what will happen with the Trust Company's historic building on the Commons?" I asked him. I knew our tenant at Gateway, the History Center, and Historic Ithaca already had their eye on it for a joint museum and administrative center for historic preservation. "Could the museum and administrative center actually materialize? Can all the pieces come together for the sale of this property to a combined historic preservation not-for-profit?"

Greg pointed out that "the bank has shareholders. We have to act prudently."

"Would TTC be generous?" I questioned.

"Certainly, with the pace and the process," he answered with a broad smile. "Would you expect anything different from us?"

**Figure 33.1** Construction of the new downtown Tompkins Financial Corporation headquarters began June 2016. The architect's rendering shows the projected building on the left and the drive-through across the street on the right. Photo of rendering courtesy of Tompkins Financial Corporation.

On June 17, 2016, the *Ithaca Journal* reported:

### *$31.3 Million HQ: Tompkins Financial Breaks Ground*

The new consolidated campus for the Tompkins Trust Company is underway, retaining up to 350 jobs in downtown. It was an important decision by the bank; it was an important decision for our downtown to keep them.

The start of construction for Tompkins Financial Corp.'s $31.3 million headquarters signals a continued commitment to downtown Ithaca, Deputy Mayor Deb Mohlenhoff said Friday. About 100 people gathered for a news conference at the construction site for the planned seven-story, 110,000-square-foot building at 116 E. Seneca St.

The headquarters will take the place of the Tompkins Trust Co.'s main office drive-up ATM. Tompkins Trust Co. is a subsidiary of Tompkins Financial Corp.

"They are not only building a beautiful new building . . . they are bringing employees and customers into the city to use the beautiful new (Ithaca) Commons," Mohlenhoff said. "By making an extremely public commitment to the downtown urban core, they are demonstrating a partnership and collaboration with the city which is extremely important, and we're very thankful to the trust company for staying in downtown."

Construction will begin immediately and end in March 2018, Tompkins Trust Co. President Greg Hartz said.

The headquarters would house more than 300 employees, with a retail branch and ATM on the first floor, according to a news release. The building would have 22 parking spaces.

The financial services holding company plans to consolidate its sprawling network of administrative offices in the new building, Hartz added.

Tompkins Financial plans to leave its offices in the Rothschild and Center Ithaca buildings, corporation president Stephen Romaine said. The main office for Tompkins Trust Co., at 110 N Tioga St. in Bank Alley on The Commons, and several other administrative buildings also would be vacated.

"We have people all over the place, and the buildings have been modified over the years, and there are lots of pockets—it's a very inefficient way for us to work," Hartz said. "This building will put all of us in one location, where there's a lot more interaction between the full staff."

All existing Tompkins Trust branches will stay open where they are now, Hartz added.

**Figure 33.2** Tompkins Financial Corp. president Stephen Romaine addressed a gathering of about one hundred at the construction site of the planned $31.3 million, seven-story headquarters at 116 E. Seneca Street. Andrew Casler/*Ithaca Journal* staff photo.

CHAPTER 34

# THE NEXT GENERATION
## They Get It!

For twenty years, Carol and I have maintained a forty-two-foot classic sailboat on the coast of Maine. For me, the thrill and challenge of sailing on the ocean directly parallels the thrill and challenge of developing a new building. Lots of risk, incredible focus—living in the moment—as you make the decisions about the set of the sails relative to the strength of the wind and the turbulence of the water. Ocean sailing mirrors the risk, excitement, challenge, and satisfaction that I experience in real estate development. When Carol can't join me, I often bring a friend or two from Ithaca as companions to introduce them to this peak experience that I find so satisfying and relaxing.

In 2010 John and Lauralee Guttridge were hardly out of their twenties. John had attended the Lehman Alternative Community School in Ithaca, and although recognized as extremely bright, he had left Northeastern University after only one year. At the age of eighteen he started his own computer business—Brightworks in downtown Ithaca—and after a few years, he and his staff of thirty tech experts could list nearly every major business in Ithaca among their clients. I invited them to join me in Maine for a few days of fun and relaxation sailing along the coast.

John had aspirations. Not only did he want to maintain and grow his computer business, he also wanted to expand into real estate development. He wanted to *own*, not rent, his offices. We had discussed this, and it made sense to me that I should be a sounding board for him, listening to and commenting on his ambitions. One could see Lauralee provided emotional grounding for John's exuberance and enthusiasm, and she provided it in a way I'm not sure he even recognized when it was taking place.

John had joined the board of the State Theatre. He had his eye on purchasing the *Ithaca Journal* building, two doors down from the State Theatre. He began telling me about his negotiations with Sherm Bodner, the

**Figure 34.1** Sailing in Maine on *Shanti,* our classic forty-two-foot Alden yawl. Photo by Brian McGovern.

publisher and representative of Gannett, the owner of both the newspaper and the building. The *Ithaca Journal* had begun as a newspaper in 1815 and had been in its current building since 1905. Frank Gannett had purchased the newspaper in 1912. John explained that the Gannett Company now wanted to sell the building, keep a smaller office in Ithaca, and move most of their production to Binghamton. I listened. I knew the story because after my trip to Cleveland with Gary and my decision to try to replicate their real estate endowment and create an ongoing income for the theater, Gary and I had also spoken at length with Sherm Bodner. I was contemplating making an offer to purchase the building on behalf of the theater. I didn't tell John of my plans at this stage.

We sailed together. John and Lauralee thoroughly enjoyed the wind and the water and the spectacular Maine scenery with its granite islands and spruce-lined shores, lobster boats, and seals playfully surfacing every so often alongside the boat. We were a long way from Ithaca, but this is often how deals are made—far from home, relaxing on a distant shore.

Carol and I had our favorite inns along the coast, where after several days' sailing we'd pull in, drop anchor, and take a room for dinner and a shower. John, Lauralee, and I sailed into Fox Islands Thoroughfare in Penobscot Bay. I called to reserve two rooms at the Nebo Lodge, a historic Maine inn, not fancy, but comfortable. We continued our conversation over dinner. I listened as John expanded on his plans to buy the *Ithaca Journal* building, rebuild the ground floor for his own use as an office for

Brightworks, and renovate the rest into additional offices and even retail through the entire block onto Green Street.

He was considering partnering with David Kuckuk, a very successful, now retired architect, who was also on the board of directors of the State Theatre. David had been one of the principals at Thomas Associates and influential in their decision twenty years ago to keep their offices downtown. John had heard me speak at the board meetings about my vision for creating an endowment for the theater by purchasing income properties, much like the Cleveland model and similar to what Carl Haynes was doing locally for Tompkins Cortland Community College. I then told him of my own research into the *Ithaca Journal* building and our conversations with Sherm Bodner. It was a perfect property for the theater to own. It had been my intention to make an offer on it.

John didn't miss a beat. He suggested maybe a collaboration would be to all of our benefit. He and David had discussed improving the entire block behind the building. Whatever was done there would certainly benefit the surrounding neighbors, in particular the State Theatre. He talked of renovating the existing building and constructing a large new building with stores and offices on what was currently a parking lot. John really had a complete vision for the area, provided Gannett would sell the property at a reasonable price.

We broke and went to our respective rooms for a welcome shower. The next morning, we met for breakfast in the dining room. I told John I had been thinking about our conversation and that I liked his vision for the use of the *Ithaca Journal* building. It was a good opportunity for him to begin assembling his own real estate portfolio. While whatever he and David did might not directly benefit the State Theatre from a financial standpoint, any improvement to the decrepit building would make the surrounding area more attractive, and the theater would benefit indirectly. I told John I would back off and not make an offer to buy the building on behalf of the theater.

Back in Ithaca, and not more than a month later, John called to let me know Gannett had accepted his offer to buy the *Ithaca Journal* property. The price at which he had it under contract was $300,000 less than what Gary and I had been prepared to offer and what Gannett had said was the asking price for the building. I was amazed and pleased for John—he really did *get it*. Not only did he have a vision, but he was a shrewd negotiator as well.

He and David did buy the building. Gannett moved their newspaper offices upstairs. John renovated the entire first floor for his Brightworks computer company. He built out the rear of the building along the Green Street frontage and rented it to Life's So Sweet, a chocolate and candy company that began in nearby Trumansburg and was delighted to find space on a busy street in downtown Ithaca. He and David redesigned the storage garages where the newspaper carriers used to drive through to pick up the bundles of newspapers for daily delivery. They put in glass facades in each of the seven bays, painted the long low building in bright colors, and rented every space to very small businesses that could operate out of 200 square feet or less. John has described it as a "microretail environment."

The following are excerpts from a 2014 interview with John by the *Ithaca Times* (used with permission):

When John Guttridge, a native Ithacan, purchased a 25,000-square foot building formerly owned by the *Ithaca Journal* along Green and Geneva streets a few years ago, he had a "lot of big dreams about the cool stuff that we can do." The "first brick in the wall" would be Life's So Sweet, a chocolate shop. However, it was the building across from Life's So Sweet's 116 West Green St. location that got Guttridge's, and his business partner David Kuckuk's, imagination racing.

That building, which once served as storage area for the *Ithaca Journal*, was assumed to be knocked down by whoever bought the property. Guttridge, however, had something else in mind.

"When we were originally looking at the property to purchase," he recalled, "we had been trying to conceptualize something to reinvigorate that side of the building, something that would be a signpost for how cool downtown Ithaca can be. When we first saw the building, the realtor told us, 'And then you'll tear this thing down to make more parking spaces.' And we were like, 'No, no, no, we'll do something cool with this.' Obviously we saw the retail potential with the south end of the building with Life's So Sweet, which was really our first brick in the wall, and we wanted to complement that with other small businesses right next door." . . .

Today, the Press Bay Alley building looks like something you'd see on the set of a *Star Wars* movie, or a place where the late Steve Jobs would feel right at home. The entire building is custom fit with glass sectional doors and a sleek design, and storefronts have the ability to pull up their doors to become "open-air retail," for the rare occasions when Ithaca weather acts accordingly. While that exact design was not always the plan, looking cool enough to get residents excited to walk through the space was.

"Our very first pass for Press Bay Alley," Guttridge said, "and the building we just completed, was that it would be almost like a farmers market. We continued to examine different ideas of how it could be just a little bit cooler than that. We wanted something that could be a presence year-round and that could be interesting, engaging and bring people downtown. From

our earliest seed of an idea to what we actually have, it is a tremendous difference. We went through a series of design iterations to get to imagining
something that looks like what we have now." . . .

Guttridge noted that the open store space that directly faces Green St. is
currently his top priority. Throughout this whole process, his team has envisioned the space becoming a café, and that remains the plan. He explained
that a good cup of coffee "creates great foot traffic," and will also offer the
opportunity to set up an outdoor sitting space for residents to enjoy. He is
currently talking to several contenders, and hopes to hash out the details
with one of them in the coming weeks. . . .

"The underlying concept," he explained, "is to create a fabric of different things that are woven together to establish a vibrant downtown area—
a little pocket of enthusiasm of excitement and energy. Obviously the scale
of Press Bay Alley (when compared to the Commons) is very different. Our
project is unique. There's nothing else like it anywhere else in town. I think
people enjoy finding these little pockets, where they can kind of tuck into
a corner and hang out.

"There's something very appealing to people about that," he continued.
"That's really what Press Bay Alley is: it's like the café tables set up behind
Center Ithaca, people love that. It's just a little nook you can hang out at,
whether it's for a business meeting or catching up with friends."

The row of stores in Press Bay Alley is small compared to a typical retailer,
with 188-square-foot and 376-square-foot units. John sees them as offering
an easy start-up environment for small retail businesses. Each unit has its own
heating and air-conditioning and a glass overhead sectional door that opens
fully, providing access for expansion onto the sidewalk in good weather.

John has since rented the remaining storefronts to Boxy Bikes, a store
selling electric bicycles; Ithaca Generator, a barbershop and community
gathering place; the Press Cafe; Bramble: Community Herbalism; and
Amuse, a craft store. In addition to Life's So Sweet and the microretailers,
he has rented ground-floor space to Circus Culture, a circus school with
150 students. He leased out the basement, where the *Ithaca Journal* presses
used to be, to individuals and businesses in need of storage space. The main
building is now 100 percent occupied. It has accomplished what he and
David set out to do when they told the Realtor, "No, no, no," in response
to his suggestion that they would, of course, tear down the garages. They
have also purchased the adjoining building between the *Ithaca Journal* and
the State Theatre. Their goal is to create something that will have a syner-
gistic use with the theater, perhaps even joining the theater and their new
building through a common wall and sharing an elevator.

**Figure 34.2** The "microretail environment" in Press Bay Alley. Photo courtesy of DIA.

In a conversation with John two years after our fateful boat trip, we were sitting alone in his conference room at Brightworks, which he offers rent-free for meetings both for the State Theatre board and the State Theatre Foundation, of which John is now president. We still share the vision for a real estate endowment for the theater, and he and Frost have together purchased the nearby Family and Children's Services building at 204 Cayuga Street, from which one-third of the income benefits the State Theatre.

John recalled the sailing trip we had made together. He remarked how improbable all this was—his now multimillion-dollar real estate portfolio, and he wasn't even thirty-five years old; his success in leasing the building; his and David's purchase of yet another building. I suggested that he *"enjoy it all." It was real. He had done it!* Through their vision and hard work, he and David had re-created and revitalized this important area of downtown.

John then repeated a perceptive comment I had heard him make once before, and which defines his approach to renting to small retailers and the effect they can have on the community: *"Little stores are like tiny threads which, woven together, create a fabric, and that fabric becomes our community."*

John and Frost and their respective development projects truly embody the vision and drive of the next generation.

# CHAPTER 35

# WHERE DO WE GO FROM HERE?

## The Road Forward

As planned for in the *Downtown Ithaca 2020 Strategic Plan*, and as I write this, a host of exciting new projects have been completed or are in the process of construction, and many more are in the planning stages.

The new Marriott hotel, at ten stories and with 159 rooms, anchoring the eastern end of the Commons, has been successful for over a year, since its opening on December 12, 2016.

**Figure 35.1** The new Marriott hotel at the east end of the Commons. Photo by author.

The Campus Advantage project on the Trebloc site never materialized; however, a regional company Newman Development Group, who were Bryan Warren's partners in Seneca Way, purchased the site and broke ground in October of 2017 for a project of 192 apartments, with a restaurant on the first floor, to be called City Center. It was not dissimilar in size and scope to the one abandoned by the previous developer, although Newman is adding seventy underground parking spaces, something not planned for in the Campus Advantage project. This gave them a decided advantage in obtaining approval for their comparably sized project. Furthermore, their targeted clientele is middle- to upper-income residents, versus the student population focused on by Campus Advantage.

**Figure 35.2** City Center foundation and underground parking during construction. Note shoring along the street. The completed Marriott hotel is in the background. November 2017. Photo by author.

**Figure 35.3** A view of City Center construction with Gateway Plaza in the background. Photo by author.

**Figure 35.4** City Center will add 192 apartments downtown. Rendering courtesy of Newman Development Group.

After several years of negotiation, title for Joe Daley's property behind the Carey Building has been passed to the Patel family, who broke ground for their new 131-room Canopy Hilton hotel in October 2017.

**Figure 35.5** Excavation begins for the Canopy Hilton hotel behind the Carey Building. Photo by author.

**Figure 35.6** Canopy Hilton hotel, with seven stories and 131 rooms, opens in fall 2018. Rendering courtesy of Baywood Hotels.

The Tompkins Trust Company's new office tower is out of the ground and scheduled for completion in the spring of 2018, at a revised project cost of nearly $40 million.

**Figure 35.7** The new TTC building will house 350 employees and keep a major financial center downtown. Photo by Jon Reis.

Out of nine developers who responded to the county's request for proposals (RFPs) to become the preferred developer of the vacant Tompkins County Library site across from DeWitt Park, Frost and Chris were selected. After working with HOLT Architects and presenting eight separate designs to the Ithaca Landmarks Preservation Commission (ILPC) over a two-year period, Travis Hyde finally received approval to proceed. The ILPC is ever the faithful watchdog for design compatibility of new buildings in our historic district.

**Figure 35.8** Dewitt House will focus on housing for seniors. Rendering provided by HOLT Architects.

The Hotel Ithaca building on Cayuga Street across from Coltivare and the new parking garage has added a new tower, new rooms, and a small conference center.

**Figure 35.9** Hotel Ithaca expansion. Photo by author.

Simeon's American Bistro, a bar and restaurant at the east end of the Commons, reopened two years after a disastrous runaway-truck collision that left the entire front facade demolished and one employee dead.

**Figure 35.10** The scene of the fatal accident at Simeon's. Photo by David Burbank.

**Figure 35.11** Simeon's opened with a rebuilt facade and interior two years after the tragic event. Photo by author.

Jason Fane, who owns the former First National Bank building on the Commons directly across from Center Ithaca, has been gradually emptying the building of tenants and recently announced his plans to convert the seven-story building into thirty-two apartments and two retail stores. The CFCU Community Credit Union has taken over the ground floor of the building in the former bank space.

**Figure 35.12** Soon to become Jason Fane's seven-story conversion to thirty-two apartments and CFCU Community Credit Union. Photo by author.

David Lubin's mixed-use project, Harold's Square on the Commons, with 16,000 square feet of ground-floor retail, 34,000 square feet of offices, and 108 apartments above, has recently received approval from the planning and development department. Demolition of the old (non-historic) buildings began in October 2017. This $38 million, twelve-story project is set to become the largest building in downtown at 168,750 square feet.

**Figure 35.13** Demolition under way on David Lubin's Harold's Square. Photo by author.

**Figure 35.14** Harold's Square. Estimated completion date is summer 2019. Rendering courtesy of David Lubin.

The county and Tompkins Trust Company have come to terms on a purchase offer for the historic bank building on the Commons, which has been home to Tompkins Trust Company for over 145 years. TTC president Greg Hartz had indicated that the bank would look favorably on making a very advantageous deal for a community use. The county will rent the entire building to the newly formed Tompkins Center for History and Culture. Eight not-for-profits will share the building, which will become a historical and cultural downtown destination—with the Convention & Visitors Bureau, the Community Arts Partnership, Wharton Film Project, and the History Center showcasing the Tommy airplane built in Ithaca in 1918 as some of the major attractions. For me this has been another lesson in community development, as three of the nonprofit organizations proposed for the new Center for History and Culture are tenants in our buildings at Gateway Center and Center Ithaca.

**Figure 35.15** Exterior of the new Tompkins Center for History and Culture with Iron Design's logo in the former Tompkins Trust Building on the Commons. Rendering by Stream Collaborative, Architects.

**Figure 35.16** The famous Tommy airplane, built in Ithaca in 1918, will be on view at the Tompkins Center for History and Culture. Rendering by Stream Collaborative, Architects.

Rod Howe, the director of the History Center, had invited me to become co-leader of the project to help bring the TCHC vision to completion. Just as I had done with competitors on earlier deals, I took the attitude that if the project is good for downtown, it will be good for us in the long run, and we should assist in any way possible for it to be built—in other words an attitude of collaboration instead of competition.

We had supported Cinemapolis in their move from Center Ithaca into the new Schon/Bloomfield project on Seneca Street. We had shared market numbers and tours of our downtown buildings with Bryan Warren and the Newmans when they built Seneca Way, and with developers Ken Schon and Steve Bloomfield when they built Cayuga Green. We had encouraged Nick Lambrou with the Hilton Garden Inn. We had collaborated with our competitors out of long-range self-interest and with the desire to strengthen and expand the downtown Ithaca market. Frost, Chris, and I would be happy to lose three tenants to the new Tompkins Center for History and Culture. We have confidence our spaces will be quickly rented to new tenants.

What has taken place over the past twenty years since the founding of the BID is the resurrection of an aging and languishing downtown. Today downtown Ithaca is flourishing. With the new Commons, with two more hotels open, and another expanding, plus the new apartments that are already in place at Gateway Commons, Breckenridge, Carey Building, and the Lofts@Six Mile Creek, and with the addition of City Center with 192 units, and Lubin's Harold's Square with 108 units, and with more apartments being planned, the foot traffic in downtown is certain to increase. Ithaca will become more and more desirable as a place to live, work, and play. Retail, restaurants, theaters, art galleries, and city and county sales and property tax will all greatly benefit.

As specialty stores develop, the downtown will continue to be seen as an even stronger contender in the retail market. Sonny Cosentini will be proved wrong. One more shoe store will not put him out of business. With the Downtown Ithaca Alliance's 2020 strategic plan, the *Tompkins County Comprehensive Plan*, and the *City of Ithaca's Comprehensive Plan*, each emphasizing the need to limit sprawl and focus density in downtown, as well as in "nodes" being planned throughout the county, where infrastructure—public water, sewers, natural gas, and transit service are already provided—there is intense focus on the downtown and the greater Ithaca area. Each one of these plans as they come to fruition will promote both downtown and greater Ithaca as a livable, walkable, and more dynamic community.

Downtown will remain the center of government and the financial center of the county, particularly with the new town hall in the old post office and the investment being made by the bank in their new Tompkins Trust Company office building. The Lubin project will add retail, offices, and apartments. Carol has opened a women's apparel store in Center Ithaca called Breathe, which carries nationally known names such as Lucky Brand and Flax. The playground on the new Commons attracts youngsters, as do Alphabet Soup, Jillian's Drawers, and Cat's Pajamas—these stores each attract parents and their children. Downtown is family friendly. American Crafts by Robbie Dein has just completed a total facade renovation. The Finger Lakes School of Massage has moved into the former Thomas Architects space in the Rothschild Building—the "second school" sought in the 2020 strategic plan. A new conference center is being proposed for the Rothschild Building adjacent to the Marriott. The city and the county are working on a plan to open up land along the inlet for development. This waterfront property is considered by many to be the most desirable development property in the city of Ithaca.

Farther out in the community, a paved walking and bike path—the Black Diamond Trail connecting Cass Park in downtown Ithaca to Taughannock Falls State Park eight miles to the north—was constructed utilizing the abandoned Lehigh Valley Railroad bed.

The 5.5-mile-long Cayuga Waterfront Trail connects the visitors bureau/chamber of commerce building and Stewart Park as it winds its way along the lakeshore and continues through Fuertes Bird Sanctuary, the Newman Municipal Golf Course, the Ithaca Farmers Market, Cass Park, the ball fields, the hockey rink, and the Ithaca Children's Garden. The two trails have done much to raise the livability and walkability index of Ithaca.

Carol and I still have hopes of walking our dogs on the expanded Creek Walk from the Commons through our Gateway site and connecting to the Six Mile Creek Nature Preserve. We have coordinated with the city in commissioning a plan for grants and funding for this project.

Surrounding Ithaca, the Finger Lakes Land Trust, a nonprofit conservation organization, has protected more than eighteen thousand acres through the establishment of thirty-six conservation areas, all accessible to the public. They have acquired conservation easements from private owners who gave up development rights on more than a hundred properties. Their goal: an "Emerald Necklace" of fifty thousand acres surrounding Ithaca with forever-wild natural areas open to the public. Ithaca is an incredible blend of the natural and built environments.

Planning is key. And the key to planning is inspirational leadership and public input. We must know what the community wants: What projects? What art? What is going to work? We must think strategically and determine what the market will support. To sustain and advance the well-rounded development of Ithaca, we must have dynamic leaders like Thys, Gary, Svante, Philly, and JoAnn, to help inspire and shape public decision-making, and we must have visionary and courageous politicians, as well as dynamic, determined developers.

The inspired planning of city and Cornell officials in the early 1970s led to the creation of the Commons in 1974, and to the vision for the redevelopment of Collegetown. This resulted in their selecting a preferred developer. Out of that came the development of Eddygate, the first major development in Collegetown. In 2000, the BID's first ten-year strategic plan kept a major employer downtown and shaped the retail and development strategy over the next decade. Enterprising developers bought into the plan and developed Gateway, Seneca Place, the Hilton hotel, Seneca Way, Cayuga Green, and the new Cayuga Street parking garage. In 2010 the second ten-year strategic plan led to the redesign, demolition, and rebuilding of the Ithaca Commons, saving the State Theatre and the Clinton House, building Breckenridge Place, the Carey Building, the new Tompkins Trust Company building, and now the City Center and Harold's Square. The resurgence of downtown has been an important influence in Novarr's decision to proceed with the development of Collegetown Terrace. If these key projects had not been implemented, downtown Ithaca could have remained stagnant, undeveloped, and languishing. It did not.

Since the formation of our business improvement district, the city of Ithaca, Cornell University, Ithaca College, and Tompkins County have all received high ratings, recognizing Ithaca as a superlative community nationwide. The following is a list of accolades, compiled by the Ithaca/Tompkins County Convention & Visitors Bureau, received by Ithaca since 2010, the second decade of our strategic plan:

- Ithaca once again ranked in "Top 100 Places to Live" by Relocate-America.com, June 2011
- Cornell ranked second in "Best Employers for Workers over 50" by *AARP: The Magazine*, September 2011
- Ithaca ranked eighth on AARP's list of "10 Affordable Cities for Retirement," *AARP: The Magazine*, September–October 2011
- Cornell ranked among the "100 Best Companies" by *Working Mother* magazine, October 2011
- Ithaca ranked one of the "10 Best Places to Retire in 2012" by *US News & World Report*, October 2011
- Ithaca ranked one of nineteen "Perfect Towns" by *Outside Magazine*, October 2011
- Ithaca ranked a top-seven retirement town in "Retire Here, Not There," *SmartMoney*, November 2011
- Ithaca ranked the "most secure" small town in the United States, Farmers Insurance study, December 2011
- Ithaca ranked in top ten "Places to Go Carless in Retirement" by *US News & World Report*, online, March 2012
- Ithaca/Tompkins County ranked a "Top 10 Small to Mid-Sized Fourth Economy Community" by Fourth Economy Consulting, April 2012
- Ithaca ranked in top ten "Great Quirky Places to Retire," *AARP: The Magazine*, April 2012
- Cayuga Lake Scenic Byway ranked among "10 Great All-American Road Trips" by Yahoo! Travel, April 2012
- Ithaca ranked third-best city for "Finding Employment Right Now" by *Forbes*, May 2012
- Ithaca ranked fifth in "The 10 Best Cities for Millennials" by 24/7 Wall St. and Moving.com, July 2012
- Cornell ranked fifth in the "Top 25 Colleges for *Outside* Readers" by *Outside Magazine*, August 2012
- Ithaca ranked one of the "Best River Towns in America" by *Outside* online, September 2012
- Ithaca named "Most Secure Place to Live" among municipalities with fewer than one hundred fifty thousand residents by Farmers Insurance, October 2012

- Ithaca ranked "#1 College Destination" by American Institute for Economic Research, October 2012
- Ithaca named best US college town in "Top 10 Best College Towns in America" by *Business Insider*, January 2013
- Ithaca named first among the "100 Smartest Cities in America" by VentureBeat online, June 2013 (based on study by Lumosity), VentureBeat.com
- Ithaca Farmers Markets ranked fourth in "8 Must-Visit Farmer's Markets around the U.S." by Zagat, July 2013
- Ithaca ranked eighth among "10 Great Places to Live, 2013" by *Kiplinger's Personal Finance*, July 2013
- Ithaca ranked third among "Best Places for Work-Life Balance" by NerdWallet.com, July 2013
- Ithaca College named among nation's best undergraduate institutions, ranking first for radio and seventh for theater, by the *Princeton Review*, August 2013
- Ithaca ranked fourth among the "10 Most Livable Cities" by MSN Real Estate, online, August 2013
- Ithaca named in "Top 25 Youngest Best Places to Live: America's Best Small Towns" by *CNN Money*, August 2013
- Cornell University ranked fifth among "Ten Coolest Schools" by *Sierra Magazine*, August 2013
- Ithaca ranked first among "10 Cities Where You Want to Walk to Work" by MSN Real Estate, online, September 2013
- Finger Lakes ranked in "America's Top 10 Lakes to Visit This Fall" by *The Daily Beast* online, *Condé Nast Traveler*, September 2013
- Ithaca ranked third among "10 Secretly Amazing Cities for Wine Lovers" by MSN Real Estate, online, October 2013
- Ithaca ranked first among "America's Best College Towns" by HomeInsurance.com, October 2013
- Ithaca named "Best College Town" by the 2013–14 AIER College Destinations Index, November 2013
- Ithaca named one of "America's Most Romantic Towns" by *Travel+Leisure*, January 2014
- Ithaca named tenth among "13 of the Best New York Art Spots That Aren't in NYC" by the *Huffington Post*, March 2014
- Tompkins County named the second "Healthiest County in New York" by CountyHealthRankings.org, April 2014
- The Finger Lakes ranked eighth on the "Wine Tour of the World: 10 Must-Visit Stops" by ABC News, April 2014
- Ithaca named ninth among the "Most Exciting College Towns" by MSN Real Estate, online, May 2014

- Ithaca ranked eighteenth among "19 Best Small Cities for Single Millennial Women" by DatingAdvice.com, March 2015
- Robert H. Treman State Park named best swimming spot in New York State by the Weather Channel, March 2015
- Ithaca ranked second among "The 20 Best College Towns in America" by *Business Insider*, April 2015
- Ithaca named "Healthiest City in New York State" by 24/7 Wall Street, September 2015
- Ithaca named the "Coffee Capital of New York State," January 2016
- Ithaca named one of the "Ten Best Places to Live" by *Men's Journal,* March 2016
- Ithaca ranked the no. 2 "Best Small College Town" by *USA Today*, April 2016

The Ithaca Commons has been at the heart of downtown redevelopment. Not everyone wanted it built in 1974; not everyone wanted it to be rebuilt in 2013. Would not downtown be better served with a street running past all the stores? There was a vote, and the pedestrian mall won. The majority of the public, the majority of Common Council, and Mayor Svante approved and followed through with construction. It showed immense confidence in downtown Ithaca on the part of public officials. The development community has responded in kind by initiating new project after new project.

**Figure 35.17** The overgrown Ithaca Commons prior to redesign and renovation. Photo by Jon Reis.

**Figure 35.18** Ithaca Commons prior to renovation (ca. 2013). Photo by Jon Reis.

**Figure 35.19** Ithaca Commons undergoing a two-year construction period (ca. 2013–15). Photo by Jon Reis.

**Figure 35.20** Ithaca's new pedestrian mall. The Commons redesigned and reopened (ca. 2015). Photo by Jon Reis.

**Figure 35.21** The new Ithaca Commons. Photo by Jon Reis.

You have had a look behind the scenes and can see why and how Cornell University, Tompkins Cortland Community College, and city officials, along with bankers, business and property owners, developers, merchants, and the public, worked together; rebuilt Collegetown; built out the downtown Ithaca Commons—twice; formed a business improvement district; and planned and developed to make Ithaca, New York, one of the *best small cities in the United States.*

All real estate is local. Hopefully, you can take these ideas and principles home to help shape your city.

# AFTERWORD

We all have mentors and important colleagues in our lives. Thinking back to the mentors and colleagues who have guided me:

Friend and contractor Ray McElwee, my father's Cornell classmate and an invaluable guide to me as I built my first major projects in Ithaca. With his encouragement I joined my first two civic boards—McGraw House elderly housing and Alpha House, a drug rehab center.

Friend and architect David Taube, founder of HOLT Architects and my guide in the conceptualization and construction of the Ravenwood and Eddygate buildings.

State senator and neighbor the late Ted Day, who several times twisted my arm unmercifully—until I joined the board of Cayuga Medical Center of Ithaca, our local hospital. (It was a nine-year education I have never regretted.)

George Gesslein, vice president of commercial lending at Citizens Savings Bank, who believed in me from my very first renovation project.

Steve Bacon, vice president of commercial lending at Tompkins Trust Company, who understands the Ithaca rental market and financed (and refinanced) many of our projects.

The late Stu Lewis, a major retailer with five stores in downtown, who sold me 407 College Avenue for no money down in 1982, and proceeded to help guide me with both real estate and downtown development advice over the years.

The late Stan Goldberg, from whom my partners and I bought Center Ithaca, albeit out of foreclosure, and who guided me in the assumption of the ownership and management role of this 144,000-square-foot building in the heart of our downtown.

My principal attorneys: Jim Kerrigan (fourteen years); Peter Walsh, who closed the Eddygate bond issue of six hundred pages with Putnam

Investments; and Elena Flash, a dear friend and counselor for over twenty-five years.

My older, more experienced investors and business partners: Tom Seaman, Norm Dykema, and Walter Noel, who guided me with sound business practices and advice for twenty-two years.

The late Andrew Dixon, who as a consultant brought a deep financial and business acumen and as a friend conceptualized the major bank refinancing that enabled me to buy out my partners in 2005.

My son and son-in-law, Frost Travis and Chris Hyde, who have taken over our company and formed Travis Hyde Properties. They run a tight ship as we move forward with our real estate development and management company with forty employees and a growing portfolio of flagship properties in the Ithaca and Binghamton, New York, markets.

And finally, but not least, my wife and partner, Carol Griggs Travis, who kept me steady with her intuition and guidance for thirty-five years.

From these people and many others who have supported and guided me, it is apparent to me that I have simply been following the normal course of life: each of us has been "advised and raised" to maturity in our line of work. We make our own way. We raise our children. We look out for them, and we guide them to make their own way. We raise our successors. We look out for them and assist them as they move into the roles of taking on the responsibility of running our society, our cities, our country. At all levels, we are continually moving younger people toward leadership positions for the next generation. It was done for us. We do it by passing on our knowledge and experience as much as possible to assure a safe and secure future for the next generation and the ones to come.

# APPENDIX

## "Growing Up and Out" by Karen Gadiel

The following article, written by the reporter Karen Gadiel, appeared in the *Ithaca Times* in January 2006 (© 2006, *Ithaca Times*, Ithaca, NY, used with permission). It is an excellent and lyrical summary of the development that took place in the first five years of the BID's strategic plan:

### Growing Up and Out

Downtown Ithaca is growing up. Literally. Each of the taller buildings—planned, under construction or already in place—creates a change in the city's visual profile, stepping ever further away from the early village that's still easy to imagine, the community seen in old photographs whose outlines are still with us in some of downtown's historic buildings.

And there are other, subtler changes like a new melody running under the surface of conversations about the city. Unlike many other locales where malls and suburban developments have emptied the urban center, Ithaca seems poised to become a model for what other cities wish they could be.

"Part of the thinking that causes all of us to think the downtown urban core is important as a place to work, to live, to be entertained during the day and the evening really harkens back to some historical traditional values that we were familiar with when we were growing up," said Michael Stamm, president of Tompkins County Area Development (TCAD). "Being able to walk around and shop, eat, live and work in a downtown urban setting—many urban centers have lost the ability to attract that kind of activity.

"Any downtown in the U.S. is certainly struggling to remain vibrant," Stamm explained. "Our downtown has always been stronger than most but it was clear the community needed to pay a little more attention to it. And it has, and the results are pretty obvious."

Among major projects initiated or moved further along in 2005 are the Seneca Place On The Commons—actually off The Commons, on Seneca and Tioga streets; the Cayuga Green developments and the Gateway II project— these last two located between Green Street and the Six Mile Creek. Each of these projects, Ithaca officials claimed, has improved the business environment for the others, in turn helping to foster a climate of growth many expect to continue gathering momentum for some years to come.

"There's no doubt about it, that positive feeds on positive, and negative on negative—and we're striving for the positive," said Gary Ferguson, executive director of the Ithaca Downtown Partnership (IDP), a business improvement district for downtown. Looking back at the year, he cheerfully found a great deal more on the positive side of the balance sheet.

"The Seneca Place project did open, after being under construction for a year and a half," he said. "The new Hilton Garden Hotel is open and functioning, Cornell [University] is using floors two to four as office space for almost 300 people, and floor five is office space for other businesses, including Solomon Smith Barney—they decided to remain in Ithaca. And they [the developers] added extra conference rooms and meeting space. That will be increasingly important to the life of downtown because of its potential to bring more people. It's been a model for people from all over the country. We've been receiving calls from all over. It's a great town-gown partnership."

The project's success is heavily attributed to Cornell's involvement. "The project wouldn't have been possible without Cornell and they knew their long-term lease for a good chunk of office space provided the nucleus," said David Chiazza, of Ciminelli Group, which developed the site. "To undertake a $30 plus-million project in a small town was a major risk." Although the complex has only been open for five months, missing much of the peak season, Chiazza said it's already modestly exceeded expectations.

He said he was told the 2006 conference and banquet component of the hotel will be strong, although it's too soon to say for certain. The group is also soon to announce the opening of a new restaurant in the facility, which it hopes will attract more people to downtown. "We're not there to compete," he said. "The purpose of this project overall was to increase the size of the pie downtown."

Mixed-use spaces have been part of the Ithaca scene for at least 30 years, since local architect Bill Downing created the DeWitt complex from the former Ithaca High School. "Had Bill not bought it, it was going to be purchased and torn down. That idea of a mixed-use approach to downtown— obviously a generation later we're picking up on and saying we like projects like that," Ferguson noted.

Another important mixed-use space was the purchase of the M&T Building in December by Tompkins Cortland Community College (TC3). College President Carl Haynes said this extension center on the top two floors of the six-story building represents a 40 percent increase from its former rented space in the Rothschild Building across The Commons. The bank will continue its operations on the building's ground floor; tenants on the other three floors will remain there, and part of the TC3 space on the fifth floor will be shared with Empire State College.

"We wanted to be as close to The Commons as possible," Haynes said. "The continuing growth and vitality of [the] downtown area is very important and we wanted to be part of that." Cornell's downtown presence at Seneca Place was also an important component, because TC3 offers workforce development courses among its menu of credit and non-credit classes. With the heaviest use of its facility in late afternoon and evenings, and a growing demand for credit course offering among those in the workforce—and now a larger working population situated just across the street—the timing and the geography couldn't be better.

Additionally, "The whole purchase was made possible by a sizeable donation of equity from the Ciminelli Group," Haynes added, with traditional mortgage financing through the Tompkins Trust Company.

Similarly, Gateway II and the second phase of the Cayuga Green projects are also mixed-use developments, which in turn will engender other projects. "It's the first real opportunity to provide housing in this market for middle and upper income," Ferguson said. "The new [Gateway] building sits up against the creek and one of the city's goals is to create a trailhead from downtown, to go through the gorge through the wildflower preserve which is quite a ways away. They will need to do some more trail-building; the city is starting to look at grant options for that."

Ferguson pointed to the IDP as a facilitator rather than a creator of projects, so his role is to encourage and assist. He and the IDP were instrumental in obtaining the nomination and the inclusion of a large section of downtown Ithaca to the New York State Historic Register, a paperwork-intensive project, which serves the area as a preservation tool. In the past year, he also obtained a Main Street grant "to help us with some of our major anchor projects to get downtown looking better." In the meantime, the "ambassador program" was expanded to year-round maintenance of landscaping and clean-up. The IDP also worked with the Ithaca Police Department to change the method and visibility of downtown policing. "One of the most visible parts of that strategy was the purchase of two yellow Volkswagen bugs," he said. "They're very cute."

The retail environment also improved with 20 new businesses opening downtown, plus at least three expansions. At the same time, six businesses closed. "It's a pretty good gain," Ferguson said. "We're going to lose a couple more, but that's why we're here. Downtown churns all the time. Nothing stays the same, and when the churning does happen, we can help. Downtowns, including downtown Ithaca, just don't stay static. We're talking to brokers, looking for prospects."

In this optimistic setting, he said he prefers to see reverses as challenges, hurdles and goals to be met. In researching successful downtown areas around the country, Ferguson discovered, "The great small-city downtowns had lots of destination attractions within easy walking distance of each other. Some had 30 or more attractions clustered together. Part of our challenge is to use our limited space to attract people and create pedestrian traffic. Food and beverage [businesses] are becoming more dominant in downtowns—we're seeing that loud and clear. You can't just spread stuff out and expect it to work. We will be continuing to advocate for dense downtown development, development that goes up. We have to use our limited space wisely."

Looking ahead, Ferguson added, "A topic for 2006 is how downtown can be more of an entertainment center for the region. One of our key goals is stabilizing the State Theatre—that's certainly one of those key assets. And Cayuga Green is very significant with its movie theater complex. We have people working with us now to try to help make us position downtown as an entertainment center—you'll be reading more about that in the ensuing few months."

Van Cort also sees the potential for future "infill" projects, utilizing currently empty or underused spaces. "We have an enormous percentage in park land already which is great but we have a very high tax burden," he said. "This will lighten the burden on existing owners and residents. There are a number of other parcels that ultimately should be developed. Land in the city center is too valuable to be used for large parking lots." He added that multi-story parking garages could be safer because they don't get snowed in.

If, as developers and planners hope, the completion of Seneca Place is a beginning, not an ending, what does the immediate and long-term future hold for downtown Ithaca?

"It needs to continue to grow and add attractions," Chiazza said. "Investment has to continue to happen. The city has to continue to redefine itself to keep itself active, interesting and dynamic."

Stamm, of the IDA, agreed. "We're going to look like a healthy, vibrant, small Upstate city," Stamm said. "To encourage appropriate development while at the same time retaining Ithaca's unique character—it's always a delicate balancing act."

**Interview with Gary Ferguson**

*BIDS: Goals and Growth*

Gary Ferguson, executive director of Ithaca's Business Improvement District (BID), has been instrumental in the success of Ithaca's downtown redevelopment. About midway through the 2020 strategic plan, I asked Gary a number of questions regarding his motivations for coming to Ithaca and what he regarded as his greatest successes and challenges in establishing and running our local BID. He went into detail:

**Why did you and Lisa choose to accept the position you were offered in Ithaca?** (Gary had been offered what were potentially much more lucrative positions in BIDS in much larger cities.)

We were looking for a community closer to our families in New England but wanted a place that could satisfy us both. Lisa wanted a farming opportunity. I wanted a city that was interested in growth and development and that had an upside potential for its downtown. We both wanted a college community. Ithaca became an intriguing option and one that we are glad we accepted.

**What is a BID? The history—when and where BIDs were first established; how many there are in the country, and how many in New York State**

BIDs are tools for community and economic development. They essentially are special districts with a twist. Whereas special districts are created for a whole host of single purposes (sidewalks, libraries, parks, water, schools, lighting, and so on), BIDs can be used for multiple purposes relating to the betterment of the district. They have become a primary tool in downtown revitalization and management across North America and indeed worldwide.

BIDs became a popular tool in the 1980s and their use grew markedly over the next two decades. Ithaca was part of that trend.

In New York State special downtown districts were already permitted in the 1980s and could be found in the major upstate cities—Syracuse, Rochester, and Buffalo. When BID law was approved by the state in the late 1980s, there was an initial push by New York City districts to adopt the format. The city was experiencing financial hardships that caused it to reduce its provision of basic services to districts. Places like Times Square and Grand Central saw BIDs as a way to supplement meager city services and better control their own destinies. In time, BIDs became extremely popular in NYC. There are currently about seventy BIDs in the city . . . ranging in size from the largest in the state to the smallest.

Elsewhere in NYS, communities also began embracing BIDs. Today there are roughly an equal number of BIDs in upstate New York. NYC BIDs have their own set of laws and an umbrella organization set up by the city to aid, support, and monitor them. No such entity exists for the rest of the state, although there is a voluntary-membership statewide organization known as the New York State Urban Council that has served to represent downtown programs and provide networking and educational opportunities.

In the United States, the use of BIDs continues to slowly increase after several decades of strong growth. All fifty states now have BID-enabling legislation on the books. In some states, such as Massachusetts, the law is especially weak and has constrained its use. For example, the original Massachusetts law enabled property owners to opt out of the BID at their choice; they were not bound by the majority like they are in NYS and most other places.

BIDs continue to slowly grow in the United States and more rapidly grow worldwide. There are growing numbers of BIDs in the UK and Australia, and South Africa. BIDs are being increasingly used in Europe, Africa, South America, and Asia. It is a fairly simple tool that can transcend culture and governing style.

**Do you have an overarching goal for what you do in your job as executive director of the BID?**

We have goals that we set in our strategic plan and our annual work plans. These are numerous and we work toward them on a daily, monthly, and yearly basis. Personally, yes, I have internal goals I strive for. Among them are:

- Wanting to make downtown Ithaca self-sustaining, and immune from sprawl and external pressures that work to erode the integrity and economic viability of downtowns.
- Making downtown Ithaca one of, if not the, premier small-city downtowns in America, or at least the Northeast.
- Blunting and reversing the trends that pulled resources, talent, and investment out of the center city.
- Growing an organization that can successfully work and thrive long after I am gone.
- Making downtown Ithaca a "must-see, must-do" place for both residents and visitors.
- Making downtown development a key and essential part of our community's economic development fabric.

**To what do you attribute the incredible growth that has taken place in downtown Ithaca over the seventeen years that you have been here?**

- Having a plan.
- Having a strong organization that daily pushes to make downtown a city and community priority.
- Having public leadership willing to stand up for downtown development, even when it is challenging and politically dangerous.
- Having local private developers and business investors who were and still are willing to tackle more difficult downtown projects, even when it would have been easier to develop or invest somewhere else.
- Creating the tax abatement program that provides incentives for development. These incentives act as gap fillers [filling in vacant lots], and they provide a visible sense of community support and priority for downtown development.
- The changes to zoning that have made it easier and more attractive to build downtown.
- The growing sense that downtown is an enduring, solid, and sustainable place to invest, develop, and start a business.

**If you were to list the most influential projects and/or policies you have been involved with, which ones would you include?**

The two earliest were most important: Gateway Plaza and Seneca Place. Both projects served as catalysts that demonstrated to the community the possibility of downtown growth and development. Being first is always most difficult. These projects were crucial in setting the tone for further development.

Creation of the Cayuga Street parking garage was likewise very significant. Without that excess parking, none of the current round of development would have been readily achievable. Demonstrating parking capacity was and remains a key to successful downtown development here in Ithaca, at least for the near term. Someday, that may change, but until it does, parking will control development.

Of course, the Commons was another key catalyst project, one that is only now demonstrating its value as more developers look to downtown as a safe and attractive place to invest for the future.

**What are the major conflicts you face?**

- Getting people in the community to support downtown growth and development. Support ebbs and rises continually, so this is an ongoing challenge.

- Ongoing work with retailers. Retailing is a tough and challenging business, and retailers necessarily have short time horizons. They don't have the time to be patient.
- Convincing folks that downtown Ithaca is deserving of special attention and grant support—whether that be from the city, county, region, or state.

**Do you foresee a limit to the growth we both want to—and can—achieve in downtown Ithaca, and if so, what are the major impediments?**

We are blessed and cursed by our geography. Being a small downtown means we are eminently walkable and can create an incredible pedestrian place. But being small also means the opportunities for development are limited and, in our case, complex.

Our growth will be dictated by two forces not necessarily working in harmony—political will and market supply and demand. The market will tell us when we have reached the limit for housing or lodging. However, we'd like to know even a bit earlier so we do not overbuild the demand and depress prices. The importance of political will is evident quite regularly here in Ithaca. Growth vs. nongrowth is an ongoing discussion and debate. If that debate tilts too strongly toward no/slow growth, downtown development will be affected.

**Where is downtown going over the next ten years? How will we map out the direction?**

I like the ten-year plans we do. They provide guidance and direction for both the DIA and the community in general. As I think about our next ten years, the following come to mind:

- Better connecting downtown with other districts (Collegetown/CU, Ithaca College, and the West End/Waterfront). This remains a key, unmet part of our second strategic plan and will be crucial in the years ahead.
- Strengthening our retail base.
- Adding more entertainment options to pull more people downtown.
- Positioning downtown to be able to compete against new districts and new nodes likely to be created—the Waterfront, East Hill Plaza, and a possible new district by Ithaca College and King Road. We can also work to help craft these new entities so that they are more complementary than competitive toward downtown.
- Continue to strategically add housing as the market warrants.

- Build a conference center to better utilize the four hotels we now enjoy.
- Work to create a downtown energy district that will make downtown development, downtown living, and downtown businesses more appealing and cost competitive.
- Expand the boundaries of our downtown district to possibly include the West End and/or the Chain Works/Emerson area.
- Examine the viability and feasibility of the DIA becoming more active in parking, since it is such an important backbone of downtown.

# BIBLIOGRAPHY

Danter Company. *A Downtown Housing Strategy in the City of Ithaca, New York*. Columbus, OH: Danter Company LLC, 2011. Revised 2016.

Downtown Ithaca Alliance. *Downtown Ithaca 2020 Strategic Plan*. Ithaca, NY, December 2010. http://www.downtownithaca.com/local/file_upload/files/ DIA%202020%20Strategic%20Plan(1).pdf. (Note: At ninety-two pages, the 2020 strategic plan is a book in itself. It encompasses the goals, strategies, and methods for continued downtown development in Ithaca—*highly recommended reading!*)

"Historic Ithaca: Reclaiming a City's Past." Editorial. *Cornell Alumni News*. May 1974.

Ithaca Department of Planning and Urban Development. *Downtown Development Guidelines for Ithaca, NY*. Ithaca, NY, 2016.

Johnson, Julee. "An Examination of Three Historic Preservation Organizations in Ithaca, NY." Master's thesis, Cornell University, 1985.

Kunstler, James Howard. *Home from Nowhere*. New York: Simon & Schuster, 1996.

*Report of the Downtown Vision Task Force*. Ithaca, NY, 1991.

Snodderly, Daniel R. *Ithaca and Its Past*. Ithaca, NY: DeWitt Historical Society of Tompkins County, 1982.

*Tompkins County Area Development Five-Year Plan, 2014*. Ithaca, NY, 2014.

# INDEX

Page numbers in *italics* refer to illustrations.